A GREEN VITRUVIUS

VITRUVIUS

PRINCIPLES AND PRACTICE OF SUSTAINABLE ARCHITECTURAL DESIGN

The European Commission
Directorate General XVII for Energy

Architects' Council of Europe

University College Dublin
Energy Research Group

SOFTECH
ENERGIA
TECNOLOGIA
AMBIENTE

JAMES
X
JAMES

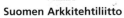

Suomen Arkkitehtiliitto

A Green Vitruvius – Principles and Practice of Sustainable Architectural Design

Published in 1999 by James & James (Science Publishers) Ltd, 35–37 William Road, London NW1 3ER, UK, for the European Commission, Directorate General XVII for Energy and the Architect's Council of Europe.

Publication No. EUR 18944 of the Commission of the European Communities

ISBN No. 1-873936-94-X

This publication was prepared within the THERMIE Programme of the Commission within a project involving the Energy Research Group (ERG) University College Dublin (Co-ordinators), the Architects' Council of Europe (ACE), Softech, Turin and the Finnish Association of Architects (SAFA), Helsinki.

THERMIE is an important EC programme designed to promote the greater use of European energy technology. Its aim is to assist the European Union in achieving its fundamental objectives of:

- improving the energy supply prospects of the European Union;
- reducing environmental pollution by decreasing emissions, particularly those of CO_2, SO_2 and NO_x;
- strengthening the competitive position of European industry, above all small and medium sized enterprises (SMEs);
- promoting the transfer of technology to Third World countries;
- strengthening economic and social cohesion within the European Union.

Legal Notice

Preparation

The material for this publication was prepared by the Energy Research Group, UCD, Dublin (Eileen Fitzgerald, Ann McNicholl, Robert Alcock and J Owen Lewis, with assistance from Maoliosa Molloy); Softech, Torino (Antonella Marucco and Giorgio Gallo) and SAFA, Helsinki, (Vesa Peltonen) with contributions from Paul Leech GAIA Associates.

Drafts were reviewed by energy experts from the Architects' Council of Europe including, Varis Bokalders (SAR), Gunilla Ronnow (PAR), Rafi Serra (CSAE), Fauto Simoes (AAP), Paul Leech (RIAI), and Michael Baumer (UNSFA).

Design

Graphic design by Caomhán Murphy and Pierre Jolivet with additional illustrations by Fergal Duff.

Acknowledgements

Illustrations and photographs in this publication are used with the kind permission of the following:

Cover: BRE Building: Fielden Clegg Architects; Dennis Gilbert, View, Photographer

Greenpeace Headquarters: Fielden Clegg Architects

Regensberg Masterplan: Sir Norman Foster and Partners Architects; Professor J Whitelegg Photographer

Schlumberger Research Building: Michael Hopkins and Partners Architects, Büro Happold Environmental Engineers

The Oxford Eco House: Sue Roaf Architect; Peter Durant, Photographer

Lichtplanung Christian Bartenbach Offices: Prof J Lackner

PV Curtain Wall Façade: Pilkington Solar International

Breathing Wall Façade, Findhorn Foundation: Keystone Architects, John Talbott

Okalux Glass: Okalux Kapillarglas GmbH

Windberg Student Residence: T Herzog and Partner Architects; Dieter Leistner, Architekton, Photographer

Design Centre, Linz: T Herzog and Partner Architects

Paul Leech GAIA Associates

Eoin O'Cofaigh

Osuna Housing Seville: Sotomayor, Dominguez & Lopez de Asian Architects

Coffee Shop Kyoto: Tadao Ando Architect

Debis Headquarters Double-façade: Renzo Piano Building Workshop

Caglic House: K Caglic Architect

Barcelona Building: BCN Cimbra Logica Architects

Skellig Interpretive Centre: Peter and Mary Doyle

School of Architecture, Lyon: Jourda and Perraudin

Arab Institue, Paris: Jean Nouvel

Material on evaluation is used with the kind permission of the Helsinki City Planning Department, Helsinki, Finland and the Building Research Establishment, Garston, Watford, United Kingdom.

Contents

The Green Building

Section 1: Process

Section 2: Issues

Section 3: Strategies

Section 4: Elements

Section 5: Evaluation

Further reading

process issues strategies elements
issues strategies elements evaluation
issues strategies elements evaluation
strategies elements evaluation
elements

Foreword

This book is intended to be a single-point general reference for architects wishing to design and realise sustainable architecture for their clients. Architects have varying levels of competence in green design. In some EU Member States, environmental preoccupations have developed over time, and the profession has a broadly-based competence in sustainability. Much of what we say will be familiar to those architects. However, this is not true for everybody. This book is for the experienced practitioner who is aware of environmental sustainability as an issue and who wishes to learn how to make more sustainable architecture but who, apart from dealing with issues raised in building regulations, has not yet acquired any particular expertise in the subject.

Environmentally friendly, environmentally conscious, energy conscious, sustainable, greener, or simply green architecture? Identifying our subject was not straightforward. There is no internationally-agreed definition for green architecture. This book offers advice in the areas of energy and water inputs, materials, indoor air quality and wastes. The rational use of energy in buildings involves maximising renewable energy inputs, minimising fossil fuel inputs, as well as general energy conservation. Materials are discussed with regard to energy-embodied, toxicity in use and optimising the use of renewable resources; however much research is yet to be done on the environmental aspects of building materials, and this book is a product of its time.

The practising architect has competency in a myriad of areas: building planning, aesthetics, construction technology, programming, building regulations... It is not easy to reconcile conflicting demands of budget, programme, site and timescale; and to optimise a respect for context, spatial organisation, functionality of layout, soundness of construction, spatial and proportional quality, and inclusive design. No one aspect of the architectural solution can be perfected at the expense of all others. Green design is one of many considerations. We recognise the reality of information overload, and have concentrated not on the 'why', but on the 'how' of green design.

Green design is place-sensitive. One of its attractions in a globalising world is the potential to make place-specific architecture by responding to the clues of a specific climate and site, and, where possible, using sustainable local materials. Most, but not all the advice in this book will be of direct use to everyone. We have striven to balance the weight of advice relevant to practitioners across the Union.

The information is organised in four independent parts. The reader may wish to seek particular advice at a given moment and not read from start to finish. The sections structure advice in accordance with the design and construction **process**, the **issues** to be considered in green design, the **strategies** to be adopted and the **elements** of green design. A short fifth section advises on design evaluation. We have sought to minimise repetition at the cost of a greater number of cross-references.

2000 years ago the Roman architect Marcus Vitruvius Pollio wrote the ten books on architecture still referred to in every European architect's education. His work has been translated into many languages and engendered many imitations, some by way of title such as *Vitruvius Britannicus* or *An American Vitruvius*, others by way of content such as L.B. Alberti's *De Architettura* or Palladio's *Quattro Libri*. The concept of the architectural pattern book offering design principles as well as solutions is universally familiar. This book is intended as a green pattern book for today.

The reference to green is not without its own resonance. To the Vitruvian triad of commodity, firmness and delight we postulate the addition of a fourth ideal: restituitas or restitution, restoration, reinstatement: where the act of building enhances its immediate and the global environment in an ecological as well as visual sense.

It would not have been possible to write and publish this book without the generous assistance of the European Commission through the THERMIE project managed by Sr. Angel Landabaso at DG XVII for Energy. Our organisations and the European architectural profession generally are indebted to the Commission for their generous financial, but also moral support in this regard.

ACE-Architects' Council of Europe Brussels-BE │ Eoin O Cofaigh
ERG-Energy Research Group, University College Dublin-IE │ Eileen Fitzgerald Ann McNicholl Robert Alcock J. Owen Lewis
SAFA-Suomen Arkkitehtiliitto, Helsinki-SF │ Vesa Peltonen
Softech, Torino-IT │ Antonella Marucco

The Green Building

THE IMPERATIVE TO GREEN DESIGN

In past centuries, the relative lack of resources to construct and maintain buildings meant energy-conservative and locally sourced inputs were the norm. From Imperial Rome until the nineteenth century only the wealthy could afford thermal baths or orangeries. Since the industrial revolution, but particularly in the present century, the twin phenomena of more widely-diffused wealth and relatively cheaper energy have resulted in widespread increases in energy use. The cost of maintaining a high-efficiency artificial light source is one thousandth of that which a tallow candle represented 100 years ago. Such reductions in proportional cost, and greater affordability, apply not only to energy but to materials produced or transported using energy - which includes all building materials. As a result, the cost of building and running buildings has fallen many times over, and for some decades it was unnecessary to consider every design issue from an energy-cost viewpoint.

In 1973 the first oil crisis prompted governments to seek secure sources of energy and reduce dependency on imported fuel. As the decade wore on, such measures became less urgent. By 1979, the time of the second oil crisis, society had again forgotten about the need to conserve energy. But reduction of dependency on oil is not the main imperative to green design.

It is now impossible to ignore the global environmental crisis, whether this be the destruction of the ozone layer by chlorofluorcarbons, the loss of wildlife habitat and diversity through pollution, desertification and deforestation, or the increasing levels of carbon dioxide caused by emissions from building heating and other inputs. It is primarily for environmental reasons that the European Union, national governments and private citizens invoke higher standards of building design. This action extends beyond buildings to cities and towns, with work on European Sustainable Cities by the Expert Group on the Urban Environment which merits study by architects. The architectural profession itself has been aware of this imperative for some years now, the 1993 'Chicago Declaration' by the Union Internationale des Architectes is a clear statement of intent in this regard, as is much of the content of 'Europe and Architecture Tomorrow' published by the Architects' Council of Europe.

Green design has other advantages also. The ongoing financial savings which energy-efficient design can achieve can be of real importance in daily life. Winter heating costs can consume a significant portion of family income, and the extra floor area afforded by a simply-constructed sunspace is welcome in many crowded households for spatial as well as economic reasons.

The other reason for architects to promote green design is that of architectural quality. Buildings with more natural and fewer artificial inputs are better. Daylit buildings are, in general, more pleasant than artificially lit ones; natural ventilation, if clean air is available from a quiet external environment, is more acceptable than mechanical; the fewer heat emitters, the better; and so on. Mies van der Rohe said that 'Less is more'; today, a better way of putting it may be, as Alexandros Tombazis says: 'Less is beautiful'. Classic design elegance is found in the complete, simple solution.

Architectural quality, quality of service

There are many facets to architectural quality. The European architectural profession promotes competition among architects on the basis of quality of architectural design and quality of service provided to the client. These two issues, building and service, are part of one process.

Quality of architecture at the scale of the fixture or fitting involves suitability for use, durability in performance, and visual delight. Suitability for use involves ergonomic considerations, especially for those who are not ablebodied or strong, and correct selection of materials, related to the functions they will support. Durability of performance involves proper length of life, taking all costs into account including the environmental. Delight derives from elegance, style and the contribution to the building's architecture made by even the smallest details.

At the scale of the building, too, quality of architecture involves suitability, firmness and durability, and delight. Suitability for use: rooms which are the correct size and scale for individual or group use; a place to sleep which is quiet, warm or cool as appropriate for the time of year, with fresh air and somewhere secure to rest; an office which is bright, practical, and which allows us to do good work; a suitable place for ritual or social interaction; a place which can adapt over time to changing functions and needs; and a place which is ecologically sound, with a healthy built environment. Durability in performance: buildings must be dry, economic in energy consumption and maintenance, last for a satisfactory life span, and function without defect. Delight: elegance of proportion, a joy in good craftsmanship, an awareness of the possibilities of colour, light and shade, form and outline, and cultural appropriateness and significance through respect for the past and for regional identity, and through belief in the cultural legitimacy of the present (ACE 1995).

This book is about one aspect of architectural quality: green design.

Over and above design is the issue of quality of service to the client. Good management within the construction project of quality, cost and time is indispensable:

The promoter's interests are: procurement of the desired accommodation at the appropriate level of quality, within an agreed time scale and as rapidly as possible; for an agreed budget and as cheaply as possible; and, for commercial owners – developers – the highest rate of investment return, in a trouble-free design and construction process where the outcome is in line with requirements and predictions (ACE 1995).

Not all clients yet want the sort of service needed to achieve environmentally friendly architecture. Owner-occupiers are generally receptive to discussion of life cycle costing and are conscious of the benefits to the building user of environmentally aware design. However, clients building for immediate disposal may believe that low initial cost is the key issue, and the most such clients may want is to comply with regulations. It is difficult to make green architecture in the face of client indifference. For this reason a part of this book deals with management issues which touch on green design: the architect-client contract, initial and life cycle cost, working with consultants and construction contract administration.

Sustainable design methods offer the architect the opportunity to re-integrate design skills which have diverged in the past century with damaging consequences. In this regard, the synthesis which the architect can make from the varied inputs of colleagues, consultants and clients is invaluable. This provides the architectural profession with a challenge and an opportunity.

PASSIVE SOLAR DESIGN

Passive solar design can improve building energy performance in three areas: building heating, cooling and lighting. The relative importance of these energy-saving contributions varies depending on the building's location and function.

Heating

South-facing surfaces receive more solar radiation in winter and less in summer when compared with surfaces with east or west orientations. This is approximately in phase with the heating requirements. Throughout the year, solar gains through west and south-west glazing are very similar to those through glazing facing east and south-east. In summer, windows facing west can give rise to overheating if they are not protected from the sun's rays, which are at a low angle of incidence.

When solar radiation strikes any material part of it is absorbed, transformed into heat and stored in the mass of the material. The material heats up progressively by conduction as the heat diffuses through it. Materials with high heat storage capacity such as concrete, brick and water heat up and cool down relatively slowly. Thermal insulating materials such as glass fibre and foam, usually because of their open or cellular structure, form poor heat stores and diffuse heat very badly.

The concept of collecting heat through use of walls for thermal mass is mainly applicable to warmer regions where there is a need for heating only at night but where thermal insulation is not necessary. In Northern Europe, more heat will be lost from inside through an uninsulated south-facing wall than can be collected from the sun. External walls must be insulated, preventing the diffusion of solar heat into the wall.

Lighting

Daylighting design involves the provision of natural daylight in the interiors of buildings to reduce or eliminate daytime use of electric lights, thereby offering substantial savings in energy use and consequent environmental damage. If skilfully executed daylighting can provide healthier and more pleasant living conditions.

Various devices are now available to capture daylight and direct it deep into buildings and to reduce excessive light levels near glazing, providing a more uniform spread of natural light. Some of these, such as atria, light shelves, roof monitors or clerestory lighting can have profound architectural design implications. Others such as prismatic glazing reflective blinds or shading systems can be more easily applied in the case of existing buildings. A wide range of specially-treated glazing materials which can control the intensity and optical properties of natural light and heat flows through windows is now available.

Cooling

The most efficient way of protecting a building from unwanted direct sunlight is to shade its windows and other apertures. The degree and type of shade necessary depends on the position of the sun and the geometry of the building. Shutters, blinds, louvres, awnings and curtains are all examples of adjustable shading devices. Some can also be used in winter to increase thermal insulation. Ideally, shading devices should be placed on the exterior.

Even when steps have been taken to shade a building, to reduce heat gains and to minimise the flow of external warm air into the building, internal temperatures in hot climates during summer can often be higher than those outside. Efficient appliances and lighting can minimise internal gains, and appropriate ventilation design can reduce their effects on comfort in summer. Where external air is cooler than the upper comfort limit, fresh air driven through the building by naturally occurring differences in air pressure can help to remedy this problem. Also, when two air masses have different temperatures, their densities and pressures are also different and this gives rise to movement of air from the denser (cooler) zone to the less dense (warmer) one. For example, by providing openings at the top and bottom of the building, warm air will rise naturally and escape from the top outlet while cooler fresh air will enter through the openings at the base.

GREEN DESIGN

While reduced consumption of energy in use is the most important factor in sustainability, strategies to reduce environmental impact are also needed in other areas of building design, construction, and use. These include waste production, building materials and systems, and consumption of natural resources including water, vegetation and soil.

Waste

Construction sector waste is an increasingly urgent issue: a substantial proportion of landfill waste is debris from building and demolition. This can be reduced by better site management, increased use of recycled materials, and conservation and reuse of old buildings.

After completion of the building, it is not the building but the people using it who generate waste. Here, too, reduction and recycling are necessary and citizens throughout the Union are increasingly conscious of this. The architect can facilitate recycling of domestic waste by ensuring adequate possibilities for production of compost, and, in many buildings, for the storage and collection for recycling of non-organic waste.

Materials

Materials have widely varying environmental impacts. Some, such as oil, hardwood timber from non-sustainably managed sources or copper are drawn from limited stocks of non-renewable resources. Others, such as limestone or sand, are more abundant but their extraction, processing and transport to site can cause significant environmental degradation. Others again, such as aluminium, are widely available but consume a lot of energy in their processing. Finally, some materials, such as softwood timber from sustainably managed forests, are relatively abundant and can be extensively and sustainably used.

Different materials have varying impacts on the quality of the indoor environment. Low ventilation rates have brought the quality of indoor air into focus. Banning smoking is a key factor in improving indoor air quality, but beyond this, selection and maintenance of finishes also matter. Finishes which emit volatile organic compounds - plastics - or which retain dust and dirt worsen air quality and can affect the health of the user.

Much research has yet to be done on the relative sustainability of different materials. Superficially similar components may have widely differing environmental impacts in their manufacture and delivery to site. For example, a brick may have been produced 10 km or 1000 km from the site. The environmental impact of the transport involved is enormously different. On the other hand, the local brick may have been less efficiently produced and so the environmental impact of the energy in production will vary. That same energy may have been produced from a sustainable source such as hydroelectricity, or from a non-sustainable source such as nuclear power.
It may yet be that the use of locally produced materials will combine with regional responses to climate and produce a new paradigm of the regionally-based architecture which many people value in Europe's historic environments.

Systems

Ventilation systems, in particular air conditioning, consume significant energy in use and need regular thorough maintenance to prevent growth of micro-organisms which can damage health. Design strategies should seek to eliminate the need for air conditioning in the first instance, and management strategies should ensure that where such systems are installed they are properly looked after.

Natural resources

There are widely varying levels of availability around the Union of water for sanitary and domestic use. In dwellings, much water is consumed by appliances which are generally not specified by the architect. However, in all building types, the architect can specify dual flushing WC cisterns, and photoelectric cell control of sanitary appliances to reduce water consumption. Less water use also implies less demand for water treatment systems.

Rainwater retention and disposal on site, and on-site or local sewage treatment, can mitigate the lowering of the water table, reduce demand for municipal pipework and waste treatment, and reduce shock loads on treatment plants. Designs to dispose of rainwater on site involve separation of polluted run-off from roads and parking areas. Designs to treat grey water on site require space provision for treatment plants or reed beds.

The conservation of indigenous vegetation and topsoil can foster environmental diversity, and provide external shelter. Where a site has topsoil which is to be removed for building, it should be reused on site or collected and re-used elsewhere. The site can be planned to conserve pre-existing vegetation and hedgerows and coppices can be reinforced by planting seedlings taken from the area.

Urban planning

The energy people consume in transport equals that used in buildings. Much research is being done on the connections between density of development, mix of uses, and environmental sustainability including land consumption and transportation, where non-motorised and public transport are to be favoured. The role of the architect as urban planner is touched on but generally lies outside the scope of this publication.

References

- Architects' Council of Europe, (1995), *Europe and Architecture Tomorrow • L'Europe et l'Architecture Demain*, Brussels. Translations have been published by professional architectural organisations in Austria, the Czech Republic, Germany, Greece, Italy, Poland, Portugal, Romania, Spain, and Switzerland.
- Union Internationale des Architectes, (1993), *Declaration of Interdependence for a Sustainable Future:* UIA/AIA World Congress of Architects, Chicago, 18–21 June 1993

Further reading

- Charter of European Cities and Towns towards Sustainability (The Aalborg Charter), 27 May 1994
- European Commission: SECTEUR: Strategic Study on the Construction Sector, DG III, Brussels, 1995
- Europe's Environment: The Dobris Assessment, European Environment Agency, Luxembourg.
- O'Cofaigh E, J A Olley , J O Lewis. (1996), Sustainable Architecture of the Past, in *The Climatic Dwelling*, London, James and James (Science Publishers) Ltd.

Section 1: Process

INTRODUCTION

Every experienced architect is familiar with the different stages of the design and construction process, and, at the time of writing, the 20 or so groupings of architects in the Architects' Council of Europe have at least a dozen documents describing its structure in their respective countries. For this book, we use the 1994 ACE breakdown, arrived at by consensus among the organisations concerned:

- Design:
- Preliminary studies
- Sketch studies
- Pre-project
- Basic project
- Execution of project

- Construction:
- Tender procedure
- Supervision
- Acceptance
- Defects period

We have decided to add a section on Inception and to extend into the period after handover, by adding a section on Refurbishment. The reader will be able to identify the stages in this book with those used in his or her day-to-day work.

The management of this process is not the architect's exclusive responsibility. In varying measures, at all stages, from pre-project, through the project and the detail design to construction and acceptance, the architect may be exclusively responsible, have shared responsibility, or merely play a partial role. However, there is always an architect-client contract, there is a project brief and the architect must work with specialist consultants, whether professional engineers or contractors with design responsibility. National building regulations are inescapable. No matter what the precise extent of the architect's responsibility on cost estimation, the definition of quality includes reasonable value for money.

The input of the architect and the other actors - client, engineering, cost and other technical specialists, contractors and subcontractors - differs greatly from stage to stage. The extent to which the architect can influence the environmental impact of the completed building varies with the stages also, but at every stage environmental performance can be improved. As landmarks such as building permit or building regulations approval are reached the potential for redesign is reduced. The potential for improvement is greatest at the initial stages.

Any list of key issues will be arbitrary. We might have chosen three, or six, or twenty. The most important issues vary with climate, and hence with project location. Key issues also vary with building size and complexity, and with building use, and hence the demand for heating, cooling, ventilation or daylight. A summary list should be treated with caution. However, the design process balances many different issues, and somehow the architect must manage to deal intuitively with all those issues, especially at the early stages. So a table of key strategies at different stages is provided (Table 1.1).

Table 1.1   GREEN STRATEGIES AT DIFFERENT STAGES

Stage	Issues
INCEPTION	• Briefing: identify green design as an issue to be considered • Agree environmental performance targets for the building • Prefer brownfield to greenfield sites
DESIGN **Preliminary Studies**	• Analyse sites for sunlight, shelter and available shading • Research the building type and analyse good practice examples • Consider what is achievable given the cost constraints
Sketch Studies	• Site layout: use passive solar strategies, including daylight • Provide solar access to residential living spaces • Use thermal mass to dampen temperature fluctuations • Maximise daylight penetration using plan and section • Consider water supply and waste handling methods • Use locally produced materials • Make iterative studies of design concepts to assess performance
Pre-Project	• Consider room heights for heating, cooling and daylighting • Consider thermal mass for building use pattern: intermittent or continuous • Optimise proportion and distribution of external envelope openings with heating and lighting in mind • Specify design criteria for services • Calculate predicted building performances and assess against targets
Basic Project	• Finalise layout (plans, sections, elevations) for statutory approvals: implications for daylight/ventilation/passive and active systems • Select materials and construction methods having regard to thermal mass, openings and shading, sourcing of materials
Execution of Project	• Develop specifications for good workmanship and site management • Detail for thermal performance, daylight, controlled ventilation • Specify window and external door frames for environmental performance • Consider internal and external finishes for environmental friendliness • Consider environmental performance in selection of heating and cooling plant, radiators, controls • Specify electrical lighting equipment and controls for lowest consumption • Specify sanitary fittings for low water consumption
CONSTRUCTION **Tender Procedure**	• Explain the requirements of green design to tendering contractors • Specify more demanding construction practices and tolerances
Supervision	• Protect the natural landscape of the site as much as possible • Ensure completeness of insulation coverings and no thermal bridging at openings • Contractor should not substitute materials or components without architect's approval • Ensure acceptable methods of waste disposal
Acceptance	• Make sure client and users understand building concepts and systems (provide maintenance manuals) • Show how to get maximum value from the active systems controls
Defects Period	• Monitor active systems for actual as against projected performance
MAINTENANCE AND REFURBISHMENT	• Use green finishes materials where these were originally applied • Use environmentally-acceptable cleaning and sanitation materials • Undertake energy audit prior to commencing project • Survey the potential for upgrading of active services • Survey the potential for upgrading of envelope • Consider indoor air quality and healthy building environment

INCEPTION

The client-architect relationship

The scope of services to be provided
In some Member States, the content of the client-architect contract is regulated by law, with the scope of the architect's appointment, fees to be charged and conditions of the architect's appointment prescribed by the State. Elsewhere, these matters are negotiated individually.

Fees for green design
Certain marketing advantages may accrue to providing what have often been seen as the 'special services' of green design at no extra cost to the client. Leaving this aside, there are conflicting viewpoints about the ethical acceptability of charging special fees for green design services.

Many architects feel that professional duty indicates that they should undertake sustainable design work as part of their standard service. No building designed at this time which ignores environmental issues can be said to be good architecture.

On the other hand, extra work is inevitably involved in a service which results in improved environmental performance, reduced energy consumption and lower life-cycle financial cost (see Table 1.2). Many architects are of the view that such work merits compensation by way of an appropriate extra fee. Until materials and component suppliers provide sustainability-related information on their products as a matter of course, a good deal of time can be spent assessing environmental performance of materials. Also, contractors may need time-consuming reassurance about innovative aspects of the work, and much time may be needed for particularly thorough site inspections.

Table 1.2	GREEN TASKS WHICH MIGHT BE IDENTIFIED IN THE CLIENT-ARCHITECT CONTRACT
Stage	**Tasks**
Preliminary Studies	• Advising on sustainability issues (environmental and life cycle cost,goal setting for the project) • Interviewing consultants for competence in sustainability • Making topographical models to study shelter and insolation • Analysing site microclimate • Above-normal levels of interdisciplinary work.
Sketch Studies and Pre-Project	• Calculations of environmental performance objectives for heating and cooling • Special research on sustainable systems, materials and components • Advising inexpert consultants on environmental issues and holistic performance • Studying alternative methods of complying with building regulations, particularly with regard to thermal insulation, heating, cooling and ventilation standards, water supply and consumption and waste disposal and treatment.
Basic Project	• Studies of room interiors to optimise daylighting and minimise glare • Redesign work and detail studies of building facades to optimise energy performance
Tender Procedure	• Pre-qualifying contractors in relation to special requirements • Checking to avoid uncompetitive loading of tenders • Preparing advice to contractors on site protection
Acceptance, Defects Period and Maintenance	• Preparing special manuals with life cycle costing advice • Advising clients on use of passive and active environmental features in the building
Refurbishment	• Making comparative life cycle cost analyses of new build as against refurbishment costs • Environmentally auditing of existing buildings

Finally, it is correct that particular expertise in any professional area, whether green design or any other, be appropriately rewarded.

Every architect will individually decide this, having regard to the individual circumstances of fee negotiation, personal and client commitment, degree of expertise available and so on. At the same time, it will never be possible to isolate fully time spent in sustainable design research and studies and recover all the extra cost involved. Where they have not done so already, national professional organisations should consider incorporating 'green design clauses' in their standard client-architect contracts.

Consultants

Scope of input

The choice of consultants is important, especially at the outset of the project. They should be competent, firstly to understand the issues involved and, secondly to give the architect the best advice. In a green design process the focus of specialist consultants will often be different (see Table 1.3). In the green building, consultants first maximise the use of passive environmental control measures, having regard to life cycle as well as initial cost. Only then should they incorporate active systems. By increasing the passive contribution, active systems can often be much smaller, and of a radically different nature, than those in a conventional building.

A second way in which the nature of some specialist inputs is different in green design is in precision of estimating. Conventional engineering, particularly in space heating, cooling or artificial lighting systems, attains to constant pre-determined design standards. The primacy of passive measures means that some degree of tolerance, or lack of fixed conditions, is to be accepted. Studies show, moreover, that building users tolerate wider environmental variation when they themselves can influence the situation, for example by opening a window or turning on a light, and significant cost and energy savings can be achieved by even small shifts in design temperatures.

Appointing consultants

In selecting consultants, the architect should specify from the outset that sustainability is a fundamental consideration in the project, and identify the consultant's level of understanding in this regard. The goal of the design process is to integrate specialist areas to achieve optimum performance of the total building, not to achieve optimum performance of the separate parts; and performance is to be considered over the project life cycle, through design, use and decommissioning.

Consultants' fees are often calculated as a proportion of the cost of the specialist work. Where mechanical and electrical engineering services are concerned, this might for commercial reasons tend to increase the scope of heating, cooling, lighting and ventilation installations. The cost of the services installations is regularly as high as 30–35% of total project cost. It may be useful to agree a different fee basis, and calculate the fee as a proportion of the total cost. This has the advantage of allowing for advice even where there may be no conventional service installations. Daylighting studies, calculation of alternative heat losses and gains and of ventilation rates, and modelling of total building performance are all indispensable to environmentally aware design, and engineers are often better equipped than architects to carry out the numerical, as opposed to intuitive, studies, necessary in any moderately complex building. An added refinement to the total building percentage fee is to pay a fee premium inversely related to the energy costs during the 12 months after handover, measured on a $kWh/m^2/yr$ index. Alternatively, the fee can be calculated on a hourly basis, or be fixed. A fixed fee can act as an incentive to minimise the scope and complexity of specialist measures to be installed.

Early consultant site visits and multi-disciplinary project meetings can contribute enormously to project success.

Table 1.3   KEY AREAS FOR GREEN SPECIALIST ADVICE

Building Structure	• Re-use of demolition spoil and use of as-found materials • Embodied energy: use of composite structures to maximise use of low embodied energy materials and systems • Structural systems using sustainable materials (timber, earth, straw) • Ease of demolition and recycling • Long-life, loose fit design (good load bearing capacity, generous floor to ceiling heights) • Relationship between mass and thermal performance
Envelope Design	• Relationship of openable area to lighting and thermal performance • Sustainable materials (finishes: paints, floor coverings; external wall openings; framing, glazing types; insulation)
Lighting Services	• Maximisation of available daylight use: daylighting studies including daylight factor studies, daylighting simulations • Selection and location of lighting components: task lighting, high efficiency fittings • Lighting management: controls to integrate natural and artificial light,
Electrical Power	• Minimisation of electricity consumption: isolation of electrical circuits at night-time, optimised cable sizing, low-energy lifts • Combined heat and power generation systems to maximise total energy efficiency
Heating Engineering	• Maximisation of passive heating techniques: Advice on building planning and on facade design to maximise useful solar gain, comparative U-value calculations to ensure effective passive contribution, modelling of heat flows through the building in different temperature situations at different times of the year • Maximum efficiency of active heating measures: Selection of heating method and fuel, combined heat and power, high efficiency heat emitters for the smaller quantities of heat involved, air and water plant size optimisation, optimisation of controls including Building Energy Management systems (BEMs), VAV air heating systems and fully ducted systems with optional free cooling • Input on life cycle costing calculations • Energy calculations to take account of passive gains • Combined heat and power on larger projects
Cooling Engineering	• Maximisation of passive cooling techniques: Thermal mass and ventilation to promote passive cooling measures Modelling of temperature changes to predict internal in relation to ambient temperatures, advice on facade design, and modelling of shading and daylight/solar gain • Active systems to minimise energy consumption including optional free cooling in ventilation systems
Water Services	• Minimisation of water consumption through component selection for water conservation, and by re-use of grey water • Small-scale self-contained waste treatment systems
Ventilation	• Building modelling to maximise through ventilation and stack effect ventilation for cooling
Cost Estimating	• Comparative life cycle cost studies, for individual components and alternative systems, to incorporate initial cost, cost in use, cost of demolition and re-use including recycling • Environmental cost accounting
Baumeister / Bureau d'études	• Inspection of construction quality but particularly for air tightness of envelope, efficiency of active systems, particularly heating
Landscaping	• Site assessment, including land contamination, methane, radon and landfill gas, hydrology • Environmental assessment, including ecological issues • Soft landscaping for life cycle winter solar access (height of vegetation, shading, light reflection,sunlight penetration) and shelter (prevailing wind directions and intensity, modelling of earth berms) • Passive cooling and urban design • Indigenous vegetation: conservation and propagation • Waste treatment plants (reed beds)

- *To develop the brief for the project, with and on behalf of the client , and with the involvement of the specialist consultants. This task involves research of the client's requirements with regard to project quality, timescale and cost.*

- *The brief includes all information and requirements produced through dialogue between the client and the design team, on the site; schedules of accommodation; room and building functional, environmental and spatial performance;project cost and timescale;post-handover maintenance;and the budget.*

Briefing

Work at the briefing stage is very important in sensitising client and consultants to green design issues.

The process of assembling a brief with the client is mutually informative. Briefs change as the client's intentions for building size, performance, cost and project timescale emerge. With sustainable design, unless the client is better informed than the architect, the architect must advise on the potential of good design to improve environmental performance. So, the process of constructing the brief becomes one of sharing information in the light of the potential for a sustainable building. Explanation of a long-life, loose-fit, low-energy strategy at this stage will help the client come to terms with much of what is involved.

There may be a choice of site available. Input regarding sustainability issues can help determine site choice. See advice on greenfield as against brownfield sites, access to public transport, solar access, overshadowing, shelter, and quality of land.

Where the client is not an expert in green issues, it is necessary to discuss the appointment of green consultants and also the extent to which the client may accept or welcome alternative performance criteria for the sake of a better building. These would include, for example, a variable internal environment and higher initial costs.

Initial and life cycle cost

A major issue with which green design must engage is that of initial as against life-cycle building cost. The construction cost of good design is often no greater than that for poor design. On the other hand it is true that increased spending on higher quality components is often worthwhile. Thicker insulation materials, low-emissivity glazing, passive infrared detector lighting switches, weather compensating controls on heating systems and photoelectric cell controls on artificial lighting are more expensive initially than conventional components. However, in many cases these cost differentials are falling, and higher initial costs can be recouped quite quickly by savings in running costs.

For the owner-occupier, the decision is easier than for, for example, the tenant undertaking a fit-out; but until external environmental costs are in some way factored into direct cost, the decision may still be difficult. Many promoters building to sell or lease will find a four-year payback time acceptable as this can be factored into a sale or letting price without total loss. Depending on the length of lease, tenants may find payback times of up to 10 years worthy of consideration. Far-sighted owner occupiers may consider payback times of up to 25 years. The public benefits of good design can endure for centuries, as the historic centres of so many European cities attest.

Table 1.4   ISSUES AT BRIEFING STAGE

General	- Will the client actively manage the environmental control systems on a day-to-day basis? This will be important in manipulating shutters, for example, unless everything is to be automated. - If there is a choice between refurbishment and new build, explore client preconceptions and see whether lower standards are acceptable in structural capacity and environmental control, to retain the existing fabric. - Review and agree design comfort standards with a view to reducing energy demand - Explain the need for climatic data on the site: macro-climate; material from meteorological stations and micro-climate; survey work may be necessary.
Building Use	- Use patterns (diurnal, weekly and seasonal) affect environmental requirements and choice of structure and systems. Is the building used intermittently or regularly? Are there long holiday periods? Construct a use profile of the building: occupants and activities at different times of day and week.

ISSUES AT BRIEFING STAGE (continued)

Architect	• What green expertise does the architect have? Don't pretend expert knowledge without dedicated training and/or substantial experience. • Explain that the subject is not yet definitively researched and that much remains to be done in researching green urban planning and materials, for example.
Consultants	• Do you recommend that environmental, daylighting or energy consultants be appointed? • Who will pay for these? • Can this cost be offset against 'normal' consultants? Does the client intend to nominate consultants? If so, do they have 'green' expertise or do they need to be supplemented by specialists? • Ensure that the scope of appointments includes the requisite environmental advice.
Heating	• Explain the possibility of passive measures: their contribution to performance. • Can the client use sunspaces if these are provided? • How does the client feel about draught lobbies? About zoning the plan? • Are weather compensating controls justified? • Will the client use 7-day programmable controls? • Would the client consider a CHP installation?
Cooling	• Will the client countenance passive cooling measures if these are judged useful? • How precise is the level of environmental control required? (Can temperatures go above comfort levels, say, 5 days per year? Or never?)
Lighting	• Is daylight maximisation a desirable goal? • Will the client pay for passive infrared switching? For individual light switching? For photoelectric override of active systems?
Ventilation	• Will the occupant operate manually operated trickle vents in windows? • Is passive stack ventilation an option (it may be in apartment buildings)? • In what areas is mechanically assisted ventilation required? • Identify the possibilities of heat exchangers, discuss capital against life cycle costs
Water	• Would the client pay for low-water WC cisterns and lavatory controls, spray taps? (depends on water tariffs, explain that these are subject to gradual increase.) Similar issues surround domestic appliances (dishwasher, washing machines.)
Waste	• Discuss disposing of surface water run-off on site, and advise on the need for treating run-off from car parks • Is composting of domestic refuse on site acceptable? • What provision might be made for recycling of paper, of packaging? Extra storage space needed?
Site Works	• Identify existing vegetation to be conserved and discuss how this affects the design. • Discuss the provision of sheltered and secure bicycle storage on site.
Materials	• Explore the possibility of alternative structural systems and materials, which might influence load-bearing capacity. • Discuss performance of finishes, especially internal wall and floor finishes, and of window and external door materials, in connection with improved indoor air quality, as against ongoing maintenance requirements.
Cost	• To what extent is the client concerned with life-cycle issues? Explain life-cycle costing: investigate the client's intention for the building: short or long-life investment? It is not yet easy to demonstrate that green design increases capital value. It may be necessary to benchmark the building cost against that of comparable non-sustainable buildings. • Try to obtain agreement that a measure of life-cycle costing may be factored into all design and specification decisions.
Timescale	• Does the design team require more time at any stage in the process to explore design issues? For example: alternative site studies, daylighting studies, and heating and cooling calculations at sketch design stage, particularly if few persons are available to undertake specialist tasks.
Contractor	• Discuss the steps needed to select the contractor and how the green design will impact on the construction process.

Preliminary Studies:
Scope of architect's services

Analysis, studies and consulta-
tions of budgetary, administra-
tive, town planning and technical
character, so as to assimilate the
legal, financial and technical
constraints necessary for the
setting up of the project
based on the client's brief.

The documents and services to be
provided include:
- *research and analysis*
- *town planning studies*
- *examination of the site to*
  take account of the chosen
  approach
- *analysis of administrative*
  constraints
- *feasibility of the brief on the*
  site.

Preliminary Studies

Preliminary studies explore the broad alternative design possibilities for the project, having investigated town planning and other regulatory constraints (such as regulations on pollution, construction, noise, waste), and weighed up cost and time considerations. Site surveys should be to hand, to include not only topographical information but also information about site environmental quality and potential. All the design team should be involved in this work.

Where town planning constraints on site density, waste treatment, or car parking seem likely to adversely affect the design, identify these issues and raise them with the Planning Authority.

Depending on the nature of the project, preliminary studies may involve alternative site development strategies, in which case issues of insolation, overshadowing of buildings and of adjoining sites and shelter come into play. At a larger scale, or where a refurbishment or extension project is concerned, alternative dispositions of layout may allow varying scope for future energy-conscious design: organising the plan to place rooms requiring heat on south-facing facades and so on. In either case the issues raised will need to be examined in greater detail at the later stages.

The Preliminary Studies will generally be accompanied by a report. It may be useful to incorporate a section to specifically identify green issues (Table 1.5). Headings which may be useful would include: Site selection, including land quality, access to building and local services; Site analysis, including overshadowing, solar access, shelter.

Table 1.5   ISSUES AT PRELIMINARY STUDIES STAGE

Site	• Obtain environmental information about the site. • Examine the environmental impact of alternative strategies. • Examine a number of alternative sites if this option is available. • Incorporate green issues into the feasibility studies reports.

Sketch Studies

Decisions at this early stage in the design are of the utmost importance, when the project acquires a provisional direction. Alternative floor plans are explored; there is a site planning and/or a building organisation strategy and a concept for the sections through the building and materials are given some thought (Table 1.6), although it is quite likely that none of these matters are yet fixed. Costs have been broadly computed.

Despite engineering imperatives, numerical evaluation can still be a hindrance at this stage in arriving at the optimum solution. To achieve holistic design quality, the architect makes decisions based on intuition, which synthesise experience, training and imagination and are based on an interdisciplinary input from consultants. Intuition, of course, is subsequently explored and tested rigorously.

Table 1.6	ISSUES AT SKETCH STUDIES STAGE
Site Plan	• Protection and use of pre-existing site characteristics: vegetation, landscaping, topography, water; site disposition for insolation, shading and shelter; proportion of hard landscaping for water run-off or conservation; vegetation and shelter; cold air drainage. • Orientation, zoning and general disposition, with impact on energy consumption.
Building Plan Section	• Section height and depth, number of floors and orientation to optimise daylighting, to enable passive ventilation using the stack effect and to reduce heat loss. Which factors can be optimised through shallow plans, high floor to ceiling heights, and roof lighting via the ceiling or an atrium.
Elevation	• Broad proportions of fenestration, with effects on daylighting, ventilation, overheating on east, west and south facades, which can be passively controlled by the use of external shading devices.
Materials	• Structural system (concrete, steel or timber) and external envelope, and their environmental impact.

Sketch Studies:
Scope of architect's services

Initiation and graphic presentation of alternative architectural solutions, enabling the client to understand the possible solutions and take decisions about their further development, involving:

* *developing the initial concept and proposing one or several general solutions for the overall forms translating the main elements of the brief;*
* *defining the general technical solutions envisaged;*
* *indicating the approximate timetable for carrying out the proposals;*
* *examining the compatibility of the proposals with the overall provisional budget;*
* *solutions which will facilitate subsequent proposals for adaptation of the programme and preparation of the complementary technical studies.*

The documents and services to be provided include:

* *an analysis of the brief*
* *a summary of the thinking behind the proposed solutions*
* *drawings to show a preliminary architectural solution in sketch form.*

Pre-Project:
Scope of architect's services

To develop the general form of the project, in plan, section and elevation, based on the preferred solution and derived from the chosen design approach, involving:

- *defining the general composition on plan;*
- *confirming the compatibility of the chosen solution with the requirements of brief and site, and with the various regulations applicable;*
- *examining the functional relationships between the different elements of the brief and the spaces provided;*
- *establishing the building's appearance, its broad dimensions and the types of materials, which, when taken together, facilitate a summary estimate of construction cost.*
- *consultations with Public Authorities;*
- *co-ordinating the work of any technical specialists.*

The documents and services to be provided include:

- *a report explaining the general concept;*
- *floor plans at 1:100 [1:200 for large projects] with significant details at 1:50;*
- *elevations and sections at 1:100 [1:200 for large projects];*
- *site and landscaping plans at 1:200 [1:500 for large projects];*
- *description of types of materials;*
- *general timetable for the execution of the project;*
- *summary estimate of provisional costs;*
- *explanation of the technical principles applied;*
- *consultation with administrative authorities and technical consultants.*

Pre-Project

At pre-project stage the provisional direction previously sketched is amended and developed through plans, sections and elevations. Earlier decisions are confirmed or modified. The building acquires a definitive form, layout, type of construction and method of servicing. Materials are proposed. The initial investigations of comfort and environment should now be confirmed by numerical studies, generally by consultants (Table 1.7). Following approvals from administrative authorities, it becomes increasingly difficult to make major changes.

Table 1.7   ISSUES AT PRE-PROJECT STAGE

Site Plan and External Landscaping	• Consider layout and orientation of building groups in relation to insolation and overshadowing. • Consider size and location of hard surfaces, in relation to desired sunlight and shelter. • Use earth berms and shelter planting to create protected and sheltered areas.
Building Plan and Section	• Provide draught lobbies at entrances where necessary. • Optimise use of daylight in habitable spaces. • In northern latitudes, zone areas such as sanitary, circulation and storage to the north. • Include air flow paths for natural ventilation in plan [if the building is shallow] and section [perhaps employing the stack effect].
Elevation	• Consider proportions of glazing to opaque facade for daylight distribution and passive heating and cooling. • Control glare and overheating, particularly on east and west facades: consider shading devices [external louvres or set backs, blinds].
Materials	• Consider use of structural thermal inertia to dampen internal temperature fluctuations. • Consider sustainability and environmental impact of materials, embodied energy, impact on habitats, toxic emissions and ease of recycling or re-use.
Specialist Consultants	• Presentations should indicate how environmental principles will be developed at detailed design stage, and how proposals will be evaluated, with maximum use of passive systems.
Technical Principles	• Consider combined heat and power to reduce primary energy use. • Provide outline illustration of environmental performance, particularly through plan and section diagrams for passive and active energy flows: heating season – day; heating season – night; cooling season – day; cooling season – night, and Sankey diagrams of energy flow.

Cost	• Consider factoring environmental and life cycle cost into initial estimates.
	• Where higher initial cost is proposed this may be for better performance, improved environmental quality, and/or lower life cycle energy and environmental cost, e.g.,
	  • high quality as against poor quality timber window frames
	  • linoleum floor finish as against petrol chemical based sheet floor finishes – more acceptable emissions and smell
	  • compact fluorescent light bulbs as opposed to tungsten, passive infra red switching
	• Design for re-cycling.

Administrative Authorities	• Consult about innovative propositions for fresh water supply, rain water disposal or reuse, grey and black water disposal. • Discuss advantageous tariffs for low consumption with utilities. • If the building generates electricity [photo-voltaic panels, wind] discuss buy-back with the utility company as necessary.

Basic project

Applications for building permit require definitive presentation of the design. Glazing proportions will need to be analysed, using sketch design evaluation tools such as the LT Method (Refer EVALUATION).

For Building Regulations approval the principal green design issues will be those of sustainable materials and calculations for energy performance, embodied energy and, sometimes, of structural design as regards thermal mass. Some States accept innovative energy calculation methods. Elsewhere, prescribed calculation methods will have to be followed.

When developing the structural design consider low energy and long life. e.g., greater cover to reinforcement, protection of structural steel. Long life design is particularly important for pre-stressed concrete, which is difficult to demolish for recycling or re-use using present technology.

The building's adaptability to future, unpredictable uses involves both structure and services. A load-bearing capacity greater than indicated in the engineering codes applicable to the function being accommodated might be useful. For example, it might be that the floor-loading capacity and hence the structural system employed for a residential building would differ from that required in an office [higher load-bearing capacity, larger spans] and the design should consider such flexibility of function. The loose functional fit afforded by a framed structure may make such a system preferable to one of load-bearing walls. Design for future services, flexibility and renewal.

The technical consultants prepare submissions for architect, client and Statutory Authorities on the building services systems and building energy performance. Energy consumption should be calculated in $kWh/m^2/yr$, this being the most widely used unit. Make calculations under the headings:
Heating • Cooling • Lighting • Fans, pumps, controls • Small power • Total

Results can be compared to normalised performance indicators for that building type in the given climate, proving a good projection of building performance and an indication of relative achievement.

Basic Project: Scope of architect's services

To obtain legal authorisation for construction and, to this end, to undertake whatever detailed design is necessary, with the integration of the work of specialist consultants where required. Beyond this stage, as changes may involve repeated consultations with statutory authorities, relatively little change will be possible to the form and many of the technical specifications. The project takes account of all applicable regulations and integrates the technical and architectural factors needed to relate the building to the site.

The documents and services to be provided include:

- *a descriptive report on the general characteristics of the project;*
- *plans of all floor levels, sections and elevations at scale 1: 50 [1:100 for major projects],*
- *an updating of the programme;*
- *a summary estimate of costs of the works, detailed by construction element;*
- *procedural documents such as construction permits.*

Table 1.8   ISSUES AT BASIC PROJECT STAGE

Site and Building Plans	• Confirm earlier decisions on site and building plans: siting and positioning for insolation and shelter; form for over-shadowing; layout and extent of hard and soft landscaping. • Consider disposal of surface water within the site. • Consider treatment of polluted water from vehicle hard standings.
Section and Elevation	• Confirm floor to floor heights to maximise daylight and natural ventilation and avoid overheating. • Confirm facade proportions, and provision and design of external shading to prevent overheating. • Consider opening sections in windows for passive ventilation. • Confirm previous decisions on sustainable materials.
Specialist Consultants	• Consider long life and loose fit building structure and the adaptability of structure and services for different building use. • Long-term adequacy of load-bearing capacity. • Ensure accessibility to ductwork, pipes and wires, with removable covers, demountable trunking. • Size conduit drops in walls for easy rewiring.
Technical Principles	• Develop design of building services systems from the principles previously enunciated. • Make calculations of building energy performance.

Project

Detail design, particularly of the external envelope; technical specification of building components and workmanship; and coordination of the engineering consultants, particularly mechanical and electrical services but also structural, have considerable implications for green design.

Detail the external envelope for best performance. (The most sustainable material for glazing frames is softwood timber; however, in a long-life building, thermally broken composite frames may also be an appropriate choice.)

Select roof and floor finishes for long life: the proportional extra cost of better sheet materials is more than offset by longer service life.

When designing mechanical services in detail, specify components for good energy performance over a long life.

Specify sanitary fittings to minimise water consumption in use.

Mechanical ventilation systems increasingly include heat recovery components. In residential buildings, proprietary components achieve about 70% heat recovery. These require ducts of typically 100mm diameter to and from living and circulation spaces to a central collection point, frequently in the roof space, from where air is expelled to the outside or drawn in.

Passive infra-red light switching is falling in cost. Compact fluorescent lighting devices are cost-effective with short payback periods. Use task lighting where possible and design for lower ambient lighting levels.

Locally produced masonry: clay bricks, concrete blocks, and tiles reduce the environmental impact of transporting heavy materials. (Refer ELEMENTS; Materials)

Table 1.9   ISSUES AT PROJECT STAGE

Site Plan	• Specify rainwater soak-aways and ponds. • Closed sewage treatment systems.
Section and Elevation	• Select glazing frames for best performance. • Glazing to incorporate low emissivity coatings. • Use trickle ventilators, and/or passive ventilation strategies. • Use heat recovery where appropriate. • Insulate beyond building regulation requirements in sustainable materials. • Detail to avoid cold bridging.
Materials	• Specify for long life and low embodied energy. • Masonry components of local origin, roof finishes for long life, greater thicknesses of sheet flooring, timber boards of low formaldehyde content, lime-based plaster mixes and acrylic and/or water-based paints are healthier. • Monitor consultants to ensure strategy agreed at earlier stages is implemented.
Technical Principles and Application	• Specify mechanical services components for good energy performance over long life:gas fired condensing boilers,best available thermostatic radiator valves, weather compensating heating system controls, underfloor low pressure hot water central heating, mechanical ventilation systems to include heat recovery components, low energy lift installations, passive infrared light switching and compact fluorescent lighting, dual flushing WC cisterns, photoelectric cell operated urinals and washbasins, energy and resource efficient domestic appliances. • Minimise hot water pipe lengths from storage to point of use.

Tender Procedure

Tender documents should take account of green principles (Table 1.10). Some contractors, particularly specialist mechanical, ventilation and sanitary engineering contractors, will be required to provide detailed design services as part of their works. If the architect wants sustainable design, this should be made clear because of the need for properly competitive bids and to see that innovation is fully taken into account by tenderers. Particular components should be specified by type or name where necessary. These would include:

- mechanical services: energy-efficient heating systems, radiators, and controls;
- electrical services: energy-efficient switching, light fittings;
- sanitary engineering: water-efficient fittings and equipment.

Where a main contractor is providing a package deal, instructions on selection of components and design of systems should be provided. Such instructions would include:

- structural system: long service life, high load-bearing capacity, low embodied energy and sustainable materials where possible;
- completion elements: window and door glazing and frame types and coatings;
- finishes: floor and wall finishes for long service life, to be specified;
- wall, floor and ceiling materials within minimal toxic out-gassing.

Apart from the design elements to be priced by contractors on a design-and-build or package-deal basis, the conventional contractual arrangements can be influenced by sustainable design. Limiting working space is important in conserving pre-existing vegetation. Specification clauses requiring contractors to protect and subsequently avoid all such areas, with drawings indicating the relevant areas, can improve levels of site protection. Clauses requiring the retention and reuse on site of all topsoil will conserve this resource.

These issues should be considered in addition to normal good construction practice.

Tender Procedure

The architect prepares and issues the tender documents, to assist the client in letting the construction contract(s). The client will choose the tendering method, whether by a main contractor, a package deal, a number of specialist contractors or a combination of these. The architect examines and verifies tenders received and takes part in any negotiations. The documents and services to be provided include:

- *provision and issuing of tender documents: contract form(s), any collateral agreements, tender forms;*
- *a report on tenders received, to include tender comparisons and analysis.*

Table 1.10   ISSUES AT TENDER STAGE

Site Plan	• Limit contractors' working space to protect pre-existing natural features and vegetation. • Specify to conserve and re-use top soil. • Give directions on materials handling and storage to minimise waste.
Specialist Contractors	• Make green design requirements explicit in all tender packages, especially in specialist packages for design and construct works. These requirements will include directives on the use of as-found material; on construction waste minimisation, handling and disposal; and on the use of environmentally-friendly cleaning materials.

Scope of architect's services

At construction stage, the architect checks the general conformity with the designs of the works being executed. Any instructions needed for the contractors to coordinate and correctly execute the works are provided.

The documents and services to be provided include:

- *preparation of contract documents, including the contract, drawings, specifications and any guarantees;*
- *programming separate contractors where applicable;*
- *monitoring the construction work in accordance with the project timetable, applicable rules and standards, and the contract documents, with regard to building dimensions, quality, standards and appearance;*
- *issuing instructions for executing the works;*
- *arranging and recording of site and progress meetings;*
- *making periodic valuations of the works.*

Inspection

On site, the main contractor deals with his own staff and with a host of specialists. Many issues come into play: construction quality, adherence to tight programmes, and efficient control of labour and materials costs, having regard to site safety and unpredictable weather. The architect checks that the specified components and materials are provided and that instructions on respecting previously existing landscape or other site features are adhered to (Table 1.11).

Environmentally-conscious construction management and the correct execution of certain items of work can considerably improve building performance. Measured studies of buildings constructed to an identical design show significant variations in energy consumption which, while partly attributable to different building users, arise also from the standard of construction. The main area of concern is the external envelope. Items to pay particular attention to include:

- quality of external facing masonry to minimise heat losses by casual air infiltration;
- installation of insulation, to avoid localised thermal bridging through omission at, for example, corners or elements of structure;
- weather tightness of opening elements such as windows and external doors;
- sealing of openings around pipes;
- installation of vapour control membranes, free from punctures.

Substitution by the contractor of less acceptable components for the ones specified may lead to incorrect specification of double glazed units, insulation, or paint. For such components, as well as for mechanical and electrical components, check delivery invoices when in doubt.

Toxic waste, including asbestos insulation, and asbestos-cement sheeting, should be disposed of off-site in an approved waste storage facility.

The contractor should perform straightforward housekeeping measures to minimise construction waste; and to store polythene and cardboard packaging materials for recycling. Correct handling and storage of materials will reduce waste.

Table 1.11	ISSUES AT INSPECTION STAGE
Check Proper Procedure	• Gathering and storage on site of topsoil for subsequent re-use. • Specified components and materials are provided. • Adequate protection of existing landscape, water, vegetation and other site features. • Correct handling and storage of materials. • Use of any as-found elements such as hardcore or earth. • Storage for recycling of polythene and cardboard packaging. • Use of environmentally friendly cleaning agents.
Check Construction Standards	• Correct installation of insulation. • Correct working of materials for health: cutting, spraying. • Quality of external facing masonry. • Weather tightness of opening elements. • Sealing of openings around pipes penetrating the external envelope. • Vapour control membranes. • Low emissivity coatings on glazing. • Correct disposal of toxic waste. • Housekeeping regarding waste materials and recycling of packaging.

Acceptance

Prior to acceptance of the building for the client, the architect inspects the building for final completion in accordance with the drawings and specifications. Hand-over can involve provision of as-constructed drawings and specifications, advice on system and component maintenance and repair, guidance on performance of services installations and, increasingly, a Safety File with advice on safe maintenance and repair (Table 1.12). Whether the design features are passive or active, the client will best optimise building performance by having the working of the building thoroughly explained and illustrated. Advice on environmentally-conscious maintenance of the building will also be valuable.

Table 1.12   ACCEPTANCE: ADVICE ON BUILDING OPERATION AND MAINTENANCE

Correct Building Maintenance	• Maintaining and renewing floor and wall finishes selected for health and environmental performance. • Regular cleaning of windows and luminaires. • Maintaining sanitary components to minimise water consumption. • Maintaining internal and external planting. • Use of sustainable, non-toxic, biodegradable cleaning agents. • Application of paint and thin film coatings in properly ventilated spaces. • Annual inspection of active systems to check continued efficiency of boilers, cooling equipment, radiator valves, infrared switching, heating and cooling controls.
Operating Energy Management Systems	• Operating systems to prevent overheating in summer: moveable shading, night-time cooling. • Operating ventilation systems: both mechanically assisted and passive: fans, natural ventilation, to optimise balance of ventilation, heating and cooling demand. • Operating the building to maximise heat gain in the heating season: control of night-time ventilation, operating blinds to maximise insolation, closing internal doors to retain captured heat, opening shutters to promote desired ventilation. • Illustrating the mechanical system controls such as programming time clocks, operating weather compensating controls, setting thermostatic radiator valves, seasonal manipulation of flow temperature in heating system. • Operating electrical installations: correct replacement of light fittings, discussion of switching on lighting and power, lighting sensors, power zoning. • Operating to maximise the use of daylight and minimise use of artificial lighting. • Avoiding peak electricity costs [typically at 7:30 and 17:30] by periodically shutting down large plant.

Monitoring completed building performance

After acceptance and practical completion, but prior to final completion of the works, some monitoring of the performance of the completed building is desirable. The degree will obviously vary with the complexity of the building, and the available budget. While not every building needs full monitoring of temperatures throughout the heating and cooling seasons, the option of monitoring buildings remotely via modem and computer is increasingly available. The auditing facilities in Building Energy Management Systems are also helpful in monitoring performance. Table 1.13 below provides examples of monitoring which might be undertaken.

Table 1.13   MONITORING ENVIRONMENTAL PERFORMANCE

• Check for air infiltration as a result of drying out and shrinkage leading to poor air tightness.

• Investigate energy consumption through an entire heating and cooling season, by reference to utilities invoices or electricity, gas, other. These can be totalled over a year and consumption in kWh/m^2 readily derived. This can be compared with reference figures for an assessment of the overall performance of the building users' comfort, particularly in relation to overheating in the cooling season, where air conditioning is not provided and natural cooling methods are employed; and user satisfaction in relation to daylight availability. Questionnaires can be helpful in this regard.

• Monitor room temperatures, either by simple maximum/minimum thermometers or by thermometer linked to computerised recording system, to establish the effectiveness of heating or cooling installations and help determine whether active installations are over-utilised.

• Water consumption, by monthly and yearly meter readings and a daily consumption in litres per head calculated from the number of building users. Data may be checked with reference to established bench marks to establish the level of performance.

REFURBISHMENT

About half of EU construction sector output is on maintenance and repair. (European Commission DG III, 1995)

In general, it is more sustainable to refurbish and re-use existing buildings than to demolish and build anew. Refurbishment involves the consumption of fewer materials and less energy for demolition and transportation. It is also usually more labour-intensive than new build. This is apart altogether from the cultural benefit of keeping familiar buildings and landmarks, and the learning possibilities of working with old buildings, many of which have lasted for many years employing sustainable materials and techniques.

Building regulations can pose a problem in refurbishment works. In most Member States' building regulation requirements are expressed in performance terms: 'reasonable thermal insulation', 'adequate structural performance'. Associated guidance is conceived in terms of new build and does not always take into account the reality of load-bearing capacity, thermal insulation performance, or other characteristics of existing building stock. It may not allow previously applicable lower standards to be maintained without extensive and often visually intrusive upgrading, even though the most sustainable act would be to conserve and refurbish the old building and not to demolish and construct afresh.

An energy audit of the building will often be worthwhile prior to determining the brief for the refurbishment work. Such an audit can be carried out by the architect, but specialists will have much to contribute by way of strategies for sustainable refurbishment which can often be startlingly cost-effective. These audits, coupled with an assessment of energy performance of the refurbished building, may provide useful indications of the potential for improvement.

The scope of refurbishment projects can vary from redecoration to part renewal of primary structure with the attendant alterations and renewals. Services equipment for heating, lighting, ventilation and cooling become more efficient, and external envelope elements such as windows, doors, shading devices and opaque elements have the potential for improved performance. Table 1.14 provides a list of works which might be usefully addressed in projects of significant scope.

Table 1.14   ISSUES IN REFURBISHMENT

Before fixing the brief for the work	• Undertake an energy audit of the building.
Identify the building's potential for environmental improvement, including	• Increasing daylighting through roof lighting. • Reducing overheating through the use of external louvres or blinds. • Reducing heating demand through installation of draught lobbies and by adding insulation to external walls and roof. • Envelope performance by better windows and doors. • Natural ventilation by adding opening sections to windows and roof lights. • Controlling ventilation and casual infiltration. • Performance of active systems through better controls: time clocks, thermostats, building energy management systems, and more efficient fittings: lights, heat emitters. • Indoor air quality by substituting natural for synthetic finishes: linoleum, water based paints.
Consider the following when refurbishing	• Improved controls on active service systems. The following will often be cost-effective: • solid state programmable controllers for heating and cooling; • automatic switching systems for lighting; • individual thermostatic room and /or radiator control; • weather compensating controls. • Improved air tightness in the external envelope. • Improved thermal insulation: not always easy, but where roof finishes are being replaced it may be possible at modest extra cost to significantly upgrade thermal insulation. External wall insulation can enormously enhance thermal performance and increase internal comfort. • If windows or external door sets are to be renewed, the best performing models available will generally be worth installing. • Secondary glazing can create small sunspaces, pre-heat ventilation air, and reduce transmission of external noise. • The best available floor and wall finishes will increase service life out of proportion to cost • Passive climate control devices, including draught lobbies at external entrances, external shading devices such as fixed or moveable louvres, and sun spaces, can be undertaken in conjunction with facade refurbishment. • Retrofitting sustainable components such as roof-mounted solar water heaters and photovoltaic cells, and low-energy lifts.

References

- European Commission DG III, (1995), *SECTEUR: Strategic Study on the Construction Sector*, Brussels

Section 2: Issues

INTRODUCTION

Defining the design parameters which need to be considered in green building design is not easy, particularly if this is to be of use to the architect at the early, conceptual stages.

In a green building the designer should take into account not only the comfort and health of the occupants but also the effect of the building on the local and global environment. We could illustrate the relationship between comfort, health and environment in a Cartesian spatial system (2.1) with three axes corresponding to these three aspects of the building's performance:

1. Occupant comfort
Comfort is affected by many factors, such as the activity, clothing, age and gender of the individual, and aspects of the internal environment such as air temperature, surface temperature, humidity, air movement, noise, light and odours.

2. Occupant health
A poor internal environment has implications for the health of the occupants:

- it may contain toxic or allergenic substances
- it may be stressful or unsafe
- it may facilitate the transmission of communicable diseases

3. Environmental impact of the building
The processes of constructing and operating a building affect the environment. Effects on the local area have always been recognised, but now it is also appreciated that buildings contribute to larger impacts, such as global warming and depletion of resources.

A green building should lie within the completely positive zone of this diagram.

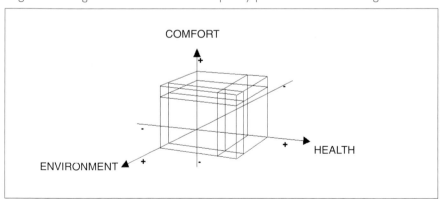

2.1 Schematic Cartesian diagram, illustrating the relationship between comfort, health and environment.

Clearly, this Cartesian system is a conceptual one, useful as a guide to thinking about the process of green building, but still a long way from being a tool for evaluating a given project. While the principal physical parameters which define comfort are known and generally accepted, those which determine the quality of the internal environment, in respect of occupant health, and the impact of the building on the external environment, are still uncertain. Also, the weight given to the various components making up the individual parameters, and their positioning on the positive or negative side of the corresponding axes, is strongly influenced by the cultural context of the building and is connected with the personal or professional perception of environmental risk.

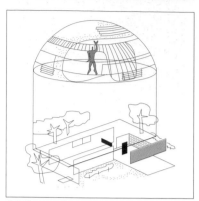

2.2 Theoretical approach to balanced shelter

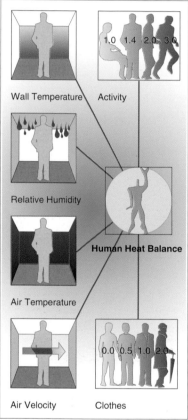

Wall Temperature   Activity

Relative Humidity

Human Heat Balance

Air Temperature

Air Velocity   Clothes

2.3 The parameters that effects thermal comfort

Units:
The unit of metabolic energy is the 'met'
1 met = 58 W/m²
where the surface area of the human body is approx. 1.8 m².
The unit of thermal resistance due to clothes is the 'clo'
1 clo = 0.155 m²K/W

COMFORT

The building modifies the external, natural environment by moderating the climate and providing protection and shelter, and designers need to understand how the external climate, the building fabric and the human body interact (2.2). Comfort is subjective and depends on age, gender, culture and who is paying the bill. In practice designers aim to provide conditions that are acceptable to a majority of users.

Conventional comfort standards, such as those given in ISO 7730, are based on studies carried out in climate laboratories. Field studies suggest that laboratory-based predictions may not be entirely reliable, because they do not allow for people's adaptive responses (taking off a jacket or closing blinds, for example) or their need for some variety in their environment (Roaf and Hancock, 1992). Consequently, optimum temperatures prescribed in standards may result in overestimated heating and cooling requirements. When one considers that a 1°C reduction in design air temperature for a heating system can save 10% in energy consumption, the benefit of carefully assessing targets for interior environmental performance is clear.

Thermal Comfort

'The comfort zone could be described as the point at which man can spend the minimum energy adjusting to his environment'. (Olygay, 1973)

Thermal comfort can be defined as a sense of well-being with respect to temperature. It depends on achieving a balance between the heat being produced by the body and the loss of heat to the surroundings.

The internal temperature of the human body is maintained at a constant level. The body has no means of storing heat and any heat generated by it has to be dissipated. The actual balance depends on seven parameters. Three (metabolism, clothing and skin temperature) relate to the individual. The other four (air temperature, relative humidity, surface temperature of the elements in the room and air speed) are linked to the surrounding environment (2.3). While the parameters may be applied in a general way, design will also need to take into account the fact that specific local conditions (sun streaming into a window, body weight, subjective factors and adaptation) are all important and will affect perception of comfort.

Metabolism is the sum of the chemical reactions that occur in the body to keep body temperature balanced at 36.7°C and to compensate for heat lost to the surroundings. Production of metabolic energy (heat) depends on the level of physical activity (2.4). Clothing impedes the exchange of heat between the surface of the skin and the surrounding atmosphere (2.5). Skin temperature is a function of metabolism, clothing and room temperature. Unlike internal body temperature, it is not constant.

Air/room temperature affects heat loss from the human body by convection and evaporation.

Relative humidity is the amount of moisture in the air as a percentage of the maximum moisture it could contain at that temperature and pressure. It affects heat loss by allowing greater or lesser degrees of evaporation. Except in extreme situations the influence of relative humidity on the sensation of thermal comfort is relatively small. In temperate regions, for instance, raising the relative humidity from 20% to 60% allows the temperature to be decreased by less than 1°C while having little or no effect on thermal comfort.

Mean radiant temperature is the average surface temperature of the elements enclosing a space. It influences both the heat lost by radiation from the body and the heat lost, by conduction, when the body is in contact with surfaces. Poorly-insulated buildings have cold internal surfaces and higher air temperatures are needed to compensate. An increase in mean radiant temperature means that comfort conditions can be achieved at lower air temperatures, and a reduction of 1°C in air temperature may save up to 10% of energy consumption. So insulation saves energy not only by reducing actual building heat loss, but also by reducing design air temperatures.

Air speed does not decrease the temperature but causes a cooling sensation through heat loss by convection and increased evaporation. Within buildings, air speeds are generally less than 0.2m/s.

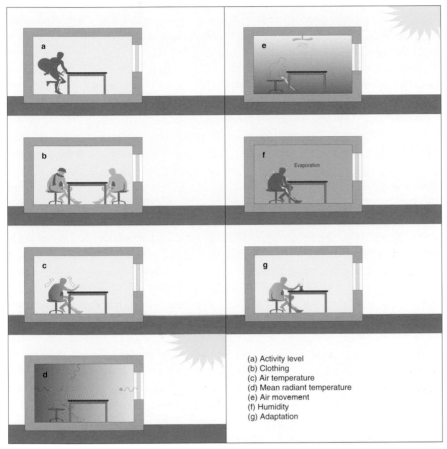

(a) Activity level
(b) Clothing
(c) Air temperature
(d) Mean radiant temperature
(e) Air movement
(f) Humidity
(g) Adaptation

2.6 Designing for thermal comfort

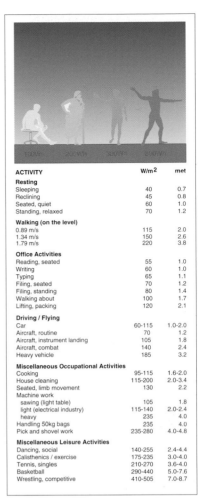

ACTIVITY	W/m²	met
Resting		
Sleeping	40	0.7
Reclining	45	0.8
Seated, quiet	60	1.0
Standing, relaxed	70	1.2
Walking (on the level)		
0.89 m/s	115	2.0
1.34 m/s	150	2.6
1.79 m/s	220	3.8
Office Activities		
Reading, seated	55	1.0
Writing	60	1.0
Typing	65	1.1
Filing, seated	70	1.2
Filing, standing	80	1.4
Walking about	100	1.7
Lifting, packing	120	2.1
Driving / Flying		
Car	60-115	1.0-2.0
Aircraft, routine	70	1.2
Aircraft, instrument landing	105	1.8
Aircraft, combat	140	2.4
Heavy vehicle	185	3.2
Miscellaneous Occupational Activities		
Cooking	95-115	1.6-2.0
House cleaning	115-200	2.0-3.4
Seated, limb movement	130	2.2
Machine work		
sawing (light table)	105	1.8
light (electrical industry)	115-140	2.0-2.4
heavy	235	4.0
Handling 50kg bags	235	4.0
Pick and shovel work	235-280	4.0-4.8
Miscellaneous Leisure Activities		
Dancing, social	140-255	2.4-4.4
Calisthenics / exercise	175-235	3.0-4.0
Tennis, singles	210-270	3.6-4.0
Basketball	290-440	5.0-7.6
Wrestling, competitive	410-505	7.0-8.7

2.4 Typical metabolic heat generation for various activities

CLOTHING	THERMAL RESISTANCE	
	m² K/W	clo
Nude	0	0
Shorts	0.015	0.1
Typical tropical clothing ensemble: briefs, shorts, open-neck shirt with short sleeves, light socks and sandals	0.045	0.3
Light summer ensemble: briefs, long light-weight trousers, open-neck shirt with short sleeves, light socks and shoes	0.08	0.5
Light working ensemble: Light underwear, cotton work shirt with long sleeves, work trousers, woollen socks and shoes	0.11	0.7
Typical indoor winter ensemble: Underwear, shirt with long sleeves, trousers, jacket or sweater with long sleeves, heavy socks and shoes	0.16	1.0
Heavy traditional European business suit: cotton underwear with long legs and sleeves, shirt, suit including trousers, jacket and waistcoat, woollen socks and heavy shoes	0.23	1.5

2.5 Thermal insulation provided by various combinations of clothing

It is common practice to design to internationally accepted fixed design temperatures, but research shows that people are not passive in relation to their thermal environment. Where appropriate they will look for comfortable conditions (shade or sunshine, wind or shelter), and change their position, activity and clothing to make themselves more comfortable.

In field studies the range of temperatures which people report as comfortable is wider than might be expected. People accustomed to high temperatures report them to be acceptable, suggesting a degree of acclimatisation which alters the level of thermal acceptability. 'It follows that there is no need for uniformity of indoor temperatures world-wide – each region of the world could adopt temperatures suitable to the prevailing climate and season.' (Roaf and Hancock, 1992).

Allowance for adaptation by both people and buildings means that definitions of comfort, too, can be broadened. Intelligent building design will provide mass to reduce temperature swings; adjustable elements such as blinds, shutters and ventilation to respond to changing conditions; and active heating or cooling systems, to maintain the desired temperature or at least ameliorate the outdoor climate.

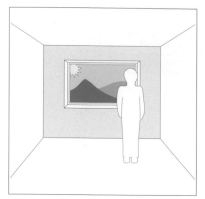

2.7 Windows have distinct advantages

Luminance (candelas/m²) is the light flux leaving a surface and reaching the eye of the observer.
Illuminance (Lux) is the light striking unit area of a specified surface.
Lux is the SI unit of illuminance produced on a 1m² surface by a luminous flux of one lumen universally distributed over that surface.
Daylight factor (%) is Illuminance at a specified point indoors, expressed as a percentage of the simultaneous horizontal illuminance outdoors under an unobscured sky.

2.8 Definitions

	Average	Minimum
Church	5.0%	1.0%
Hospital ward	5.0%	1.0%
Office	5.0%	2.0%
Classroom	5.0%	2.0%
Living room	1.5%	0.5%
Bedroom	1.0%	0.3%
Kitchen	2.0%	0.6%

2.9 Recommended daylight factors (CIBSE, 1987)

Luminance ratio

background of visual task : environment
3 : 1

background of visual task : peripheral field
10 : 1

light source : adjoining fields
20 : 1

interior in general
40:1

2.10 Recommended luminance ratios

Visual Comfort

Poor lighting can cause eyestrain, fatigue, headaches, irritability, mistakes and accidents. Comfortable lighting conditions in a space are dependent on quantity, distribution and quality of light. The source of light may be natural or artificial or a combination of both, but windows have distinct advantages. In schools, hospital wards and factories the absence of a view out produces psychological discomfort. In offices the psychological benefits of windows have been found to be even greater than the physical benefits of which the occupants themselves were aware.

Almost all spaces need artificial lighting after dark. Some spaces and activities will need it during daylight hours. Where this is the case, the light spectrum of the artificial light should be as close as possible to that of natural light.

Quantity
Recommended lighting levels for particular tasks are well defined and if specified and implemented in accordance with standards are unlikely to cause problems for occupants. Establish the lighting requirements for the specific occupants and activities planned for the building through reference to tables of recommended illuminances for different activities (2.9), such as the CIBSE-UK Guides or equivalent sources (CIBSE, 1984 and CIBSE, 1987).

Distribution
Distribution of light in a space is often more important than quantity. The perception of brightness is influenced by the evenness of lighting levels. Where there is too great a difference between the daylight levels beside windows and at a distance from them, people in the area which is relatively darker tend to switch on lights, even though the daylight illuminance in their part of the room may be functionally adequate. The perception of the distribution of light can be defined in terms of either contrast or glare.

Contrast is the difference between the appearance of an object against that of its immediate background. For comfort, there are limits to the amount of contrast which can be allowed between different parts of a visual field (2.10). Contrast can be defined in terms of luminance, illuminance or reflectivity compared between adjacent surfaces. The amount and distribution of light (and hence the amount of contrast) in a room is influenced by the reflectivity of the surfaces.

Glare is excessive contrast, usually caused by the introduction of an intense light source into the visual field, causing a feeling of discomfort and fatigue. The result may be anything from mildly distracting to visually blinding for the occupant. Glare can be caused directly, indirectly or by reflection.

Direct glare results when a light source with high luminance enters directly into the field of view. It can be experienced with interior light sources, sun or sky. Indirect glare occurs when the luminance of surfaces is too high. Reflected glare is caused by reflection from light sources on polished surfaces.

Quality
Visual quality is harder to define, but includes direction, colour and variation over time. Daylight provides excellent quality in terms of direction and both colour appearance and colour rendering. People enjoy daylight and sunlight, and the views that come with them. They tend to accept greater variation in light intensity in naturally lit spaces than they are prepared to tolerate from artificial lighting systems.

Indoor Air Quality

Compared with the other parameters of comfort this is the one about which there is the most uncertainty. Provided that the outdoor air is of acceptable quality the traditional problems of stuffiness and odour can usually be resolved by ensuring adequate air change rates, efficient air distribution and control of interior pollution sources. Where clean outdoor air is not available, or the building's particular use makes heavy demands on the ventilation system, other steps may have to be taken (Refer HEALTH; Indoor Air Quality)

Acoustic Quality

Although acoustic quality is not a primary issue in sustainable design, 'green' design strategies should take acoustic consequences into account (2.11). For example, natural ventilation may imply open windows or ventilation openings between interior spaces; obtrusive noise or loss of acoustic privacy are not acceptable by-products. If carpeting or other absorbent floor finishes are omitted to allow the structure to act as a thermal store, other measures may have to be taken to reduce the transmission of impact noise and provide enough sound absorption in occupied spaces.

Standard environmental parameters include acceptable and recommended noise levels.

Sources of noise discomfort include:

*   external: traffic noise or loss of acoustic privacy from open windows (may conflict with natural ventilation requirements);
*   internal: loud or disruptive noises generated by activities within the building;
*   building construction and finishes: impact noise from hard surfaces (possibly resulting from use of structure as a thermal store);
*   building services: noise created by building services (e.g. mechanical ventilation).

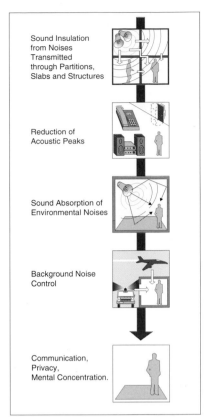

Sound Insulation from Noises Transmitted through Partitions, Slabs and Structures

Reduction of Acoustic Peaks

Sound Absorption of Environmental Noises

Background Noise Control

Communication, Privacy, Mental Concentration.

2.11

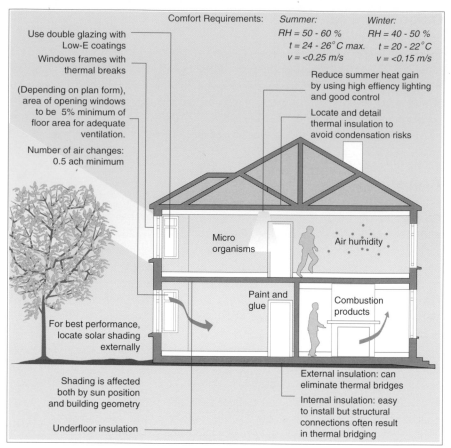

Comfort Requirements: *Summer:*   *Winter:*
                        RH = 50 - 60 %   *RH = 40 - 50 %*
                        t = 24 - 26°C max. *t = 20 - 22°C*
                        v = <0.25 m/s   *v = <0.15 m/s*

Use double glazing with Low-E coatings

Windows frames with thermal breaks

(Depending on plan form), area of opening windows to be 5% minimum of floor area for adequate ventilation.

Number of air changes: 0.5 ach minimum

Reduce summer heat gain by using high effiency lighting and good control

Locate and detail thermal insulation to avoid condensation risks

Micro organisms

Air humidity

Paint and glue

Combustion products

For best performance, locate solar shading externally

Shading is affected both by sun position and building geometry

Underfloor insulation

External insulation: can eliminate thermal bridges

Internal insulation: easy to install but structural connections often result in thermal bridging

2.12 *Thermal comfort and indoor air quality in the home*

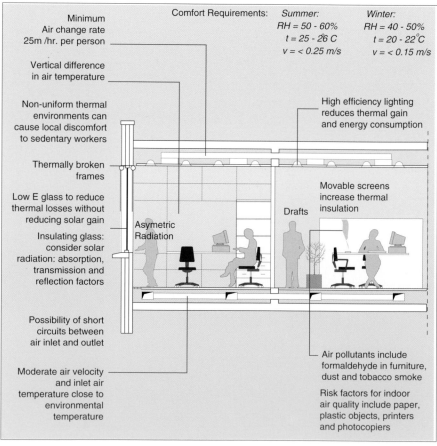

Comfort Requirements: *Summer:*   *Winter:*
                        RH = 50 - 60%   *RH = 40 - 50%*
                        t = 25 - 26 C   *t = 20 - 22°C*
                        v = < 0.25 m/s   *v = < 0.15 m/s*

Minimum Air change rate 25m /hr. per person

Vertical difference in air temperature

Non-uniform thermal environments can cause local discomfort to sedentary workers

Thermally broken frames

Low E glass to reduce thermal losses without reducing solar gain

Insulating glass: consider solar radiation: absorption, transmission and reflection factors

High efficiency lighting reduces thermal gain and energy consumption

Movable screens increase thermal insulation

Drafts

Asymetric Radiation

Possibility of short circuits between air inlet and outlet

Moderate air velocity and inlet air temperature close to environmental temperature

Air pollutants include formaldehyde in furniture, dust and tobacco smoke

Risk factors for indoor air quality include paper, plastic objects, printers and photocopiers

2.13 *Thermal comfort and indoor air quality in the office*

Objectives

Shelter occupants from the elements

Gathering information on climate is part of the development of any healthy building strategy. It enables designers to evaluate a site so as to anticipate adverse weather conditions or natural hazards which could affect the building.

- Buildings should be planned and located in relation to topography and prevailing winds.
- The building should be designed and constructed to keep out damp (rising, penetrating, condensation).
- Structures and roofs should resist high wind speeds and snow-loads.
- The envelope should prevent excessive air infiltration.
- In cold climates envelopes and service pipes should be protected against frost damage.
- Specific measures should be taken to prevent local flooding.
- Tall buildings should be provided with lightning conductors.

Maintain a comfortable thermal environment

Thermal comfort is the state in which no significant strain is imposed on the thermo-regulatory mechanism of the body. Maintaining an indoor thermal equilibrium should therefore prevent undue raising or lowering of body temperature, while at the same time assisting physiological functions to proceed.

- The ambient temperature should provide thermal comfort to occupants. (20–22°C winter, 24–26°C summer are reasonable starting points, but allow for activity and adaptive behaviour.)
- Optimal temperature should be achieved at knee height (0.5m from the floor).
- Mean radiant temperature should be less than 3°C below assumed optimum indoor air temperature.
- There should not be any excessive air movement in rooms (acceptable levels 0.1–0.15 m/s for winter; 0.25 m/s for summer).
- Relative humidity should be kept at an acceptable level (40%–70% at northern latitudes; 50–60% in summer and 40–50% in winter in Mediterranean climates).
- Heating systems should be easy to control.
- An average ratio of window to wall of 30% for the building as a whole makes a good starting point for design. Then adjust to account for climate, orientation and building use. In warm climates consider limiting window area to about one tenth of floor area.
- Shading devices such as venetian blinds, shutters and screens, deflectors, or photo thermo electro-chromic glasses can be used to control sunlight penetration.
- Light-coloured paint on external walls will reflect solar radiation.
- Green belts, trees, climbing plants, as well as water reservoirs, can be used to reduce temperatures of walls and roofs in warm conditions.
- In warm climates buildings should be oriented to take advantage of prevailing summer winds.
- Natural night ventilation is effective in reducing air temperatures during hot weather.

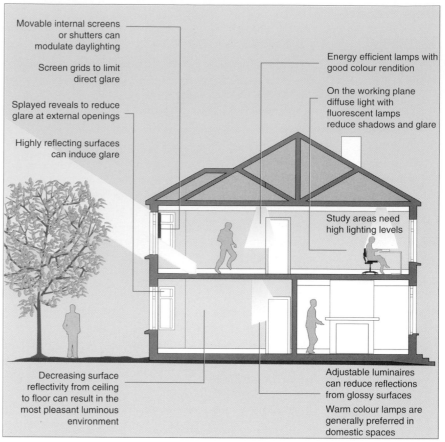

Movable internal screens
or shutters can
modulate daylighting

Screen grids to limit
direct glare

Splayed reveals to reduce
glare at external openings

Highly reflecting surfaces
can induce glare

Energy efficient lamps with
good colour rendition

On the working plane
diffuse light with
fluorescent lamps
reduce shadows and glare

Study areas need
high lighting levels

Decreasing surface
reflectivity from ceiling
to floor can result in the
most pleasant luminous
environment

Adjustable luminaires
can reduce reflections
from glossy surfaces

Warm colour lamps are
generally preferred in
domestic spaces

2.14 Visual comfort in the home

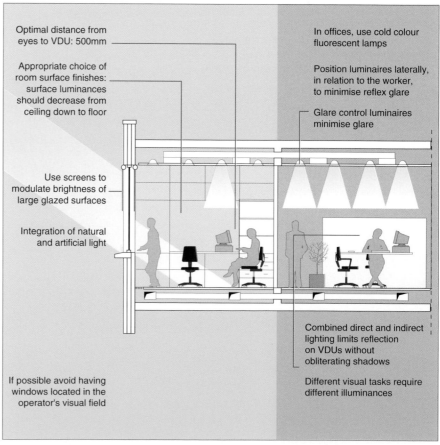

Optimal distance from
eyes to VDU: 500mm

Appropriate choice of
room surface finishes:
surface luminances
should decrease from
ceiling down to floor

Use screens to
modulate brightness of
large glazed surfaces

Integration of natural
and artificial light

If possible avoid having
windows located in the
operator's visual field

In offices, use cold colour
fluorescent lamps

Position luminaires laterally,
in relation to the worker,
to minimise reflex glare

Glare control luminaires
minimise glare

Combined direct and indirect
lighting limits reflection
on VDUs without
obliterating shadows

Different visual tasks require
different illuminances

2.15 Visual comfort in the office

Provide visual comfort

The aim of good lighting practice should be to provide lighting which is both qualitatively and quantitatively adequate. In all climates a balance needs to be maintained between natural lighting requirements and the requirement for thermal comfort.

- Good orientation and correct spacing of buildings can enhance natural lighting.
- Glazing ratio and window design should ensure that building interiors receive adequate natural lighting.
- To ensure an appropriate distribution of daylight, aim to have some sky visible from most places within the room.
- The spectrum of daytime artificial lighting should resemble that of daylight.
- Natural and artificial lighting should both meet physiological and health requirements: optimum intensity, similar brightness, protection against glare, avoidance of shadows, adequate contrast.
- Wherever feasible rooms should have rooflights or windows, giving occupants some visual contact with the outdoor environment.

Provide sufficient ventilation

The importance of adequate ventilation in maintaining good indoor air quality is becoming more widely recognised, not least because of the tendency towards lower ventilation levels as a result of changing construction styles and techniques and/or deliberate action to reduce heat losses.

- Ventilation rates should comply with air quality standards and sanitary recommendation; average 25m³ per person per hour (offices).
- Air filtration alone may provide an acceptable level of air exchange. However, all buildings should have provision for additional controlled ventilation, designed to be effective and easy to use.
- The openable area of windows should extend close to ceilings to allow hot air in the upper part of the room to escape.
- Windows should incorporate 'trickle ventilation' features such as two-position casement fasteners.
- Windows should allow for easily operated and controllable ventilation.
- Air inlets and outlets to mechanical systems should be situated to avoid acoustic nuisance to neighbouring properties.
- If air-conditioning is unavoidable, it should be designed to facilitate regular cleaning and maintenance.

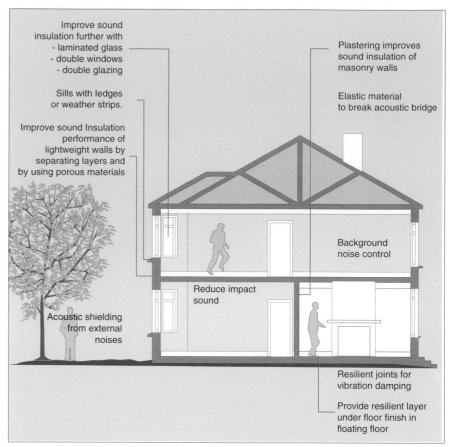

Improve sound
insulation further with
- laminated glass
- double windows
- double glazing

Sills with ledges
or weather strips.

Improve sound Insulation
performance of
lightweight walls by
separating layers and
by using porous materials

Plastering improves
sound insulation of
masonry walls

Elastic material
to break acoustic bridge

Background
noise control

Reduce impact
sound

Acoustic shielding
from external
noises

Resilient joints for
vibration damping

Provide resilient layer
under floor finish in
floating floor

2.16 Acoustic comfort in the home

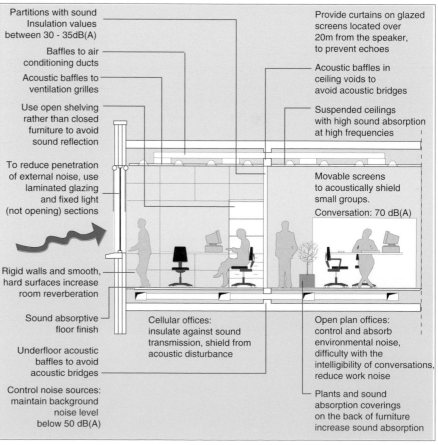

Partitions with sound
Insulation values
between 30 - 35dB(A)

Baffles to air
conditioning ducts

Acoustic baffles to
ventilation grilles

Use open shelving
rather than closed
furniture to avoid
sound reflection

To reduce penetration
of external noise, use
laminated glazing
and fixed light
(not opening) sections

Rigid walls and smooth,
hard surfaces increase
room reverberation

Sound absorptive
floor finish

Underfloor acoustic
baffles to avoid
acoustic bridges

Control noise sources:
maintain background
noise level
below 50 dB(A)

Provide curtains on glazed
screens located over
20m from the speaker,
to prevent echoes

Acoustic baffles in
ceiling voids to
avoid acoustic bridges

Suspended ceilings
with high sound absorption
at high frequencies

Movable screens
to acoustically shield
small groups.
Conversation: 70 dB(A)

Cellular offices:
insulate against sound
transmission, shield from
acoustic disturbance

Open plan offices:
control and absorb
environmental noise,
difficulty with the
intelligibility of conversations,
reduce work noise

Plants and sound
absorption coverings
on the back of furniture
increase sound absorption

2.17 Acoustic comfort in the office

Provide acceptable acoustic conditions

Many human activities, concentrated intellectual work, conversation, music and sleep, for example, demand controlled noise levels and/or acoustic privacy.

*   Buildings can be protected from outdoor noise by orientation and by the use of barriers such as walls, earth mounds or vegetation.
*   Noise-generating activities or equipment within the building should be located as far as possible in unoccupied spaces.
*   Spaces with shared walls and floors should preferably be of similar use.
*   Reduction of sound transmission is best achieved by increasing the mass of structural building elements. This is particularly effective at lower frequencies.
*   Air-borne sound transmission is minimised by eliminating gaps in the external envelope and in internal partitions.
*   Window openings are one of the main sources of noise infiltration. Depending on the environment, they may be sealed or incorporate insulated glazing components such as laminated glass. Ventilation grilles should be provided with sound baffles.
*   Resilient layers under floating floors and suspended ceilings reduce impact noise transmission in multiple-housing schemes.
*   Indirect sound transmission through cavity walls should be reduced by sound-absorbing materials in the cavity.
*   Where excessive interior noise pollution is expected, specify sound absorbant building components and materials.
*   Reduce noise transmission in office environments, by incorporating high level baffles, which reflect sound back into the space.
*   Drain-pipes should not be carried in ducts next to living rooms or bedrooms.
*   Lift and other motors should be mounted on resilient supports.
*   Ventilation fans should be as large as possible so as to run at the lowest possible speed.

HEALTH

Conditions inside a building clearly affect not only the comfort but also the health of the occupants and users. Poor air quality, toxic materials, lack of daylight or excessive noise can have lasting consequences for health.

Indoor Air Quality

More than most environmental issues, indoor air pollution has a direct impact on health and, by implication, on productivity. Health effects ascribed to indoor air pollution include allergies and asthma, infectious disease, cancer and other genetic damage. Widespread, chronic, low-level effects in particular buildings are referred to as 'sick building syndrome' (SBS) (Levin, 1996). Indoor air quality is determined by air quality outside the building, pollutant emissions within the building and the ventilation rate, as well as by the efficiency of filtration and standard of maintenance of mechanical systems, and so on.

People spend 80–90% of their lives inside buildings and the impact of constant exposure to low level emissions from the wide variety of materials commonly found in buildings today is unknown. Most of these pollutants originate in the building itself (2.18). With an increase in the use of organic solvents, interior finishes emitting VOCs (volatile organic compounds), cleaning agents, and office appliances, indoor air pollution has become a serious concern.

Making buildings more airtight to conserve energy has an effect on air quality. There is less incidental, unplanned ventilation, and dust and emission concentrations in the air rise. One view is that lower ventilation rates are creating unhealthy conditions. Another is that the increase in indoor pollutant sources is the real problem. According to Baker the phenomenon of sick building syndrome is observed almost exclusively in mechanically ventilated buildings (Baker, 1995). What is certain, however, is that in under-ventilated spaces mould spores and house dust mites thrive, and VOCs reach higher concentrations. It is also well established that where artificial systems are installed a healthy indoor environment will only be achieved if systems are correctly installed, fully commissioned and properly maintained.

These factors increase the need for care in the specification of materials and in the design of ventilation systems.

Three main approaches are used to control indoor air pollutants:
* removing the source of pollution from the building;
* controlling pollutant emissions at source;
* expelling the pollutants from the building through ventilation measures.

Materials

A number of toxic chemicals and materials are used in building materials, finishes and consumer goods (2.19). Some of these products pollute indoor air or water supplies; others cause damage by contact or ingestion. These can affect the workers who make them or install them in a new building, the building's users, and/or the workers who demolish or refurbish the building at the end of its useful life.

Lead and asbestos are well-established health hazards. Some synthetics such as PVC can also lead to hazardous emissions in use. Paints, preservatives and adhesives are common sources of toxic emissions. For information about the impact of different categories of materials on health and the environment. (Refer ELEMENTS; Materials)

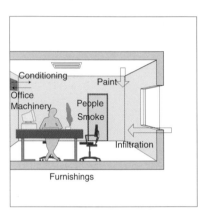

2.18 Principal sources of pollutants in an office building

COMMON INDOOR AIR CONTAMINANTS

* Asbestos fibre

* Formaldehyde vapour

* Volatile Organic Compounds (VOC's)

* Tobacco smoke

* Radon gas

2.19

Daylight

Windows and daylight are beneficial to health. The absence of daylight can cause depression (known as Seasonal Affective Disorder), bone disease (due to Vitamin D deficiency) and disturbances of sleep and concentration. There is also evidence that daylight is particularly necessary for children. At a school in Alberta, Canada, students in classrooms with full-spectrum light were healthier, attended school 3.2–3.5 days more per year, had nine times less dental decay and grew an average 2.1cm more over two years than students in rooms with average lighting (SunWorld, 1996). In a comparison of schools in Johnston County, North Carolina, USA, school attendance was higher in 'daylit' schools, and after three years in these schools students scored 14% higher in final exams than students in conventional schools. The longer the students were in the daylit school the greater the effect appeared to be (IAEEL Newsletter, 1996).

Noise

Exposure to excessive noise levels can produce stress-related illnesses and hearing loss (2.20). Sources of noise nuisance are listed in COMFORT; Acoustic Quality above.

Objectives

Protect against outdoor air pollutants
The interior environment has a continuous but variable influx of air pollutants from the outdoor air. Included in this category are suspended particulates, sulphur oxides, nitrogen oxides, hydrocarbons, carbon oxides and lead.

- Where possible site buildings away from roads and other sources of pollution.
- Provide internal and external planting to absorb pollutants and reduce dust.
- Avoid gaps in the external envelope which allow unplanned infiltration of external air.
- Where outdoor air is of unacceptable quality provide sealed windows and mechanical ventilation.
- Locate windows and air inlets to mechanical ventilation systems so as to avoid intake of contaminated air.

Control pollutants from processes within the building
The occupants and activities within a building are a source of emissions. Common pollutants include carbon and nitrogen oxides, odours, tobacco smoke, water vapour, airborne pathogens and toxic emissions from appliances and machinery.

- Most cases of carbon monoxide (CO) poisoning are caused by incomplete combustion of heating and cooking fuels. Appliances and flues must be properly maintained and ventilation adequate.
- Provide local extract ventilation for smoking areas, and for spaces housing emission-generating appliances or equipment.
- Provide adequate natural ventilation to rooms to dilute airborne micro-organism concentrations.
- Allow direct sunlight to enter all rooms.
- Provide sufficient natural and artificial lighting to enable inspection and cleaning.

Protect against radioactive emissions
In ordinary circumstances the largest contribution to radon exposure arises from inhaling decayed radon products in indoor air.

- When high levels of radon are suspected, radiological monitoring should be undertaken.
- Increase ventilation rates in buildings both under the floor and within rooms.
- Provide a vapour barrier between the ground and the living space, or seal floors and walls to reduce radon emissions.

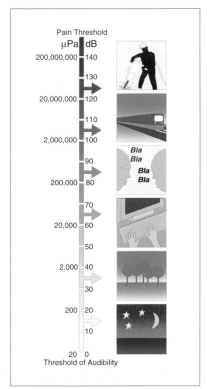

2.20

Specify non-toxic building materials, finishes and equipment

- Require manufacturers or suppliers to indicate the content of any materials or components it is proposed to incorporate in the building and select the least injurious.
- Minimise the use of VOC-emitting finishes which will be exposed to the indoor air.
- Design for easy access to services so as to facilitate proper maintenance of any air-conditioning or mechanical ventilation equipment.
- Seal or remove, after evaluating condition, any asbestos-containing materials in existing buildings, provided that this will not create more hazard from dust and fibre release than would occur by leaving it in place.
- In existing buildings replacement of lead piping and lead-lined water tanks should be considered where chemical attack from water represents a problem.

Design for adequate daylight

- Rooms in which occupants spend any substantial part of their day should be provided with windows/rooflights if the function of the space permits.

Protect against excessive noise and vibration

Actions to avoid excessive noise or vibration are listed in COMFORT; Objectives above.

ENVIRONMENT

The range of impacts of buildings on the environment is diverse. Problems which result from construction-related processes, such as global warming, ozone depletion, loss of natural habitat and biodiversity, soil erosion and release of toxic pollutants are now well known. It is useful to think of the proposed building as a new, living, healthy entity. The building is an integral part of the site. The two diagrams (2.21a, 2.21b) illustrate the linear, open systems of conventional buildings and the closed, cyclical, sustainable systems which represent the alternative.

A building is a physical structure composed of different elements and also a kind of 'living machine'; a place where people go about their lives, appliances use electricity, temperature must be regulated, and so on. There are two main headings under which the environmental impact of the building must be analysed:

1. As a physical structure, a building is dead, the mere 'sum of its parts'. These parts are individually extracted, manufactured, assembled, maintained, demolished, and finally disposed of. Each part has a set of effects associated with these processes, and the total environmental impact of the building is the sum of these effects.

2. As a 'living machine' the cost to the environment is that of running the building during its lifetime: the inputs that will be required, such as energy and services, and the outputs, such as CO_2 and wastes.

To establish the true environmental impact of a building, the analysis may be carried out in a way that reflects the relative importance of different building elements and processes, and the priorities for reducing environmental impacts. This is called life cycle analysis. The information required to carry out this task comprehensively for a whole building is substantial, and so detailed as to render the task impractical to undertake in most circumstances. It is possible, however, to analyse selected building elements or components. While the idea of cradle-to-grave analysis may be out of reach for all but the specialist, understanding the concept will help rationalise choices (2.22).

While various factors exert their influence upon the different stages of a building's lifetime, it is during planning and construction that almost all of them are fundamentally fixed. Decisions at this time determine the extent of resource and energy consumption during future stages, such as maintenance, renovation, conversion and restructuring.

Issues which need to be considered fall into five main categories: control of energy consumption • use of materials • water use • waste management • noise control

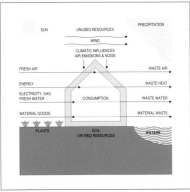

2.21a Wasteful use of resources in a conventional building

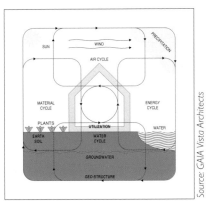

2.21b Cyclical use of resources in a sustainable building

Source: GAIA Vista Architects

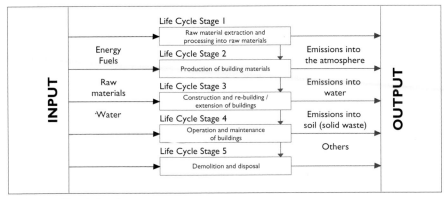

2.22 Building life cycle flow charts

Energy

The use of energy in conventional buildings impacts on the environment through the consumption of non-renewable resources and by contributing to global pollution through CO_2, NO_x and SO_2 emissions.

Design for sustainability means that one of the clear design objectives is to minimise the effect of pollution from energy use in three ways:

- Use passive design principles to ensure that the building needs less energy
- Supplement conventional energy sources with renewable ones such as solar, biomass, wind, etc.
- Where conventional systems are employed specify the most efficient and least polluting types

In a conventional building, the amount of energy consumed in use (and where that energy comes from) is still the single most important consideration from an environmental point of view. However this situation is changing as buildings become more energy-efficient. The UK Building Research Establishment has noted that in some new, well-insulated buildings, the energy embodied in their fabric could amount to as much as 50% of the energy used to run them over a 25 year period.

Materials

Criteria for the selection of materials and components include cost, aesthetics, performance and availability. Environmentally-responsible specification of building materials and components, and of the manner in which they are assembled, means that consideration of embodied energy (2.23) and local and global environmental impacts must be added. Effects on the building interior and the broader environmental impacts of various categories of materials are covered in HEALTH; Materials above.

The choice of materials and components has an important role in determining energy performance. The embodied energy in a concrete structure may be high, but if it is designed to use passive solar heating and cooling, it can easily produce an equal reduction in energy consumption over a few years of use. Other components, such as low-emissivity windows and efficient heating and lighting installations, are so important to energy efficiency as to greatly outweigh any increased impact from their manufacture and disposal.

Materials and their embodied energy value (kWh/m³)	A	B	C	Variation between sources
Lightweight blocks	417	600	(-)	144%
Lightweight concrete	833	(-)	480	174%
Concrete	625	600-800	368	217%
Timber (imported)	694	754	(-)	108%
Timber (local)	(-)	110-220	53 (assumed local)	415%
Bricks	1222	1462	2100	172%
Plaster	1806	900	730	247%
Plastics	9300	47000	12000	500%
Glass	23000	15000	15000	153%
Steel	63000	103000	78330	163%
Aluminium	195000	75600	151200	258%

A - The Architects Journal, 8.6.97
B - BSRIA, Env.Code of Practice 1994
C - Environmental Science Handbook quoted S V Szokolay 1980

2.23 Embodied energy of common building materials

Water

The careless use of water causes a variety of environmental problems. This covers both the supply of water for use in buildings and handling of surface and waste water in built-up areas.

Under most building codes almost all water used in buildings must be of drinkable quality. This is drawn from the natural environment, often reducing groundwater levels and water levels in streams, lakes and marshlands. Its treatment requires the construction and running of water treatment plants, with all the use of materials and energy that that implies.

After use, waste water must be routed through sewers to be treated again before being released, more or less purified, back into the natural environment.

In addition, impervious urban surfaces speed up rainwater run-off, reducing natural evaporation, causing soil erosion in landscaped areas and the banks of natural waterways. More construction – drains, culverts, embankments – is needed to prevent flooding. Under storm conditions surface water is often mixed with untreated or partially treated sewage in overflow systems, discharging pollutants into the environment.

Even where water is not a scarce resource, effects on natural habitats and bio-diversity can be widespread and long-lasting.

Waste

Household and commercial refuse, street litter, construction debris, industrial process and other wastes together with sewage sludge present environmental problems. Even though existing waste handling systems in most European countries tend to minimise local impacts, eventual disposal has significant effects, including contamination of land, air and water sources, at the regional and global scale. The EU Waste Management Strategy lists a four-stranded waste management system:

- reduce waste at source
- sort wastes
- re-use or re-cycle
- dispose of waste safely

The design team can contribute to sustainable practices on the part of building owners and users by planning safe and adequate storage for different categories of waste. This is the preliminary to recycling or to safe and efficient disposal.

The only time at which the design team has direct influence on the generation of wastes is during the construction phase. Waste reduction through careful handling of materials, and sorting of waste for re-use or re-cycling is within the contractors area of control. In Sweden it has been calculated that the construction of a ten-storey building generates waste equivalent to one full storey. However, the development of more sustainable practices for construction and demolition wastes is heavily dependent on the existence of handling facilities and of a market for recycled materials. In The Netherlands, fixed processing sites for construction and demolition wastes recover for re-use an estimated 60% of material. Denmark, in 1993, achieved an 80% recycling rate for construction and demolition waste through landfill and materials tax incentives (World Resource Foundation, 1995). There have been discussions about an EU Directive on Construction Waste.

Noise

The increase in high-density schemes together with mechanisation and urbanisation means that noise is a serious problem in most human settlements throughout the world. The effects are local rather than global, but do have a significant impact on the quality of life in affected areas.

Objectives

Use renewable energy sources
Renewable energy sources can be integrated as design features in most new or existing buildings. This leads to a reduction of fossil fuel consumption for heating and air conditioning, minimising the environmental impact of buildings and contributing to the reduction of the CO_2 emissions.

- Minimise the energy demand of buildings for heating, cooling and lighting purposes, by making use of passive solar systems and technologies (atria, sun spaces, solar walls, solar chimneys, ventilated roofs and walls, daylighting, etc.).
- Use air solar systems and collectors for providing adequate ventilation exchange rates to the indoor environment.
- Make use of water solar systems and collectors for basic hot sanitary water requirements and low temperature space heating of building settlements.
- Integrate photovoltaic modules and cells within roofs and southern-oriented façades, appropriate in size and peak power, for electricity production and load management.
- Integrate low emission wood-chip furnaces and other biomass for local district heating, incorporating low cost electrostatic filters.

Specify low energy systems and appliances
The successful application and implementation of innovative measures in energy technologies calls for cooperation with energy suppliers at the building design stage. Design should incorporate energy conscious solutions at the building and district level. This can result from an accurate integration of different technologies and design concepts at the early design phase.

- Time shifting of electricity peaks should be introduced wherever practicable, using suitable thermal properties of building and equipment technologies.
- Equipment design should include load management systems with control devices that optimise the electricity tariff.
- Heating and cooling systems should incorporate building energy management systems (BEMS).
- Artificial lighting should use energy-efficient lamps and ballasts, and automatic lighting control systems.
- Spot radiant systems can reduce the energy consumption of large spaces at low occupancy.
- Low temperature local district heating/cooling systems can be integrated with renewable energies or waste energy cascading from technological equipment.
- Air equipment design should incorporate heat exchange and recovery on exhaust air extractors.

Use materials wisely
Building design should consider the choice of materials, and the deconstruction and dismantling of the building at the end of its life cycle, as key design issues. This will minimise the use of resources and the generation of emissions, and facilitate re-use and recycling.

- Select materials with their environmental effects in mind.
- Design for durability of materials and components.

- Design for flexibility, allowing for change in building use over time
- Facades and internal partitioning should permit removal and replacement without structural disturbance.
- Incorporate a methodology for dismantling buildings, re-using or recycling building components through their easy separation into constituent elements at the end of their lifespan.
- Design should focus on easy maintenance of components and systems for long life and low emissions.
- Require contractor to use eco-friendly cleaning materials during construction and at final clean-up.

Provide sufficient clean water

In EU Member States, between 40–97% of the rural population is connected to a good quality water supply system, and 30% to a sewerage system. In urban areas 95–99% are connected to a satisfactory water supply system and 70–75% to a sewerage system (World Health Organisation assessment).

The qualitative aspects of water supplies are also important. Toxic products can pollute water supplies, making it unfit for consumption. Control measures at this level are of paramount importance to public health and to the safety of our environment.

- In new developments water supply, water distribution, waste water disposal, drainage and sewerage should form an integral part of a master development plan.
- Piped water supplies need to be protected against contamination from harmful bacteria or chemicals in the ground.
- External or internal water storage tanks should always be covered to discourage algae growth due to its exposure to sunlight and to prevent the entry of rodents, while facilitating regular cleaning operations.
- Materials used for water services should not represent a source of bacterial or chemical contamination to supplies.

Provide for water conservation and re-use

Design should minimise the consumption of water, and reduce the environmental impact of new and existing settlements, by using water-saving technologies and other measures.

- Install water meters to facilitate measurement and control of water use.
- Incorporate water saving technologies for WC, showers and other water-using appliances, to reduce water consumption.
- The principle of grey water usage should be planned at the design stage.
- Landscapes should be designed for minimum irrigation.
- Site planning and building design should incorporate provisions for storage of rainwater for exterior use.

Provide sanitary means of waste and surface water disposal

Adequate water disposal contributes to health and environmental improvement. Inadequate surface-water drainage can cause periodic flooding of roads, wells and housing, creating safety and environmental hazards.

- Design and construction of drainage systems should conform with health principles. Ensure that effluent does not leak into surrounding ground, contaminating water supplies.
- Specify preference for enclosed pipes protected with access points for maintenance. Ensure that open rainwater-drainage channels are regularly checked for blockage.
- Plumbing should be easily accessible for maintenance and avoid back pressure that might lead to contamination of the water supply system.
- Materials for plumbing systems should be selected for strength, durability, and the ability to resist to the corrosive action of wastes.

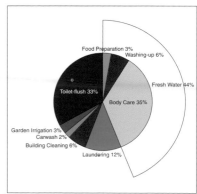

2.24

Provide for reduction, sorting, storage, collection and disposal of waste

Careful design and management can reduce construction wastes. Facilities for storage, collection and disposal of domestic waste after the building is occupied are essential. Methods of disposal depend largely upon the availability of suitable sites, cost of transport, socio-economic factors and local conditions.

- Design for standard sizes to reduce on-site cutting and require contractor to use off-cuts to feasible maximum.
- Enforce specification requirements for handling, storage and protection of materials.
- Require contractors to plan careful estimating and ordering of materials.
- Specify separation, storage and collection or re-use of recyclable materials, including packaging.
- Facilities for handling waste should provide adequate space for on-site treatment, combined with convenience for the occupier and waste collector and high standards of hygiene, safety and amenity.
- Provide spaces for individual storage containers for each dwelling in residential developments.
- Provide designated access routes to all containers for the waste collector, without passing through any part of the building.
- Consider the refuse shelter as a properly designed integral part of the building complex.

Control outdoor noise

- Industrial buildings should be insulated to prevent noise transmission at source.
- Urban main streets should be widened with protective belts of greenery to separate different zones.
- Vehicular traffic should be prohibited or reduced in residential areas, particularly at night.
- Avoid paving and other hard surfaces where possible so as to minimise ground reflection. Use vegetation and grass areas to absorb noise.

References

- Anink David, Chiel Boonstra and John Mak. (1996) *Handbook of Sustainable Building: An Environmental Preference Method for Selection of Materials for Use in Construction and Refurbishment.* James & James (Science Publishers) Limited.
- ASHRAE/DOE/BTECC (1992) *Thermal Performance of the Exterior Envelopes of Buildings* Conference Proceedings, Clearwater Beach, FL. USA.
- Baker N., A. Fanchiotti and K.A. (1995) *Daylighting in Architecture: A European Reference Book.*, London. James and James (Science Publishers) Limited for the Commission of the European Communities, ISBN 1-87 3936 21
- BS 8206: 1992 Part 2: Code of Practice for Daylighting, London, BSI, 1992.
- CIBSE (1984) *Code for Interior Lighting.* London. Chartered Institution of Building Services
- CIBSE (1987) *Applications Manual: Window Design.* London, Chartered Institution of Building Services Engineers (CIBSE).
- Crisp V.H.C., P.J. Littlefair, G.T. McKenna and I.Cooper. (1985). *Daylighting as a Passive Solar Energy Option* (BR 129). Garston, Building Research Establishment,
- Den Ouden C. and T.C.Steemers (Eds). (1992) *Building 2000 (Vol. I and Vol. II)* Dordrecht (NL), Kluwer Academic Publishers,
- Energia Demo. Collection of technical reports. Istitut Català d'Energia, Barcelona
- Energy Efficient Lighting in Buildings (1991) A I Slater and P J Davidson, Garston, BRESCU-OPET for the European Commission.
- Energy Efficient Lighting in Schools, 1992; Energy Efficient Lighting in Industrial Buildings, 1992. Energy Efficient Lighting in Buildings, 1993. Energy Efficient Lighting in Offices, 1993. Energy Efficient Lighting Practice, 1994. Garston, BRECSU-OPET for the Commission of the European Communities
- Evans, Barrie. *Green report highlights priority issues.* in Architects' Journal, vol. 197, no. 14, 1993 Apr 7 p6
- *Green buildings: ideas in practice - debating natural ventilation.* in Building Services, January 1994, pp. 18–22
- *Guidelines for Ventilation Requirements in Buildings,* (Report 11, European Collaborative Action - Indoor Air Quality and its Impact on Man.) Brussels, European Commission, Directorate General for Employment, Industrial Relations and Social Affairs, 1992.
- IAEEL Newsletter, (1996)
- Levins Hal. (1996) Best sustainable indoor air quality practices in commercial buildings in Environmental Building News, http:www.ebuild.com/Greenbuilding/halpaper.html.
- Littler, John and Randall Thomas. *Design with Energy: the conservation and use of energy in buildings.* Cambridge, Cambridge University Press 1984. ISBN 0 521 24562 1
- Matteoli, Lorenzo. (1981) Energia Progetto. Torino, V.V. Celid,
- McNicholl Ann and J. Owen Lewis, (Eds.) *Daylighting in Buildings.* Dublin, UCD - OPET for the European Commission, 1994.
- Olgyay. (1973) *Design with Climate.* Princeton. Princeton University Press
- Potter, I. N. (1988) *Sick Building Syndrome.* (Technical Note 4/88). Bracknell, The Building Services Research and Information Association (BSRIA)
- Project Monitor. Series of case studies illustrating passive solar architecture in the European Union. European Commission, European Commission, DGXII, 1987.
- Ranson R. (1991) *Healthy Housing: practical guide.* World Health Organization Regional Office for Europe. London, E & FN Spon,
- Research Digest : *Solar Energy in Architecture and Urban Planning,* Nos. 1–8. Dublin, ERG-UCD for the European Commission, 1987 –1997.
- Roaf S. and M. Hancock (Eds) (1992) *Energy Efficient Building: a design guide.* Oxford, Blackwell Scientific Publications. ISBN: 0-632-03245-6
- *Sick Building Syndrome: A Practical Guide.* (Report 4, European Collaborative Action - Indoor Air Quality and its Impact on Man.) Luxembourg, European Commission, 1989.
- SunWorld (1996) Vol 20 No.3 September 1996 pp13–15
- World Resource Foundation (1985) *Construction and Demolition wastes* (Information Sheet) Tonbridge, Kent

Section 3: Strategies

URBAN AND NEIGHBOURHOOD SCALE

Urban form is the result of the complex interaction of interdependent pressures and influences: climatic, economic, social, political, strategic, aesthetic, technical and regulatory. Many planning decisions have a pervasive and long-lasting impact on social cohesion and the quality of life of the individual, as well as on the global environment. On an urban scale the issues of conservation of fossil fuel and energy resources, and the need for more environmentally friendly energy sources are magnified. However, energy efficiency is not a goal in itself, but part of an integrated search for sustainable development which recognises the local, regional and global impact of cities on air, land, water, vegetation, wildlife and the human population.

3.1 Urban fabric of Athens

The architect rarely has the power to make decisions about the location of the project within the urban fabric. In many cases the site, whether urban, suburban, brownfield or greenfield, will have been selected before the architect becomes involved in the project. At the scale of the city block, however, architects are more often involved in the planning process, and the design decisions they make have significant consequences for sustainability.

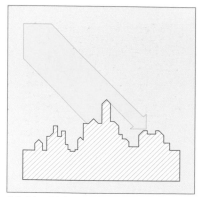

3.3 Urban fabric traps solar gain

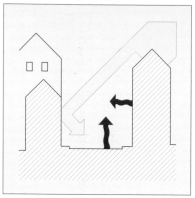

3.4 Dense materials store and radiate heat

Microclimate

The urban climate differs from that of its surrounding territory, and there is a strong relationship between urban forms and spaces and strategic energy-efficient urban design. At block and neighbourhood scale design decisions can improve local microclimate through creating shelter from excessive exposure to sun or wind, for example, or ameliorating the negative effects of urban conditions such as noise and atmospheric or visual pollution. Different layouts result in differing microclimates, providing greater or lesser comfort.

Temperature
Large towns tend to be considerably warmer than the surrounding countryside (3.2). Typically, daily mean temperatures are 1–2°C higher; more on a still summer evening. This is caused by several factors which together constitute 'the heat island' effect.

- Heat is given off by buildings, transport systems and industry
- Dense surface materials in ground and buildings store and conduct heat more effectively than do soil or vegetation (3.3, 3.4).
- Buildings impede wind flow, reducing its potential cooling effect.
- Impervious surfaces, which induce fast water run-off, and mechanical snow-clearing reduce evaporation, so there is less cooling effect.

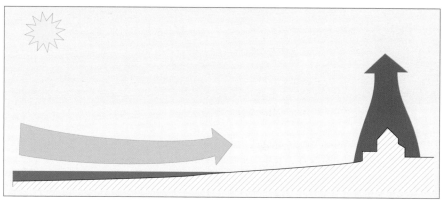

3.2 The 'heat island' effect

Wind
Because of the obstacles to wind flow presented by buildings and other structures, air movement in towns tends to be slower on average but more turbulent than in the countryside (3.5). It has been calculated that wind velocity within a town is half of what it is over open water. At the edge of a town it is reduced by a third (Meiss, 1979) (3.6).

Sunlight
It is obvious that buildings and other urban structures obstruct direct sunlight to some degree (3.7). Whether this is a benefit or disadvantage depends on other parameters of the microclimate. Depending on latitude, exposure to or protection from summer sun can be the more important.

Air quality
Pollutants from traffic, heating systems and industrial processes absorb and scatter sunlight, weakening direct solar radiation but increasing diffuse radiation on cloudless days. Air quality has implications for solar energy applications and for natural ventilation. In addition, pollutants contribute to the faster decay of building materials. Air quality, especially concentrations of CO, CO_2, SO_2, NO_x and particulates, also affects human health. It is estimated that there are ten times more particulates in city air than in the countryside (Hough, 1995).

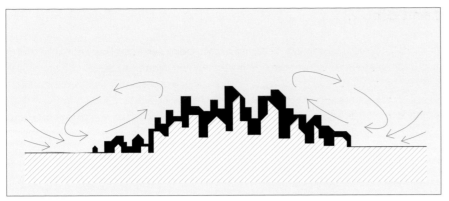

3.5 Air movement in towns is more turbulent than in the countryside.

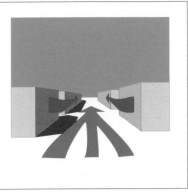

3.8 Prevailing wind funneled through a city street

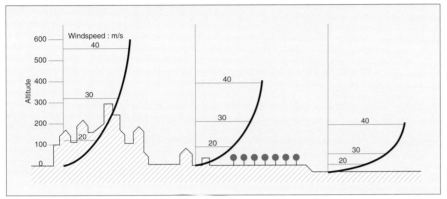

3.6 Wind speed at a given height is lower in towns than over open land.

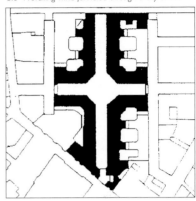

3.9 Site plan of the galleria in Milano, Mengoni

Air pollution has to be considered in two ways: firstly, the effect of pollutants on building design and performance and on the occupants' health; and secondly, the need to ensure that the buildings do not themselves contribute to more air pollution.

- Take account of prevailing winds in street layouts and orientations (3.8.) Lay out buildings to shelter public spaces, unless cooling or dispersion of atmospheric pollutants is needed (3.9).
- In cool climates choose favourable solar orientations for streets and open spaces. Where possible, prevent surrounding vegetation or structures from overshadowing solar collection areas in the heating season. In warm climates, on the other hand, existing shade can be exploited.
- Remember the effects of surface materials at ground level. Stone, brick, concrete and similar materials with high thermal capacity form a heat store which can contribute to high air temperatures. Water can have a cooling effect through evaporation, as can vegetation through shading and evapo-transpiration.

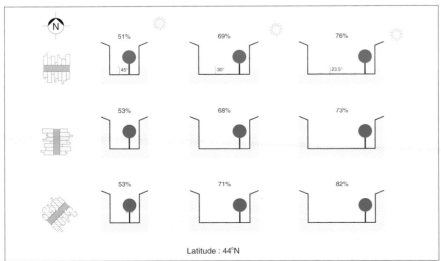

3.7 Solar access to buildings related to distance of obstructions

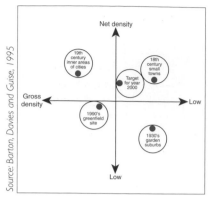

Source: Barton, Davies and Guise, 1995

3.10 Comparison of different periods of housing in terms of net and gross densities, suggesting a shift from the prevailing 1990s pattern towards the ideal of the eighteenth century town; compact, mixed use developments, surrounded by green areas for recreation, garden farming etc.

For neighbourhood developments an average net density per hectare of 100 people [or about 40–50 dwellings] is recommended (Barton, Davies and Guise, 1995) on the basis that:

- *it is the necessary density to support a good bus service*
- *it is the lowest density viable for district heating schemes*
- *it is the highest density capable of allowing good solar access with appropriate layout and it is the average level that permits a wide variety of dwelling and garden size.*

Land use

Land use is a highly significant factor in sustainable urban form. During much of the twentieth century, zoning regulations have resulted in the separation of the places where citizens work from the districts in which they live or shop or find recreation. This results in many people travelling great distances on a daily basis, diminishing the quality of their lives and, in addition, increasing levels of global pollution through emissions from the transport systems they are forced to use.

In the effort to build more sustainable cities these policies are beginning to change. City or neighbourhood centres, multi-purpose buildings and spaces with a mix of civic, office, retail, leisure and residential uses encourage multi-purpose trips. Housing developed within reach of school, work, shops, social and health facilities reduces travel, giving people easier access to jobs, and businesses, easier access to potential customers and workers.

A wide mix of house types should be provided within a given urban area, so that people can find suitably designed and priced accommodation within short commuting distance of work. Such areas can attract a wide range of skills and professions for local employment. Mixed age groups can even out-peak demand for leisure facilities, public transport and other services.

Infill urban sites, already serviced and part of an accessible infrastructure, should be exploited wherever possible. Re-using an existing brownfield site avoids many of the service and infrastructural costs of developing a greenfield site and, in addition, raises environmental and aesthetic quality in its immediate neighbourhood.

Density

It is generally argued that sustainable urban development patterns rely on the intensification and renewal of the existing fabric, and the application of bio-climatic principles to all of the activities carried on there. However, there are arguments for both high and low density (3.10).

Higher densities can mean lower energy consumption in buildings, less wastage of greenfield sites, greater use of public transport and increased potential for district and other forms of common heating. It can also have socio-economic benefits. For example, the commercial survival of many services depends on relatively high population densities for their customer base. The UK Department of the Environment encourages 'concentrating higher density residential developments near public transport centres, maintaining existing densities, and where possible increasing them' (Barton, Davis and Guise, 1995). Quoted in the same publication Friends of the Earth suggest that, overall, densities in towns and cities ought to be at the level equivalent to the three or four storey urban street. However, while high density areas are associated with more efficient provision of services and accessibility, negative impacts such as lack of public space and pollution can result. Low density may result in higher quality of life, larger houses, the possibility of working from home, and a garden or green space for vegetable growing and composting, but can also mean inefficient use of transport.

While most Western countries now urge greater density and mixed land uses in urban areas, there are cities in southern Europe which could benefit from lower densities and stricter segregation of land uses. Each individual city must be evaluated for its own character and in its own context. There are no universal answers (Athanassiou, 1996).

Large or high buildings tend not only to use more energy inside, but also to have a more severe impact on the immediate external environment in terms of shade, wind turbulence and rain shadow. Reducing size or density can improve microclimate, but if it increases investment costs profits are reduced, or housing, for example, becomes less affordable for low income people. A study which involved redesigning representative sectors of Buenos Aires concluded that 'it is possible to maintain the same densities but adopt different building forms to create better climate conditions outdoors and indoors without affecting initial or urbanisation costs.' Having studied different densities the authors concluded that 'density is not the basic factor to be considered; building form is more important' (Murillo and de Schiller, 1996). This is easier to achieve in large integrated developments with central control than in situations where individual owners are restricted only by planning codes.

Transportation

Land use, density and urban transportation systems are closely interdependent (3.11, 3.12). Cheap road and rail transport and specialised land-use zoning have encouraged dispersed settlement patterns. These require citizens to make many journeys and also make public transport systems uneconomic. The private car is the most wasteful user of energy and source of emissions today, so sustainable architecture needs to be combined with measures to reduce and restrict its use. Success partly depends on public policies for traffic calming, parking restrictions, road pricing, bus/taxi priority and other factors outside the control of the architect.

At block scale, the detailed planning of access to public transport and the provision of convenient pedestrian and cycle pathways which tie into the broader urban systems is critical. Significant development should be within easy walking distance (approximately 400m) of public transport. (Barton, Davis and Guise, 1995) For cyclists and pedestrians, routes should be continuous, reasonably direct, and free from heavy traffic, noise or pollution. Such systems encourage cycle and pedestrian travel for both functional and recreational purposes.

Design can emphasise:

- *accessibility to services for all citizens, regardless of age, ability, and economic status*
- *reduced dependence on car transport*
- *use of public transport, bicycle paths and pedestrian corridors*
- *teleworking*

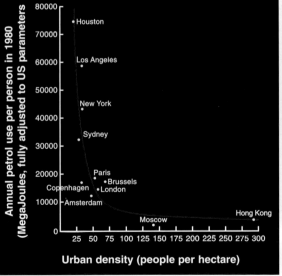

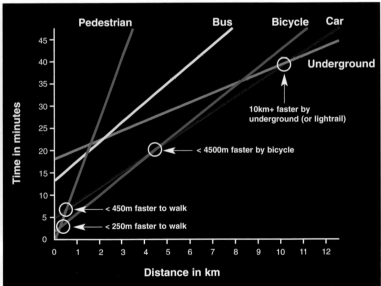

3.11 *Relationship between petrol consumption and urban density.*   3.12 *Travel times from door to door for different modes of transport in urban areas.*

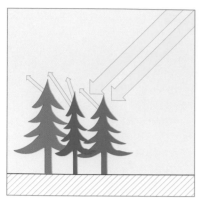

3.13 Vegetation modifies air temperatures near the ground.

Green Space

An important aspect of sustainable urban planning is the provision of green space at a number of scales. Play space, public parks and gardens in urban areas, and multi-purpose open spaces on the perimeter reduce pollution, create wildlife zones, and give access to the countryside for urban dwellers. They also contribute to the social, physical and psychological health of individuals and the community.

The green spaces in a neighbourhood can moderate local microclimate. Vegetation and water modify humidity, air temperature, wind, sunshine, noise and air pollution (3.13, 3.14, 3.15). They also have a role in the management of surface water and, potentially, of effluent (3.16). At the scale of the city parkland has a significant effect on microclimate. Temperatures can be lower by 5–10°C in urban parks than in densely built areas around them. The effect on pollution is also significant.

A particularly beneficial strategy is to connect green spaces and wildlife habitats by linear or circular green links into a city-wide network. These links can be quite narrow and still facilitate the free movement of pedestrians, cyclists and animals throughout the system. Designers can set industry in parkland, or re-claim brownfield sites for open space. Try to ensure that recreational and pedestrian spaces have some protection from noise, traffic and pollution. However, uncultivated marginal land or the strips of land bordering railways or motorways or on industrial sites can be just as effective as parkland in fostering flora and fauna.

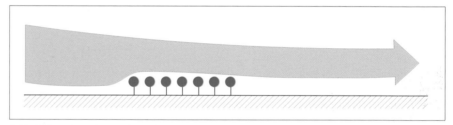

3.14   Shelter belts reduce wind speed

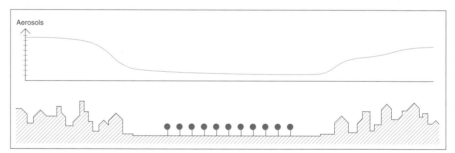

3.15   Vegetation absorbs or filters pollutants

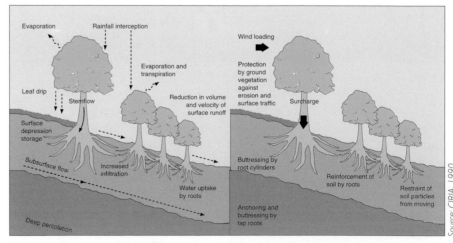

3.16   Vegetation reduces surface run-off

Source: CIRIA, 1990

Water and Waste

Waste handling and water conservation are closely linked. Poor handling of waste can irretrievably compromise the quality of water, with consequences for human and animal populations. Clean water is a resource to be protected at all times. (3.17)

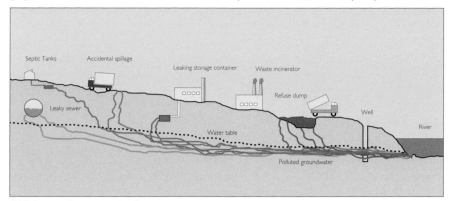

3.17 Impact of poor waste handling on water resources

Avoid designing landscape features which use water taken from the public drinking water supply and also any actions which might lead to its contamination.
Policies and designs should:

* minimise the demand for water suitable for drinking;
* minimise the amount of waste water to be handled by mechanical treatment;
* minimise the production of solid wastes, particularly unsorted wastes.

These steps will reduce the capital and running costs of public water supply, drainage and waste handling systems.

Systems which separate surface water from foul water are essential. Those separating grey water from black water are highly desirable. Filter strips of permeable ground cover and holding ponds allow rainwater to percolate back into the soil. Grey water can be treated on site using reed beds before being released into waterways. Then only black water remains to be handled by conventional treatment plants. Constructed wetlands, combined with effluent treatment, can reduce sewage treatment costs by 60–90% compared with conventional mechanical systems (Rocky Mountain Institute, 1998).

Communal provision at neighbourhood or block scale may make separation, collection and re-use of solid waste more economic. Organic waste can be composted. Combustible waste may be burned to provide district heating, but the scale of operation must be large enough to pay for the flue-gas cleaning equipment and controls which prevent the release of other pollutants into the atmosphere.

Energy

Energy efficiency at the urban scale is promoted by attention to land-use, density, transportation, water and waste, and by two additional strategies. The first is to ensure that every new or refurbished building minimises the energy embodied in its construction and used over its lifetime.
The second is to use economical and environmentally friendly energy sources to make good any remaining energy deficit. This clearly depends on local climate and conditions: renewable energies such as hydro or wind-power, ground water or biomass, active solar or PV may or may not be practical options. However, even at neighbourhood or block scale, opportunities for use of renewable energies and the more efficient use of conventional energy sources (eg. combined heat and power or district heating) present themselves more often than might be expected (Refer ELEMENTS; Components). In the case of industrial projects, educational or hospital campuses, or even large housing developments, these possibilities are well worth investigating.

Site and layout factors influencing microclimate

Outside designer's control:
Area and local climate
Plan shape of the site
Large-scale topographical features:
form, shape and aspect of the ground
Retained existing buildings
Road access
Services access
Planning constraints:
densities, building heights, tree preservation
Covenants restricting the form or character of development

Within designer's control:
Arrangement of buildings on site:
spacing, orientation, juxtaposition, courtyards, road pattern and access, location of open spaces, gardens, utility areas, garages and stores.
Design of buildings:
form, height, roof profile, orientation, fenestration and type of glass, insulation and thermal capacity
air permeability
cladding materials

Other site features
Tree cover:
major wind shelter planting
local wind shelter planting
decorative planting
Ground profiling:
mounds and banks
Walls and artificial wind breaks
Snow barriers
Ground surface:
paving, grass

BRE Digest 350 April 1990, Climate and Site Development Part 3

In most projects the site has been selected before the architect is appointed. Where this is not the case, and the architect has a role in the selection process, the issues discussed in this section can be added to those usually considered when alternative sites are being investigated. The purpose is to transfer down to the level of the individual site the sustainable approach to microclimate, land use, density, transportation, green space, water, waste and energy that the previous section addressed at the urban and block scale. This should result in a choice which offers better conditions for the building user, a more benign effect on the global environment and, very possibly, lower development costs

Site Selection

'Decisions on how to use the site, if indeed it should be built on at all, establish the base on which all later design decisions rest. The site provides the context for the buildings, but the buildings in turn modify the site. The local ecosystem is altered, habitats changed and flows of energy, water, nutrients and pollutants modified. Neighbouring buildings and distant communities are affected.' (McNicholl, 1996)

Site selection checklist
- Is the land suitable for the intended purpose (does it have cultural, historical, archaeological or scientific significance?) and for development?
- Can it be developed without being destroyed?
- Are there better uses for the land, such as agriculture?
- Is there any potential for renewable energies or district heating?
- Does the site have solar access?
- Are there lakes, ponds or streams, or wetlands? Can groundwater be tapped?
- What is the condition of air, water and soil ? What about noise?
- Is public transport available nearby?
- Is there a pre-existing infrastructure of power, water supply, communications, waste handling, and drainage?
- Depending on the intended use, are there appropriate commercial or community services nearby?
- Can existing structures be re-used?
- How might future developments on adjacent land affect the project?

It is important to emphasise that in sustainable site selection the site is considered not in isolation, but rather in its context, with a view to its place in and its contribution to the wider environment.

Site Analysis

'Careful site assessment can enable developers to capitalise on the land's potential - views, solar access, natural drainage opportunities, natural shading through vegetation, cooling from prevailing winds - while minimising or avoiding damage or disturbance to the site and surrounding areas' (Rocky Mountain Institute, 1998).

At the macroscale, the general climate of the region sets the stage with characteristic temperature, humidity, precipitation, cloudiness, wind speed, wind direction and sun path. Normal maxima and minima are used to define the amount of rainwater that must be drained away; the directions of the favourable and unfavourable winds; when solar radiation should invited or avoided and from which direction; and when the temperature moves outside the comfort zone.

At the local scale this climate will be modified by particular conditions. Drainage will affect humidity; industrial smoke or waste gases may reduce solar radiation; topography will affect wind speed.

At the microscale of the site itself available solar energy, wind speed and temperature are all subject to modification by topography, vegetation and existing buildings, walls and fences. The microscale is the scale at which most can be done to manipulate the environment around the building. The objective is to exploit the naturally occurring benefits and minimise any negative effects.

Site analysis checklist
- Air temperatures / monthly mean temperatures for day and night
- Daylight: obstructions on or near the site can affect the availability of light (3.18).
- Sunlight: slope and orientation of the site; maximum potential hours of sunlight based on climate data; sun angles based on site latitude; any overshadowingm(3.19, 3.20, 3.21).
- Wind: the wind rose for the area will give the directions and frequencies of the prevailing winds, but note the degree of exposure and local effects due to topography (3.22).
- Topography: obstructions on the site can deflect the wind and provide shelter, but they may create overshadowing.
- Structures: details of any structures which can be re-used and soil, stone or timber on the site that can be used for construction, landscaping or shelter.
- Vegetation: note the type and condition of trees, shrubs, shelter belts, crops, ground cover.
- Water: note the level of the water table and the existing pattern of water movement.
- Soil type: this will affect foundations, drainage and planting.
- Air quality and noise levels: these will have an impact on ventilation options.
- Space for on-site waste recycling or digestion, for permaculture, for biomass or food production?
- Hazards: contaminated soil or ground water, radon or electromagnetic radiation sources.
- Views: views from, of or through the site may deserve preservation or exploitation.
- Human and vehicular movement patterns.

In particular note,

Sunlight
- A south facing slope receives more solar radiation than a level site, which is important during winter when the sun angle is low.
- Slopes over 10% and facing within 45° of north are generally unsuitable for passive solar applications. Even small structures such as boundary walls may result in solar obstruction (Barton, Davis and Guise, 1995).
- Any overshadowing by hills, trees or existing buildings will affect the amount of light available. Define large or nearby obstructions, even those to the north of the site.

Wind
- Wind speeds on the crest of a hill may be 20% greater than on flat ground.
- At night time the cold air will tend to move downwards on exposed slopes, while the air is warmer higher up.
- A slight wind even on calm days is characteristic of sea-coasts or lake shores.
- Deep valleys or long straight avenues can funnel and accelerate wind speeds.
- High buildings can create localised high wind speed and turbulence.

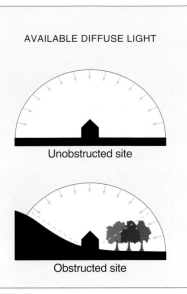

AVAILABLE DIFFUSE LIGHT

Unobstructed site

Obstructed site

3.18 Effect of obstruction on daylight availability

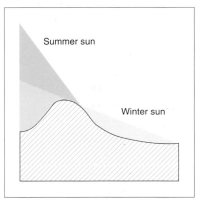

Summer sun

Winter sun

3.19 Effect of topography on solar access

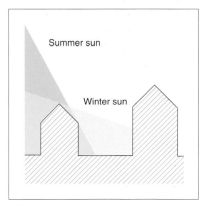

Summer sun

Winter sun

3.20 Effect of buildings on solar access

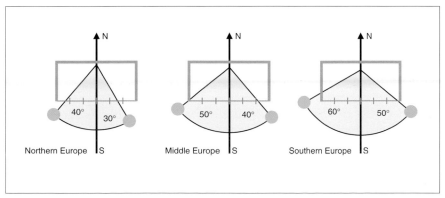

Northern Europe — 40° / 30° — S

Middle Europe — 50° / 40° — S

Southern Europe — 60° / 50° — S

3.21 Best orientation for solar gain varies with latitude.

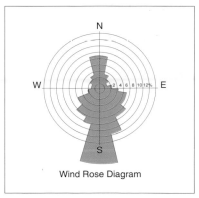

Wind Rose Diagram

3.22 Local wind patterns

SITE PLANNING

Urban and Neighbourhood Scale considered primarily the impact of development on the regional and global environment and on the community in which it sits. At the level of the site these continue to be of concern, but the designer begins to consider also the implications for the owner and for the users of the buildings which are to be built. The value of interdisciplinary team work at this stage cannot be overstated.

'Good design should exploit or manipulate site characteristics to reduce energy consumption in the building. The objective is to create the best possible conditions for the building and its occupants, and the most positive interaction with the wider environment' (McNicholl, 1996).

Site planning typically involves the evaluation of a number of site characteristics, but some of the natural characteristics of the site and the potential of alternative energies are often ignored. There are a number of critical relationships: those between the buildings themselves; between the buildings and the topography of the site; and the overall harmony of behaviour between buildings, vegetation and natural and artificial land forms. When internal and external spaces are designed with bioclimatic aims, buildings and the space surrounding them react together to regulate the internal and external environment, to enhance and protect the site, local ecosystems and bio-diversity. (3.23, 3.24).

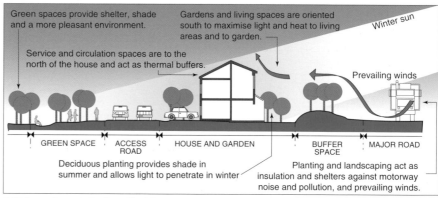

3.23 Some site strategies for residential areas

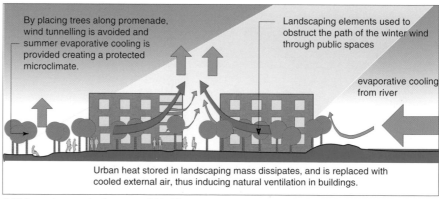

3.24 Some site strategies for commercial buildings

Microclimate

At the level of the individual site we consider microclimate from two viewpoints. We are concerned to modify site microclimate so as to create optimum conditions within the building while consuming the minimum of energy. We also want to design and locate the buildings so as to provide pleasant exterior spaces to be enjoyed by occupants and passers-by.

Density

Site coverage is usually determined by the interaction of financial objectives and local ordinances. Preserve and reinforce what you can of natural landscape and topography or, where this is inappropriate, try to ensure that the new buildings do not compromise conditions in nearby buildings or neighbouring streets and urban spaces. Remember that large buildings, in addition to using more energy in construction and in use, have a more radical effect on the immediate microclimate.

Transportation

Pedestrian and cycle routes should generally follow the contours of the site, to a normal maximum gradient of 1:20. Absolute maxima are 1:12 for pedestrians over very short distances or 1:14 for cyclists over distances not exceeding 30m (Barton, Davis and Guise, 1995). In planning these routes take advantage of landmarks, views and existing vegetation, but try to ensure that pathways are sufficiently busy or overlooked that users are safe (3.25). Where parking is needed it can be integrated into the overall landscape. Parking areas do not need to have an impervious surface. Perforated blocks allow them to be grass-covered when not in use for parking, the parking area can form part of the landscaping.

Green Space

Gardens and other green spaces provide visual and physical release from the enclosure of the building. Where site space is limited, a diversity of options such as balconies, terraces, roof gardens or courtyards can be explored. In residential areas, gardens allow the opportunity to grow food and should ideally be provided in a variety of sizes. In green spaces design will exploit landscape, water and vegetation to modify wind and shelter, light and shade, noise and air quality to provide the best conditions for the users of the building and the site.

Existing trees and vegetation should be protected and used in conjunction with new planting to create a desirable microclimate. Natural, indigenous planting has many advantages, and selecting the right varieties of trees, shrubs and ground cover can greatly reduce maintenance costs (3.26).

Avoid planning landscape features which will need irrigation in summer, unless provision is being made for the storage and re-use of rainwater or grey water.

3.25 Plan safe pedestrian routes

Type of open space	Index
Woodland	100
Shrubs	118
Groundcovers	475
Roses	1075
Rose gardens	1291
Annuals	6855
Perennials	1842
Hedges	1303
Lawns (overall maintenance)	210

Source: Aanemerij Plantsoenen vande Gemeete, Rotterdam, Dept of Parks, Rotterdam, 1980

3.26 Plants: comparative costs of maintenance

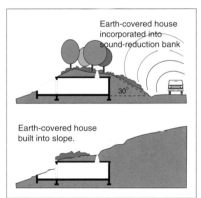

Earth-covered house incorporated into sound-reduction bank

Earth-covered house built into slope.

3.27

Indigenous Planting
While significantly reducing maintenance costs, indigenous planting also:
- promotes long-term landscape stability and sustainability;
- increases biological diversity;
- enhances groundwater recharge through increased absorption;
- regenerates organic soil layer through decomposition of above-ground growth;
- reduces soil erosion with soil-holding root systems;
- reduces downstream flooding by virtually eliminating surface water run-off;
- preserves and/or restores existing plant and seed banks, maintaining genetic memory;
- improves air quality through permanent carbon fixing in the soil;
- improves water quality through filtering of dirty water and slowing of surface water velocities;
- reduces maintenance impacts through reduction or elimination of herbicide, pesticide and fertiliser applications, motor mowing emissions and irrigation.
  (Rocky Mountain Institute, 1998)

Earth
- Earth berms will provide shelter and deflect noise (3.27).
- On a sloped site the building should be terraced rather than the land flattened.

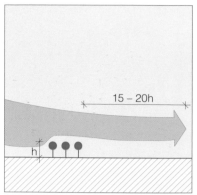

3.28 Natural shelter belts: extent of sheltered zone

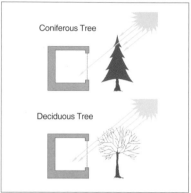

3.29

3.30

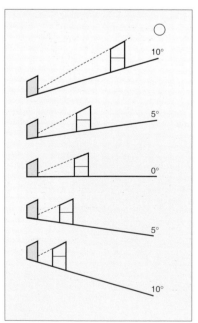

3.31 Effect of slope on solar access

Trees and Shrubs

- Tree and shrub belts can reduce wind velocities by up to 50% for a distance downwind of 10–20 x their height (3.28).
- Trees in leaf reduce the amount of available light to 10–20% of its unobstructed value; even in winter deciduous trees reduce it by 40 or 50% (3.29).
- Dense shelter belts of trees and shrubs act as a sound barrier
- Trees and shrubs absorb CO_2 and can remove up to 75% of dust, lead and other particulates from the air.
- Trees and shrubs can lower summer temperatures by shading and evapo-transpiration (3.30).
- Trees and shrubs can increase winter temperatures by slowing wind speeds and reducing radiation to the night sky.
- Trees with tall trunks and high canopy provide shade from the sun and, at the same time, permit cooling air circulation near ground level.
- Shrubs or small trees can be used to shade any air conditioning or heat pump equipment which is located externally. This will improve the performance of the equipment. For good airflow and access, plants should not be closer than 900mm to the compressor.
- Carefully evaluate existing plants on site to identify those which can play a role in an energy-conserving landscape. Mature trees will require less effort to maintain and will generally be of a larger size and more established than newly planted varieties.
- If large trees need to be planted, it is best to select varieties that have a moderate rather than fast growth rate. These are sturdier against storm damage and generally more resistant to insects and disease.

Surface Cover

- Ground-cover planting and/or turf has a cooling effect through evapo-transpiration (the loss of water through the soil by evaporation and transpiration of the plants growing on it).
- The temperature emitted by ground-cover will be 10–15° cooler than that of heat-absorbent materials such as asphalt or a reflective material such as light coloured gravel or rock.
- A heat-absorbent material will continue to radiate heat after sunset.
- Vines can be used to provide shading on walls and windows. Trellises placed close to the walls can be used to support growth without touching the walls.
- Deciduous vines will allow winter sunlight to penetrate, while providing welcome summer shading. Evergreen vines will shade walls in the summer and reduce the effects of cold winds in the winter.

Water Features:

- In southern Europe water features can help moderate microclimate through evaporative cooling of outdoor spaces.
- Where possible, try to isolate the space to be cooled from the surroundings, so as to concentrate the benefits of the cooling presence of water in a limited area. The courtyard is a classic form.
- The effect of a fountain on relative humidity extends to a distance of 2m radius only, unless it is surrounded by a green area with plenty of planting (Romero, 96).
- In sustainable landscape design the site's natural drainage patterns can be used to create water features.

Water and Waste

At present, most developed sites deal with rainwater run-off by channelling it into sewers. In storm conditions rainwater mixed with sewage overflows into streams. A natural drainage system mimics nature, eliminates sewage treatment concerns and costs substantially less to build. Try to follow the natural drainage patterns on the site. Minimise the extent of impervious surfaces such as driveways, parking and paving. This slows run-off, reducing damage to neighbouring land and waterways and the load on the district sewage system. Ensure that as much rainwater as possible finds its way back into the soil in as clean a condition as possible. Consider also the possibility of collecting and storing rainwater for irrigating vegetation, cleaning exterior surfaces and other outdoor uses. As for foul water, there are a wide range of treatment plants available, including septic tank, rotating bio-disks, reed beds, dry toilet systems. Separation of grey water and black water offer the possibility of re-using site-treated greywater for irrigation and other uses.

'Carefully designed storm water infiltration systems, natural wastewater treatment systems and water-efficient landscaping strategies all can save the developer money' (Rocky Mountain Institute, 1998). However, remember that even such natural systems need proper maintenance to function effectively.

Provide on-site facilities for separation, storage and collection of solid waste, where possible. Organic waste can be composted for use in site landscape or, in residential areas, for private gardens.

Energy

Creative use of the site to reduce heating and/or cooling loads within the building represents one of the greatest opportunities in site design. The best position for the building is found by assessing the interior demands of the building in relation to data gathered in the course of the detailed site analysis (Refer STRATEGIES; Site Selection and Analysis).

Heating

In northern latitudes, where heating load is the dominant factor in many buildings, the 'ideal' orientation for passive solar design is a south-facing principal facade. In residential buildings large window openings on the south facade allow the sun to flood into the building in winter-time and openings on the northern facade can be reduced to the minimum. In the United Kingdom, ETSU studies have shown that for a given site with given houses, simple site replanning and dwelling reorientation can almost halve energy demand per house.

In non-residential buildings at these latitudes the daylight gained through larger windows on the north facade may more than balance the heat losses through them, and overheating must be prevented by shading on south facades. In these buildings windows on east or west facades are often the cause of overheating and are difficult to shade effectively. In either case it is wise to site the proposed buildings in the zone with the least overshadowing during the most important hours of the heating season. South-facing slopes receive more sun than ground sloping north (3.31). Place taller buildings to the north, so they do not overshadow the lower ones. When assessing the potential solar gain, take account of any shade or partial shade from trees, and thermal radiation from adjacent buildings walls and surfaces.

As stated in earlier sections, site topography will affect wind speed and direction. In many areas of Europe the wind blows predominantly from one direction and design should attempt to deflect or reduce this without reducing solar gain.

Wind speed or direction can be modified by new land forms, structures and vegetation, and the form of individual buildings can be designed to block or divert winds (3.32, 3.33, 3.34). Using or creating shelter on the site can cut heat loss from buildings, through convection and infiltration, by up to 15% (Barton, Davis and Guise, 1995). It can also improve the comfort of outdoor living spaces.

Cooling

In southern latitudes orient the building and use its fenestration to minimise solar overheating, taking advantage of any existing shade. But do not forget the need for adequate daylight.
In the south, especially with light-weight, low thermal inertia buildings, specific measures may be required. In the cooling season, it may be useful to direct the prevailing wind flow, using building form, vegetation or topography to funnel cool breezes around or through the building, reducing the cooling load (3.35).

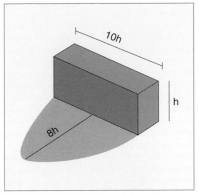
3.32 Solid barrier: maximum sheltered zone

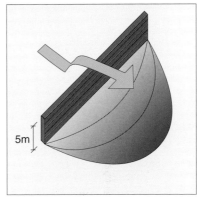
3.33 Calculated areas of protection behind a permeable windbreak

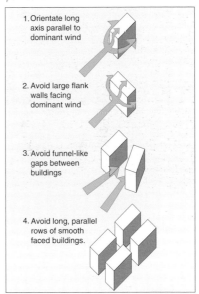
1. Orientate long axis parallel to dominant wind

2. Avoid large flank walls facing dominant wind

3. Avoid funnel-like gaps between buildings

4. Avoid long, parallel rows of smooth faced buildings.

3.34 Choose form and arrangement of building clusters to avoid downdraughts and shelter external spaces

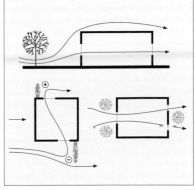
3.35

When hard surfaces are used, pale colours are more effective in reflecting solar radiation and consequently keeping down surface temperatures, but they may cause glare. For cooling, it is best to minimise the use of heat absorbent and reflective materials near buildings and/or shade them from any direct sunshine.

Use vegetation in the form of trees or vines, and ground cover planting instead of hard surfaces. Both will lower temperatures through shading and evapo-transpiration.

Consider the use of water features to provide evaporative cooling.

Ventilation

Air quality and noise affect the extent to which opening windows can be used for ventilation.

Sound is reflected by surrounding objects and hard surfaces. It is reduced by distance and barriers (such as walls, buildings and earth berms), and absorbed to some degree by soft ground surfaces and walls.

Trees can play a double role in this regard. Dense shelter belts act as a sound barrier and, in addition, absorb CO_2 and can remove up to 75% of dust, lead and other particulates from the air.

Daylight

The amount of daylight available in the building will be affected by the placement of the buildings on the site, the amount of overshadowing, the external landscaping and finishes. Pale surfaces on the ground and on neighbouring buildings will increase the amount of light available to the interior.

The location of trees in relation to buildings needs careful consideration, because they reduce light transmission even when leafless in winter. One rule of thumb is to locate only smaller trees (5–10m high, depending on distance) to the south of the building.

BUILDING FORM

Building plan and form emerge in a complex process. Functional, technical and aesthetic considerations all contribute to a synthesis. Wind, solar availability and direction, shelter and exposure, air quality and noise conditions will inform the relationship of the building to its external environment and effect the form and the design of the envelope. Bioclimatic heating, cooling, daylighting and energy strategies should be meshed at an early stage with the architect's other priorities. Simply making the building the right shape and the correct orientation can reduce the energy consumption by 30–40% at no extra cost.

Getting the form and spatial organisation right first time is important. Changes once the building is built are difficult if not impossible, and both financially and environmentally costly.

Zone and orient spaces, both in plan and in section, in relation to their heating, cooling, lighting and ventilation needs so as to minimise the total energy demand of the building (3.36).

Where possible, locate spaces requiring continuous heat on southern façades so that they can benefit from solar gain; buffer them to the north with spaces which do not need it. Rooms needing only intermittent heating can occupy less favourable orientations. For optimal performance of passive solar heating, daylighting and natural cooling, the heat gaining spaces should all face within 15° of due south.

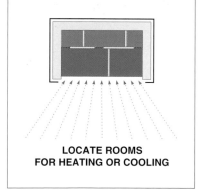

**LOCATE ROOMS
FOR HEATING OR COOLING**

3.36

Conversely, spaces needing cooling should be located on northern façades. Spaces where daylight is important clearly need to be located near to the walls or roof of the building. For natural ventilation the depth and section of the building are critical.

Meeting these objectives for every space, while also satisfying the normal functional demands of any building, is not easy, and heavily influences its form (3.37).

In terms of heating and cooling the optimum shape of a building is one which loses the minimum amount of heat in the heating season and gains the minimum amount in the cooling season. This of course will vary according to the climatic zone in which the building is located.

A building elongated along the east-west axis exposes the longer south side to maximum heat gain in the winter months, and the shorter east and west sides to maximum heat gain in summer. At European latitudes the south facade of a building receives at least three times the solar radiation in winter as the east and west. In summer the situation is reversed. In both in summer and winter, the north side receives very little radiation. Consequently a building elongated along the east-west axis is held to be the most efficient shape in all climates for minimising heating requirements in winter and cooling in summer, but the extent of elongation depends on the climate (Olygay, 1973).

In all climates, attached units like row houses or terraced houses are the most efficient because only two walls are external, and the opportunity for cross-ventilation is available. For a given floor area, apartments use less energy than terraced houses; terraced less than semi-detached; and semi-detached, less than detached houses (3.38).

Two formal elements often used in conventional buildings, the sunspace and the atrium, can play a useful role in passive solar design.

Familiar in the form of the traditional domestic conservatory, glazed balcony or loggia, the sunspace has, over time, proven to be a practical and versatile element of passive solar heating. Employing a combination of both direct and indirect gain approaches, it can be incorporated into the design of a new building, or can be a valuable addition to an existing one (3.39).

The atrium has the power to transform both functionally and climatically what might have been seen as an anonymous street or a drab, lifeless courtyard into a sheltered, functional amenity, an asset to any development. For this reason, the covering of open spaces between buildings with glazed roofing has become a common feature, but exploitation of the potential to reduce heating, cooling and lighting demands tends to be overlooked. A correctly designed atrium will improve indoor comfort and reduce payback time (3.40).

Most European buildings, of course, have both a heating and cooling season, so must provide for some degree of adjustment to meet changing conditions. In addition, on many sites the microclimate conditions create their own conflicts, such as severe wind exposure on the southern facade for example. Furthermore, constricted sites, difficult boundary conditions or local regulations may place further restrictions on the designer's ability to achieve optimum response to climate.

Finally, energy considerations alone can never determine building form. Design for flexibility and 'loose fit' to encourage re-use in the future, but remember also that in terms of environmental impact the expression 'small is beautiful' is a useful guide.

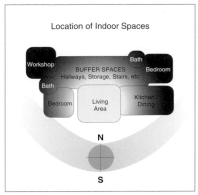

3.37

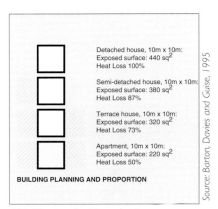

3.38 Heat loss for different housing types

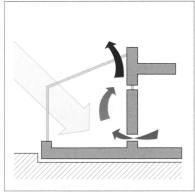

3.39 A sunspace will effect solar energy and reduce heat loss.

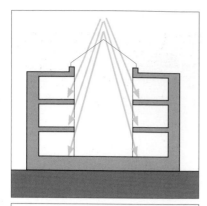

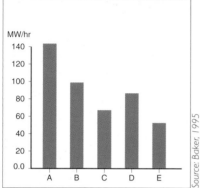

3.40 Annual heating energy consumption for a building with an atrium: A - No atrium; B - Atrium present, but no ventilation coupling with the building; C - Ventilation pre-heating, D - Ventilating air expelled into atrium, raising its temperature; E - Recirculation of air between building and atrium.

Source: Baker, 1995

3.42 Overhangs and canopies shade envelope.

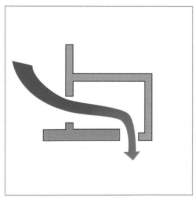

3.43 Locate openings to catch prevailing winds

Northern Latitudes

Where heating is the dominant requirement the following strategies can be effective:

- low surface to volume ratio;
- maximising solar gain;
- reduction of the surface area facing north, or exposed to prevailing winds
- insulation of building envelope;
- control of ventilation and infiltration;
- use of draught lobbies to separate heated spaces from unheated spaces and from the outside;
- location of entrance doors away from corners and from prevailing winds;
- use of 'buffer spaces' on northern or exposed facades, and unheated conservatories or 'sunspaces' on the south. The less the temperature difference between internal and outdoor temperatures, the lower the rate of heat loss through the envelope;
- use of atria and courtyards to act as thermal buffer space and introduce daylight into deep plans;
- use of thermal mass to store heat produced by solar gain and release it as interior temperatures fall (3.41).

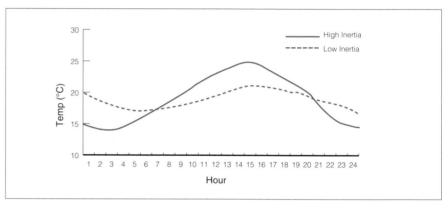

3.41 Internal temperatures on a hot day in buildings of high and low thermal inertia. Thermal mass can help in both hot and cold climates

Southern Latitudes

Where cooling is the dominant need the following strategies may apply:

- low surface to volume ratio;
- reduction of the surface area facing south;
- provision of overhangs, arcades, shutters and canopies to shade building envelope (3.42);
- insulation of building envelope, particularly the roof;
- control of ventilation and infiltration when exterior air temperatures are high;
- provision of solar chimneys to encourage stack ventilation where outdoor temperatures are sufficiently cool;
- location of openings on shaded side of building or so as to catch prevailing winds. (3.43)
- use of 'buffer spaces' on southern facades;
- use of thermal mass to store heat produced by solar gain thus reducing overheating in interior spaces;
- use of courtyards to form reservoirs of cool air close to building and introduce daylight to deep building plans;
- use of water features for evaporative cooling.

ENVELOPE

In sustainable architecture the link between building performance and the design of the envelope is critical. Any well-built building enclosure is expected to keep out wind, damp and rain, to let in light and air, to conserve heat and to provide security and privacy. In a sustainable building we may also expect it to mediate the effects of climate on the energy systems of the building, collect and store heat, redirect light, control air movement and generate power.

A better envelope may sometimes be more expensive to build, but if it improves the balance between heat gain and heat loss, reduces the size of heating plant, eliminates the need for perimeter heating, or cuts fuel bills, the extra cost may be balanced by savings.

Apart from any ventilation openings they may contain, the opaque areas of walls, floors and roofs are static elements. The functions include thermal functions such as heating and cooling through shelter and insulation and by reduction of temperature swings through use of thermal mass; as well as acoustic and energy production functions (3.44).

The glazed elements of the building may be more dynamic to respond to short- and long-term changes in interior and exterior conditions. They have more complex functions such as daylighting, as well as providing views and communication with the outside; heating through controlled use of solar gain and cooling by shading and ventilation (3.45).

Sustainable strategies for envelope design

- Respond to orientation. The world about the building is not symmetrical. Modify the envelope to respond to the problems and opportunities presented by different façade orientations (3.46).
- Keep the fabric warm. Place insulation as close as practicable to the exterior face of the envelope. This allows the envelope to contribute to the thermal mass of the building, helps to even out interior temperature fluctuations and raises the radiant temperature of the interior.
- Design for durability. Specify for long life and low maintenance to minimise the use of energy and materials over the life of the building.
- Keep it simple. Do as much as possible by architectural means before resorting to service installations to fine-tune the indoor environment.

3.44

3.45 Active façade

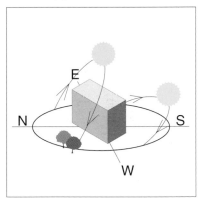

3.46 Respond to orientation

Considerations for façade design include:

- *Thermal, solar and light transmission properties of the elements*
- *Control of openings, for heat losses and gains*
- *Potential for thermal collection and storage*
- *Glazing ratios*

The role the envelope is asked to play in any particular building will depend on the heating, cooling, ventilation and lighting strategies adopted.

The following checklist may help to prioritise decisions in relation to envelope design and specification:

- *Is it to be a slow or fast response building?*
- *Is the envelope to be used as a heat store?*
- *Is the primary objective to exploit daylight, to maximise heat gain, or to minimise heat loss?*
- *Are there particular problems of use, site or orientation to be overcome?*

Choices about materials will be influenced by issues of embodied energy and of health.

Architects: Sottomayor, Dominguez and Lopez de Asian

3.47

Opaque / Solid Elements

The solid elements of the building envelope can perform both heating and cooling functions through use of thermal mass, insulation and protection of the internal environment from air infiltration.

HEATING AND COOLING

Efficient thermal performance of the envelope in northern Europe means heat conservation. Buildings lose heat through their external fabric and by uncontrolled ventilation and infiltration.

In southern Europe walls may facilitate the undesirable transfer of heat to the inside. Traditionally, solid, brightly painted walls are used to reflect solar radiation, while the thermal inertia of masonry walls slows down unwanted gain and dissipates it at night keeping the interior cool (3.47).

For both heating and cooling functions, the thermal properties of an opaque wall can be controlled by:
- thermal conductivity and thermal storage capacity of material (thermal mass);
- thermal insulation;
- good detailing.

Thermal Mass
Recent studies analysing passive solar design of non-domestic buildings (HGA 1994) found that:
- high thermal mass is desirable to stabilise daytime temperatures and for night cooling, but may marginally increase heating cost;
- thermal mass is best increased by maximising surface area, increase in thickness is relatively ineffective;
- thermal mass should not be thermally isolated from circulating air (e.g. under a raised floor or above a suspended ceiling);
- secure and controllable night cooling should be provided where exposed thermal mass is intended to moderate day-time temperatures.

Walls
Wall materials can be categorised in terms of low or high thermal mass. For example masonry construction has good thermal inertia qualities, which slow down the building's response to changes in external conditions and limit internal temperature swings. Clay bricks, concrete blocks and rammed earth are examples of this kind of construction.

A low thermal mass building is one with a timber- or steel-framed structure and lightweight cladding panels. This gives a fast thermal response to changes in external conditions and results in large temperature swings. Timber frame construction, which is one example of this type, is becoming more widespread and acceptable, and lends itself to high levels of insulation (Talbott 1993).

In buildings occupied by day, thermal mass will absorb heat during the day and release it at night, reducing peak day-time air temperatures. Thermal comfort depends as much on mean radiant temperature as on air temperature, and the surface temperature of thermally massive elements will be lower than air temperature at peak times, contributing further to comfort.

Floors
Suspended timber floors have less embodied energy than concrete floors (Refer, ISSUES, Environment), but a concrete slab, provided that it is not covered with a lightweight finish, can act as a thermal store, as the cross-section through the floor construction of the BRE building in the UK illustrates (3.48).

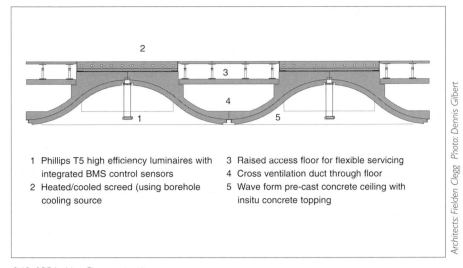

1 Phillips T5 high efficiency luminaires with
   integrated BMS control sensors
2 Heated/cooled screed (using borehole
   cooling source
3 Raised access floor for flexible servicing
4 Cross ventilation duct through floor
5 Wave form pre-cast concrete ceiling with
   insitu concrete topping

Architects: Fielden Clegg Photo: Dennis Gilbert

3.48 BRE building, Floor construction.

Insulation

Walls, roofs and other opaque parts of a building must be provided with thermal insulation, both to reduce heat loss and to maintain internal surfaces at a higher temperature than would otherwise be the case, thus improving comfort levels.

Reduction of heat loss by means of increased levels of insulation is still the most effective conservation measure, but it should be remembered that the law of diminishing returns applies in specifying insulation thickness. For example, savings achieved by increasing thickness from 4 to 6cm are comparable to savings when thickness is increased from 6 to 12cm (3.49, 3.50).

Walls

Insulation may be placed on the outside face of a wall, on the inside or within the wall without altering the overall insulation properties. Occupancy patterns, the response time of the heating system and its controls, and the optimal thermal mass of the building will determine the appropriate position (Achard, Gicquel 1986).

Internal insulation
Internal insulation will separate the thermal mass of the walls from the space, and reduce both the response time and the energy required to bring the room up to comfort levels. There may be thermal mass available in other elements in the space which will dampen temperature fluctuations. Otherwise the application is appropriate only for intermittently heated buildings.

The disadvantage of internal insulation is that it is prone to detailing problems such as thermal bridging and condensation.

External insulation
The higher internal thermal capacity available as a result of locating the insulation on the outside of the building means that fluctuations in air temperature are reduced, but the space will take longer to heat up and cool down. Thus the application is most suitable for continuously heated buildings.

The disadvantage of locating the insulation externally is that the layers of finish on the outside of the insulation will be subject to large temperature fluctuations, resulting in thermal stress and movement.

Cavity insulation
In some parts of Europe cavity wall insulation is a standard form of construction. The cavity may be either partially or fully insulated depending on the details of construction,

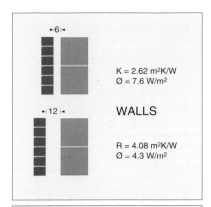

K = 2.62 m²K/W
Ø = 7.6 W/m²

WALLS

R = 4.08 m²K/W
Ø = 4.3 W/m²

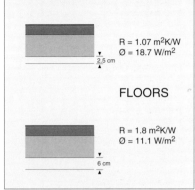

R = 1.07 m²K/W
Ø = 18.7 W/m²
2.5 cm

FLOORS

R = 1.8 m²K/W
Ø = 11.1 W/m²
6 cm

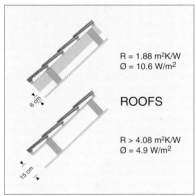

R = 1.88 m²K/W
Ø = 10.6 W/m²
6 cm

ROOFS

R > 4.08 m²K/W
Ø = 4.9 W/m²
15 cm

3.49 Types of thermal insulation

Materials	Thermal Conductivity W/mK
Expanded polystyrene board	0.036–0.038
Expanded polystyrene cavity wall partial fill board	0.025
Glass fibre quilt	0.040
Glass fibre partial fill cavity slab	0.034
Mineral fibre quilt	0.037
Mineral fibre partial fill cavity slab	0.032–0.033
Polyurethane board	0.023–0.025

3.50 Thermal conductivity of some common insulating materials

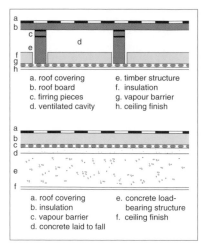

a. roof covering   e. timber structure
b. roof board   f. insulation
c. firring pieces   g. vapour barrier
d. ventilated cavity   h. ceiling finish

a. roof covering   e. concrete load-
b. insulation   bearing structure
c. vapour barrier   f. ceiling finish
d. concrete laid to fall

3.51 Section through typical 'cold roof' (top) and typical 'warm roof' (bottom)

and the climate. Cavity insulation makes available some of the thermal inertia within the wall and substantially reduces the risk of condensation within the building. It also reduces problems from thermal bridges.

Roofs

Generally the position of insulation in the roof will offer similar advantages and disadvantages as mentioned for walls.

Pitched roofs are usually insulated just above ceiling level leaving the attic space unheated (if it is not occupied). The unheated space is well ventilated and risk of condensation is low. Insulation can easily be upgraded by adding another layer.

Flat roofs may be one of two types: the 'cold roof' is ventilated above the insulation, while in the 'warm roof' the insulation layer lies immediately below the roof covering and is unventilated. The warm roof is recommended and has less risk of condensation, but as with external insulation, the layers of finish on top of the insulation will be subject to large temperature fluctuations, and to thermal stress and movement (3.51).

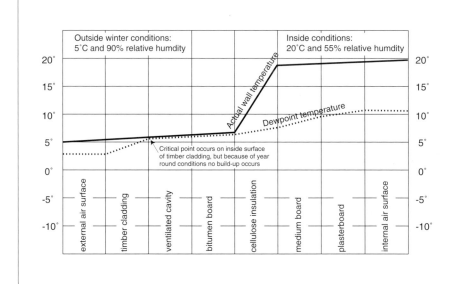

Breathing walls

Breathing wall construction is a type of timber frame construction that is attracting attention among architects interested in green or ecological issues. The houses at Findhorn (Talbott, 1993) (3.52) are constructed using this technique. Breathing walls are porous to air and water vapour. It is postulated that modern building methods lead to air-tight enclosures giving rise to extremes of internal humidity and lack of ventilation, and that breathing wall construction methods can overcome this. Studies carried out at the Martin Centre in Cambridge (Crowther, Baker 1993) sought to discover whether breathing walls could be shown to provide energy-efficient background ventilation. The results showed that no actual air-flow was taking place, but that internal humidity was related to that outside. The testers suggested that a variation in the results could be obtained by varying materials used and construction techniques.

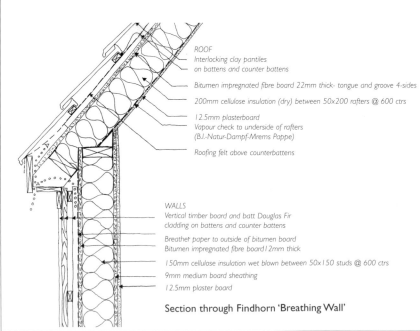

ROOF
*Interlocking clay pantiles
on battens and counter battens*

Bitumen impregnated fibre board 22mm thick- tongue and groove 4-sides

200mm cellulose insulation (dry) between 50x200 rafters @ 600 ctrs

*12.5mm plasterboard
Vapour check to underside of rafters
(B.I.-Natur-Dampf-Mrems Pappe)*

Roofing felt above counterbattens

WALLS
*Vertical timber board and batt Douglas Fir
cladding on battens and counter battens*

*Breather paper to outside of bitumen board
Bitumen impregnated fibre board12mm thick*

150mm cellulose insulation wet blown between 50x150 studs @ 600 ctrs

9mm medium board sheathing

12.5mm plaster board

Section through Findhorn 'Breathing Wall'

3.52 Breathing walls

Floors

There is evidence that heat losses through ground floors are greater than standard calculations suggest. Heat loss from the slab is not constant over the whole area of the floor, the greatest being from the edge. Insulating the edges of the slab will have as good an effect as overall insulation (BRE, 1994) and the U-value calculation for the ground floor slab must take into account both the size and edge conditions of the slab.

Additional insulation of a suspended timber floor is usually provided in the form of either a continuous layer of semi-rigid or flexible material laid above the joists (and below the floor finish), or else semi-rigid material between the joists. The U-value is calculated as a combination of the floor finish, the air-spaces and the overall insulation above the structural floor.

Superinsulated construction

This technique is used widely in Canada and in Scandinavian countries. It uses a combination of high levels of insulation in combination with timber frame construction. It is more air-tight, has less thermal bridging, and is built more carefully.

Superinsulation has less impact on the architectural character of a building than other sustainable strategies. It is less demanding of plan layout, section, orientation and window design than a passive solar strategy. High insulation levels are the main way of saving energy, but beyond a certain point increased insulation will bring diminishing levels of return, and this point will vary in relation to climate and fuel cost. Great care must be taken to avoid air leaks; moisture in the cavity will affect the performance of the insulation and rot the structure.

Superinsulation is primarily a cold-climate construction technique. In hot humid climates increasing the building's thermal resistance involves adding radiant barriers. The radiant barrier should face into an air space, and should not be sealed or it would then act as a vapour retardant and lead to condensation within the wall (Fisher, 1985).
(Refer ELEMENTS; Radiant Barriers)

Section showing diagrammatically the construction of a transparent insulation wall.

1
A pane of low-iron content glass in glazing bars.

2
Cavity containing a motorised blind which can be raised to admit solar radiation, or lowered to reflect unwanted solar radiation in summer to conserve heat at night.

3
Transparent insulation material and supporting clips.

4 (dotted)
Backing sheet of transparent polycarbonate to prevent convection losses through the insulation from the heated wall

5
Cavity to prevent conduction losses through the insulation from the heated wall. Cavity is closed horizontally at intervals to reduce air circulation leading to higher convection losses.

6
Layer of dark blue paint to increase heat absorption.

7
Wall of dense concrete blocks to store heat with internal plaster finish.

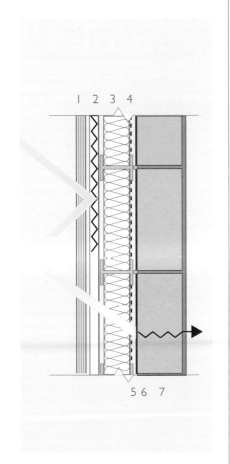

3.53 Superinsulated wall construction

Source: Okalux Kapillarglas GmbH

3.54 Okalux glass with transparent insulation

Translucent Elements

HEATING

Transparent insulation material (TIM) can admit daylight but without the heat loss associated with conventional glazing. In addition, its composition still allows useful solar gain. Studies show that the heating load in both new and retrofit applications can be reduced by up to 75% with the application of TIM (O'Cofaigh, 1996). However care is needed to avoid overheating problems.

DAYLIGHTING

Transparent insulation material sandwiched between sheets of glass in a conventional frame can replace traditional windows where light but not vision is required (3.54, 3.55). There are several categories of TIM, and light transmission ranges from 45–80% with a reduction of approximately 8% for each sheet of protective glass used. Thermal insulation values are very much better than for glass: 98mm hexagonal honeycomb polyamide TIM has a light transmission factor of 61%, combined with a thermal resistance value five times that of a double-glazed window. Costs currently are about three times those of conventional double-glazed windows.

Architect: Thomas Herzog

3.55 Hostel at Windberg with transparent insulated facade.

Transparent Elements

In a sustainable building the glazing elements are often the most interesting and complex. Glazing and window design are the areas in which there have been the greatest technical developments in recent years, with new materials emerging from research laboratories. It is now possible to specify the make-up of a glazing unit to meet the requirements for heat gain, heat conservation, light transmission and light direction, at different latitudes and for different orientations (3.56).

Good window design means finding a balance between demands which are often conflicting such as passive heating and cooling functions, e.g. allow solar gain but keep out excessive solar heat, provide sufficient daylight without causing glare, allow controllable ventilation into the building but keep out excessive noise, allow visual contact with the surroundings but ensure sufficient privacy and ensure safety.

HEATING

Direct heat gain through correctly oriented windows is the simplest and often the most effective manifestation of 'climatic' architecture. Glazing design and orientation should optimise useful solar gains and minimise heat losses during the heating season.

The design of glazed areas must balance heating, cooling and daylighting needs. (Refer EVALUATION; The LT Method).

Description	Thickness mm (italics denote cavity)	% Direct Radiant Heat Transmission	U-value W/m²K	% Light Transmission
Single clear glass	6	0.83	5.4–5.8	88
Double	6,*12*, 6	0.72	2.8–3.0	78
Double with Low E coatings	6,*12*, 6	0.52	1.7–2.0	74
Triple	6		1.9	69
Triple with two low e coatings	6,*12*, 6,*12*, 6	0.45	1.0–1.2	65
Double low e and partially evacuated space	6,*12*, 6	0.5–0.75	0.5	74
Double low e and argon	6,*12*, 6,*12*, 6	0.5–0.75	1.5	74
Triple 2 low e 2 argon	6,*12*, 6	0.45–0.65	0.8	65
Double with reflecting outer pane (antisun float)	6,*12*, 6	0.3–0.49	2.7–2.8	36–61
Double with heat absorbing outer pane (suncool float)	6,*12*, 6	0.16	2.3–2.6	9–35
Glass block	100	-	2.9	75
Glass block	80	-	3.24	75
Electrically powered sealed insulating glass unit with low e inner pane and argon cavity	6,12, 6	0.72	1.48–0 when operating	72

3.56 *The optical and thermal characteristics of a range of glazing materials. (Figures assembled from product literature of various manufacturers)*

Double clear glass: 6:12:6mm

3.57 *Transmission through standard double glazing system*

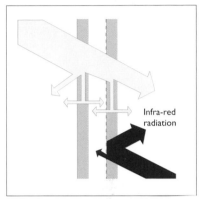

Infra-red radiation

3.58 *Transmission through typical Low E glazing*

If south-facing glazed areas are to be larger than the size required for daylighting so as to increase solar gain, their U-value must be improved. But lower U-values in glazing are usually associated with some reduction in lighting transmittance. On the other hand improving the U-value of the glazing will raise the mean radiant temperature in the space and so reduce the air temperature required for comfort (3.57, 3.58).

An alternative approach is to use glazed areas no larger than those required for daylighting, but to install very high levels of insulation, taking particular care to eliminate cold bridges and minimise infiltration losses. In such a building, the solar gains from conventionally sized windows should meet a significant proportion of the heating demand.

Thermal insulation

Glass is a poor thermal insulator. There are a number of simple ways to decrease heat lost through glazing:
- double-glazing (two panes of glass with an air-gap between) is the most commonly specified energy efficient glazing;
- a low-energy coating on the glass (Low E) decreases radiation heat loss through glazing; it is expensive but its specification may be rationalised on the basis of comfort alone;
- gases such as argon or krypton may be substituted for the air in the cavity to further decrease the convective heat loss of the pane;
- double glazed units from which some or all of the air is extracted are being developed. See Figure 3.59 for notional U-values of different pane types.

In addition to the thermal conductivity qualities of the glass itself, energy is lost through and around the fenestration by infiltration and radiation. Infiltration gains and losses are equivalent to 39% of the loss or gain through the glass itself (Hammer, 1991). Well-fitting frames and weather-stripping will reduce infiltration gains and losses. Since the overall percentage of the area of framing in elevation can be 10–20% of the component area, the thermal insulation value of the frame is important (3.60).

Type of Pane	U-Value W/m²K	light transmission %	solar transmission %
Clear glass			
Single glass, 4 mm	6.0	88	83
Double glass with air (4-12-4)	3.0	80	76
Double glass with Low E coating & argon (4-12-4)	1.5	77	65
Triple glass with air (4-12-4-12-4)	2.0	72	67
Triple glass with Low E coating & argon	1.2	70	60
Vacuum pane with Low E coating (4-12-4)	0.5	77	65
Reflective glass			
Double medium reflective glass with Low E coating (6-12-6)	1.6	29	39
Double glass, bronze + low E coating with argon (6-12-6)	1.6	9	13

Source: EC2000 Information dossier.

3.59   Example of key values for different pane types

Frame material	U Value W/m²K
Wood: average thickness >80mm	1.6
Wood: average thickness 50–80mm	2.0
Wood: average thickness <50mm	2.8
Plastic: without metal reinforcement	2.8
Plastic: with metal reinforcement	3.6
Aluminium: with thermal barrier: thermal path length >10mm	3.6
Aluminium: with thermal barrier: thermal path length <10mm	5.0
Aluminium or steel without thermal barrier	7.0

Source: Button and Pye, 1993

3.60

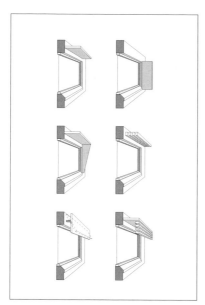

3.61 Typical fixed external shading devices

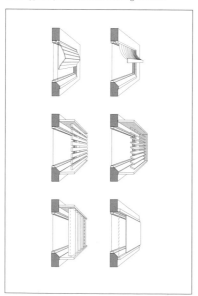

3.62 Typical adjustable external shading devices

COOLING

Overheating in the cooling season is one of the most serious problems related to window design. The principal passive cooling techniques include the use of solar shading and ventilation

Solar shading

Heat gain through conventional windows can be significant. Depending on the orientation and geographic location, if sensible glazing ratios are adopted, the need for shading may be reduced. However, where solar radiation is excessive for parts of the day in summer, the most effective way to reduce heat gain is to prevent or block solar radiation by using shading. A wide and ever-growing competitive range of shading devices is available to the architect, including blinds, shutters, louvres and structural or add-on devices.

If external shading is not possible, the closer the shading is to the outside of the building the more satisfactory it will be. Use of plants for shading should also be considered (Refer STRATEGIES; Landscape).

Shading devices can be classified as fixed or movable, internal or external (3.61, 3.62). Overhangs, loggias and arcades are examples of fixed shading favoured in southern Europe for their provision of shade against hot summer midday sun, and are among the traditional built approaches. Louvres and overhangs can be fixed directly onto the facade. These systems, while maintaining air movement, are limited in that they provide adequate shading for only part of the day in particular seasons, and limit the amount of daylight entering the space at other times of year when natural light would be most welcome.

Moveable shading devices include shutters, which are widely used. Insulated shutters are an energy-efficient option. Manually or automatically controlled louvres can provide optimal light levels at all times of year, provided they are operated correctly. For large areas of glazing, semi-transparent, opaque or reflective external curtains have proved effective. Some shading systems can incorporate photovoltaic panels to generate electricity (Refer ELEMENTS; Shading, Light Directing Chromic Glazing and Photovoltaics for further information).

Ventilation

Ventilation air may be supplied by natural or mechanical means, or a hybrid system containing elements of both. Natural ventilation is driven by wind or buoyancy forces caused by temperature differences between the inside and outside air. To encourage cross-ventilation, there should be vents or openable windows on opposite sides of the building, without major obstructions to air flow in between. An open-plan layout is good in this regard.

Well-designed naturally ventilated buildings are generally shallow-plan, with the distance from facade to facade (or atrium) not greater than five times room height. For cellular rooms with single-sided ventilation, natural ventilation will be effective only to a depth of about twice room height. Room heights may need to be higher than those in a mechanically ventilated building. The space saved through not needing ducting in the ceiling or floor will offset any required increase in storey height.

Vents should be located so as to avoid cold draughts. A number of well-distributed trickle vents in window heads are better in this regard than a single open window. Proprietary self-regulating vents which provide the same air flow rate regardless of external wind speed are available. Vents which attenuate outside noise are also available, though their flow resistance is higher.

In climates where night-time air temperatures in summer are significantly lower than day-time temperatures, night ventilation can be used in combination with thermal mass to provide cooling. There should be good thermal contact between the ventilation air flow and the thermal mass. Windows or vents used to provide night ventilation should not present a security risk. The duration of night cooling should be controlled in order to avoid over-cooling, which could result in the occupants feeling cold the following morning, or even the heating being turned on.

DAYLIGHTING

Artificial lighting accounts for about 50% of the energy used in offices, and a significant proportion of the energy used in other non-residential buildings. In recent years, use of daylighting combined with high performance lighting means that between 30–50% savings can be easily achieved while 60–70% savings are possible in some cases.

Thus, substituting daylight for artificial light will lead to substantial energy savings. Daylit spaces are more attractive and more economical to work and live in. In addition, a deficiency of daylight in our living and working environment can lead to health problems such as Seasonal Affective Disorder (SAD) and Vitamin D deficiency (Refer ISSUES; Health, Comfort and the Environment).

Good daylight design of the envelope depends on:

- *position, form and dimensions of the openings;*
- *characteristics of the glazing materials;*
- *position, form and dimensions of shading.*

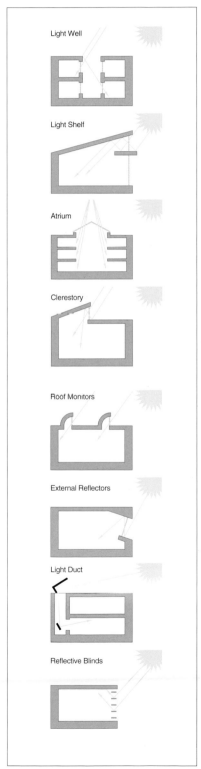

Light Well

Light Shelf

Atrium

Clerestory

Roof Monitors

External Reflectors

Light Duct

Reflective Blinds

3.63 Transparent elements - daylight systems and devices

Daylighting requirements will depend on the function of the building, the hours of use, type of user, requirements for view, need for privacy and ventilation requirements as well as the energy and environmental targets (3.63).

Windows

As a rule of thumb, daylighting within a building will only be significant within about twice the room height of a windowed façade. Thus shallow-plan buildings provide more opportunities for daylighting (as well as natural ventilation and cooling) than deep-plan ones.

The level of daylighting at a point in a room depends to a large extent on the amount of sky visible through the window from that point. Thus the provision of a significant amount of glazing near the ceiling is beneficial from a daylighting point of view. For example, tall narrow windows will provide a better daylight distribution in a room than low wide ones. For rooms at corners or on the top floor, windows in more than one façade or rooflights will also improve daylight distribution.

The shape and size of the window will depend on factors such as the depth of the room, and the orientation of the window. High windows will ensure good daylight penetration into the back of the space, wide ones will give better view. Often the window may be divided to cope with differing demands, a lower window may be provided for view and a higher part for daylight requirements. These may be even shaded differently. Studies have found that dual aspect spaces with high window head heights and lightshelves provide particularly uniform daylight levels across the depth of the space (HGA 1994) (3.64).

Rooflighting is a highly effective source of daylight in low-rise buildings and on the top floor of buildings.

Daylight systems and devices

Daylight devices can be used to distribute the light more evenly. They are designed to reflect light onto the ceiling and to the back of the room while reducing excessive light levels near the windows, thus saving lighting energy. Because of the eyes, adaptive response, the perceived need for artificial lighting is less in conditions of uniform lighting. Light shelves and reflective blinds are the most commonly used systems (3.65). Other examples are:

- passive systems e.g. lamella, reflective structures, prisms, patterned glass, films, laser cut panels;
- tracked systems e.g. holograms, heliostats.

Some of the more complex systems are designed not merely to shade the front of the room, but to increase overall lighting levels at the back. Tests carried out at the UK Building Research Establishment (Littlefair, 1996) assessed the ability of a variety of systems to increase lighting, improve uniformity, and cut down glare. The results were mixed. All systems improved uniformity, but the ones which also raised rear-of-room light levels only did so during direct sunlight, and for certain sun angles.

Shading

If windows have fixed overhangs to minimise solar gains in summer, these will also reduce daylight entry throughout the year. Movable shading or blinds will reduce daylight only while they are in place. While direct sunlight can be an attractive feature in a room (particularly in winter), if it falls directly on occupants or worktops it may be undesirable. Venetian blinds may be used to reflect sunlight towards the ceiling, thus avoiding discomfort due to direct sunlight and achieving greater penetration of daylight at the same time. Occupants may need instruction on how the use such blinds to best effect.

Ventilation

Where opening lights in windows present problems, operable vents, whether located in opaque elements or integrated in a window assembly, are worth considering. With air

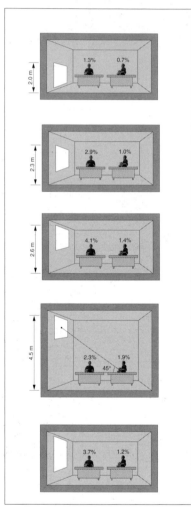

3.64 Window position and size

Source: N. Baker, Optimising daylight design

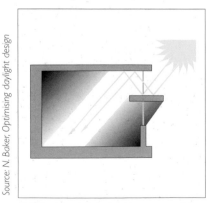

3.65 The light shelf shades the main part of the window but allows light to reach the back of the room by reflection between the shelf and the ceiling

flow control, insect and dust screens or acoustic baffles, they can provide a relatively inexpensive solution where noise or air pollution create difficult site conditions. Openable opaque panels can enhance ventilation rates in summer while avoiding excessive glazed areas.

Insulation

Insulating shutters which are closed after dark can be useful in reducing heat loss. Creating a well-sealed air-gap between shutters and glazing increases their effectiveness, but can be difficult to achieve. External shutters are preferable; internal shutters may lead to condensation on the glass during cold conditions, or, if left closed while the sun shines, set up thermal stresses which cause the glass to break. However, managing the operation of external shutters is not easy; in cold weather the occupants are unlikely to open windows to close the shutters. A louvred shutter operated from the inside can overcome this problem, but it may also interfere with light penetration during the day.

Energy Production Elements

PHOTOVOLTAICS

Photovoltaic cladding is now becoming feasible although at present the cost is prohibitive. Over the past ten years the cost of electricity production through this method has halved and efficiencies have doubled. The panels may be located on the roof or walls of buildings. Integrating PV panels into conventional cladding systems is relatively straightforward (3.66, 3.67). As panel temperature rises, efficiency falls, so the panels are more effective as rainscreen over-cladding, with a ventilated cavity, than as cladding per se.

Photovoltaic roofs, in which the photovoltaic panels themselves serve as the roofing material, present a very different sustainable solution. In the Sue Roaf House, Oxford, the PV panels are integrated into an aluminium glazing bar system, together with Velux roof lights and solar water-heating panels (3.68).

SOLAR THERMAL PANELS

A typical solar panel consists of a collecting plate sandwiched between an insulating backing and a glazed front. Within the panels are tubes through which the water is pumped. The optimum orientation is south-facing on roof or walls, though any orientation within about 30° of south will perform almost as well as a south-facing collector. The optimum inclination depends on application. For water heating an angle with the horizontal of less than the latitude of the site is usually best, to make good use of energy from the high-altitude summer sun. For space heating a higher inclination angle is best, since the sun is lower in the sky during the heating season. The path of the sun is not the only consideration in choosing collector inclination – diffuse solar radiation from the sky is also important.

(for further information Refer ELEMENTS; Photovoltaics, Solar Thermal Panels)

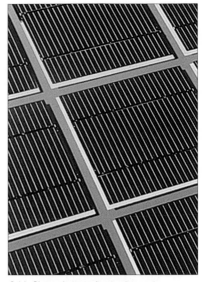

3.66 *Photovoltaic application in practice*

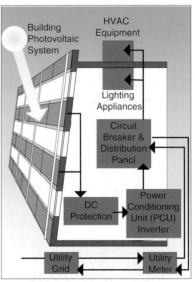

3.67 *Building-integrated photovoltaic system*

Architect: S. Roaf

3.68 *Photovoltaic roof, Roaf House, Oxford*

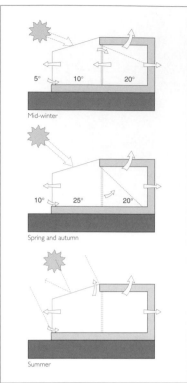

Sunspaces

Familiar to many in the form of the traditional domestic conservatory, the sunspace is a combination of both direct and indirect gain approaches to passive solar heating.

HEATING AND COOLING

The sunspace acts as a buffer zone for a house, dramatically reducing heat loss. Even in the absence of direct solar gain it is a functional energy efficient device (3.69).

Sunlight entering the space via the glazing is stored in the solid elements as heat energy. The distribution of this heat can be achieved in a variety of ways. A masonry wall, forming a partition between the sunspace and the rest of the house, can provide sufficient thermal mass to store absorbed heat and release it later. A natural convection loop will be encouraged by inserting vents at floor and ceiling level. Likewise, a fan coupled with a thermostat will allow heat exchange between the sunspace and the rest of the house, when desired.

Where a sunspace has been added to the external wall of an existing building, it is not necessary to double glaze, insulate or tightly seal the external envelope. Likewise, the thermal properties of the chosen framing material, are not important. At least two thirds of the fenestration must be openable to avoid summer overheating. If possible, provide movable insulation to cover the sunspace glazing at night or when the sky is overcast.

Sunspaces should be separated from adjacent heated spaces by tight-fitting doors or windows. When heat from the sunspace is available and needed, convected heat can quickly be admitted to the main spaces. At night-time or in cold weather, the sunspace can be cut off to serve as a thermal buffer.

A sunspace fitted with a heating system will be a source of energy loss instead of energy gain.

Atria

HEATING AND COOLING

Atria function as intermediate buffer spaces, and their ambient temperature levels depend on the specific losses from the glazed space to the outside, and the specific gains from the buildings to the glazed space (3.70).

Thermal gain from solar radiation has to be carefully evaluated because a large amount

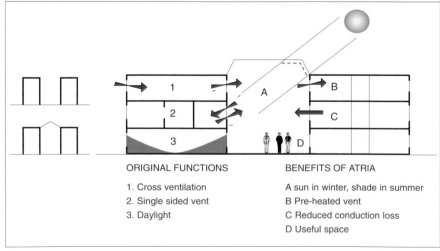

ORIGINAL FUNCTIONS

1. Cross ventilation
2. Single sided vent
3. Daylight

BENEFITS OF ATRIA

A sun in winter, shade in summer
B Pre-heated vent
C Reduced conduction loss
D Useful space

3.70 *The environmental benefits of atria evolved from open space*

of thermal radiation can be re-transmitted to the outside, especially in the case of low absorbent opaque surfaces. An atrium may retain between 30–85% of transmitted radiation, depending on the adjacent building colours and geometry, and on the glazing transmission properties.

VENTILATION

Solar shading and ventilation is an effective combination to reduce atrium temperatures during summer, but natural cross-ventilation has to be carefully evaluated in order to ensure comfort on critical days. Appropriate ventilation systems can achieve a higher temperature in the atrium without increasing the building's energy consumption. For example, exhaust air from the building may be used as an air supply for the atrium, and likewise exhaust air from the atrium can pre-heat the supply air to the building via a heat exchanger.

DAYLIGHTING

Atria can noticeably improve the quality of the adjoining internal spaces, which can enjoy all the advantages of daylight, without the accompanying climatic extremities. Improved technologies allow the architect greater freedom regarding the choice of construction, design and materials, even where longer payback periods are indicated there may be a strong case for employing such a system (3.71).

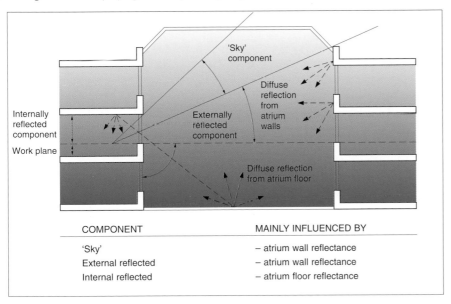

COMPONENT	MAINLY INFLUENCED BY
'Sky'	– atrium wall reflectance
External reflected	– atrium wall reflectance
Internal reflected	– atrium floor reflectance

3.71 The atrium as a source of daylight

FINISHES

3.72

Architect: A Campo Baeza

Building Research Establishment ISBN No. 011 721155, Publ.No. 737645 CI09/94

Material	Density kg/m3	Conductivity (k) W/m C	Resistivity (1/k)mC/W
Asbestos insulating board	750	0.12	8.3
Carpet			
• wool felt underlay	160	0.045	22.2
• cellular rubber underlay	400	0.10	10.0
Concrete	2400	1.83	0.55
Cork flooring	540	0.085	11.8
Fibre insulating board	260	0.050	20.0
Glasswool	25	0.04	25.0
Linoleum to BS 810	1150	0.22	4.6
Mineral wool			
• felted	50	0.039	25.6
	80	0.038	26.3
• semi-rigid felted mat	130	0.036	27.8
• loose, felted slab or mat	180	0.042	23.8
Plastics, cellular			
• phenolic foam board	30	0.038	26.3
	50	0.036	27.8
• polystyrene, expanded	15	0.037	27.0
	25	0.034	29.4
• polyurethane foam (aged)	30	0.026	38.5
PVC flooring and Rubber flooring		0.40	2.5
Wood			
• hardwood		0.15	6.7
• plywood		0.14	7.1
• softwood		0.13	7.7
Wood chipboard	800	0.15	6.7
Woodwool slab	500	0.085	11.8
	600	0.093	10.8

3.73 Thermal properties of some flooring materials

In specifying the finishes for a building there are a number of issues to take into consideration. Many of these have already been raised in earlier sections and some will be treated in detail in later ones.

Low energy and environmentally friendly design strategies will inform the selection and specification of finishes. In general however, materials may be assessed under three main headings:

- The effect of the materials' production on the global environment; the environmental impact per kilogram of the processes of extraction, transportation, manufacturing, installation, demolition and disposal.
- The effect of the use of the material on building energy consumption; thermal and daylighting performance.
- The effect of the use of the material on the indoor environment; indoor air quality, visual and accoustic characteristics.

The first has already been covered in some detail elsewhere, as the information applies to strategies for the selection of all materials, and it is not intended to deal with it here. (Refer ISSUES; Comfort, Health, Environment and ELEMENTS; Materials)

Building Energy Performance

At the early stages of a building design, targets for the energy performance of the building will be determined and agreed. During construction and completion it is important that the finishes specification be consistent with these targets. The finishes selected will have a positive or negative effect on the energy and environmental performance of the building. It is important that the client and design team all be aware that the theoretical performance of a low-energy design will in practice depend on the rigorous implementation of supportive strategies at later stages.

The role of finishes in the energy performance of buildings will relate in particular to thermal and daylight (light reflection and redirection) performance.

HEATING AND COOLING

The passive solar design of the building may anticipate the use of elements such as walls or floor as a passive thermal store for either heating or cooling purposes. For these elements to function as designed they should be exposed to the source of heating or cooling and in direct contact with air current (3.72).

The finishes used may help or hinder the thermal function. Using a dark finish on floors will increase their capacity to absorb heat and act as a thermal store. Light coloured finishes will reflect light and also heat. Low density finishes such as timber or carpet act as insulating layers and inhibit heat absorption (3.73). Raised floors and suspended ceilings will counteract the use of thermal mass.

However some flexibility is possible. As has already been discussed (Refer STRATEGIES; Envelope) an interior with high thermal mass would be slow to warm, surface temperatures will remain depressed and ensure a cooler internal environment. This is ideal in summer in hot climates, but may be less attractive in the winter. Application of alternative finishes such as timber will alter the thermal response time and the thermal capacity. In *The Climatic Dwelling* the example is used of tapestries in medieval buildings: 'in summer the wall hangings could be removed to reveal the heavy thermal mass of the masonry walls and their lower surface temperature' (O'Cofaigh, Olley 1996).

DAYLIGHTING

Illuminance

Illuminance is a function of the amount of light entering a room and the colour and finish of the surfaces. When daylight enters a room it is reflected off the internal surfaces (walls, floor, ceiling, interior fittings). The colour and finish of the surfaces will affect both the quantity and quality of light in that space. In general, light colours have more reflectance while dark colours have more absorption. Use of light-coloured finishes on the ground and vertical surfaces will reflect light, thus contributing to higher levels of daylight while reducing the contrast between bright window areas and the surrounding surfaces (3.74). Conversely, darker surfaces cause a loss of light.

Reflectance

Values of reflectances to be achieved have to be agreed at an early stage. Basic lighting calculations will use assumed surface reflectances for walls, ceiling and floor. The final decision on finishes frequently takes place much near the completion of the project. Actual reflectances may differ markedly from those used in the lighting calculations, normally to the detriment of the illuminance. Reducing the reflectance factor of the walls of a room from 50% to 10% could reduce the horizontal illuminance on the working plane by up to 25%. 'Because the eye is very adaptive such changes in illuminance may be acceptable for the task, but may no longer meet the specification. This emphasises the need for true multi-disciplinary designs' (Roaf, Hancock, 1992).

For working planes, or surfaces in the view of any work space, shiny finishes should be avoided. As surfaces with very highly reflecting finishes may cause distracting reflections, semi-matt or matt finishes are better.

Improving the reflectance of a ceiling benefits light distribution and improves both horizontal and vertical plane illuminance.

Colours

The colours used will affect light absorbance and reflectance of surfaces as well as their thermal performance as discussed earlier. Colours should be assessed in regard to their relative absorbtance and reflectance and selected accordingly.

Internal fixtures and fittings

At the design stage, interior surfaces are often conceived as planar and monochromatic, but once occupied this is rarely the case. Walls may have pictures or shelving on them, while floors will be covered by furniture whose finishes will affect the daylight distribution. Office partitions, VDUs and artificial lighting systems will all introduce further shading/modelling effects.

Indoor Air Quality

Conservation of energy often means highly insulated, and well sealed internal environments. Choice of materials in energy efficient buildings affects indoor air quality to an even higher degree than in conventional buildings. Where materials with toxic ingredients are specified and there is out-gassing, the effects will be magnified by reduced air movement and ventilation, resulting in a wide range of impurities in the indoor environment. High concentrations of chemicals such as formaldehyde from fabric, furnishings, and particle-boards may be particularly hazardous for a sleeping or desk-bound person in a confined space (Refer ISSUES; Comfort, Health, Environment and ELEMENTS; Materials).

Careful selection of building finishes is one way to improve indoor air, although it should be part of a broad strategy looking at ventilation systems, indoor plants, maintenance, and other factors.

3.74

Some typical reflectances of matt paint finishes:	
White	.85
Pale yellow	.82
Bright yellow	.70
Pale orange	.54
Pale blue	.45
Bright orange	.28
Bright red	.17
Dark green	.09
Black	.05

(Table Esbensen 1997)

Materials / Products	Range of Formaldehyde emission rates µg / m² / day
Medium - density fibreboard	17,600 – 55,000
Hardwood plywood panelling	1,500 – 34,000
Particleboard	2,000 – 25,000
Urea - formaldehyde foam insulation	1,200 – 19,200
Softwood plywood	240 – 720
Paper products	260 – 680
Fibreglass products	400 –- 470
Clothing	35 – 570
Resilient flooring	<240
Carpeting	NP* – 65
Upholstery fabric	NP – 7

*None Present

Source: Balaras, 1993

3.75 Formaldehyde emissions from a variety of construction materials, furnishings and consumer products (Data from ASHRAE)

The highest levels of pollutants are often found during construction and in the first weeks of occupation, as toxins diffuse out of the source materials (3.75). Other materials such as carpet and wall coverings may need to be protected during this phase to prevent them absorbing toxins and becoming sources of pollution themselves. The most toxic materials tend to be those that are unstable or that are applied in a wet state. Paints, sealants, preservatives, glues, cleaners and plastics such as PVC are among the worst offenders. Often, less damaging alternatives to standard products exist but may not be widely known or available. Materials present in small quantities may have a disproportionate impact on air quality. It may be a good idea to delay the installation of soft furnishings such as carpets until solvent-based products are dry. This prevents VOCs and other air pollutants being absorbed by the soft furnishings and released again.

FINISHES SPECIFICATION

The science of materials and their specification is a complex area. Finishes are selected on the basis of many criteria such as cost, durability, appropriateness, function, aesthetics and so on. Impact on the indoor environment is only one of these issues. No publication of this type can hope to give a full discussion of the environmental advantages and disadvantages of the uses of common materials. There are many specialist publications and periodicals which do just that. However, there follows a brief resume of some generic types of commonly used finishes and the environmental effects of their use, with particular regard to indoor air.

Walls and Ceilings

Plaster
Most walls and ceilings are finished with plaster unless the structural materials used are self-finishing. Plaster is available in a number of forms, 'wet' trowel applied, 'dry-walling' board, tiles. The raw material for plaster may either be gypsum (whose processing is highly energy intensive), or lime mortar. Flue gas gypsum is a by-product of electricity production and its use avoids disposal of the material as waste. Natural gypsum is extracted with some environmental effects but the material is non-toxic and benign. Phosphogypsum is a by-product of fertiliser production and may be radioactive: for this reason it is the least attractive of these plaster products. Lime mortar is a natural compound with a low energy manufacturing process.

Plasterboard may contain additives, and the jointing compound used to cover the seam between two boards contains a range of chemicals which can continue to outgas for some months after setting. An alternative is to use low-toxicity compounds (Talbott, 1993).

Paint
Paint contains a wide range of toxic ingredients and solvents. The function of paint is both decorative and functional. An environmental objective might be to reduce the need for painted finishes of any kind, especially in little used, residual or service spaces. Where paint is used it should be water-based and contain the minimum of toxic or polluting ingredients. Where polyurethane paints are specified the application should be with brush or roller rather than spray.

The number of suppliers of 'natural' paints is growing as a result of increased demand. However at the time of writing, these paints are still substantially more expensive than the conventional types. In addition, the solvents in organic paints can be as hazardous to health as those in conventional paints (Green Building Digest, 1995) (Refer ELEMENTS; Materials for more detailed information on paints and wood finishes).

Paper
Paper is widely used, especially in domestic applications. Un-coated paper is preferable to vinyl coated, but harder to maintain. Vinyl wallpaper is increasingly popular because it is washable but the coating is PVC, with the attendant indoor air implications.

Ceramic tiles

Tiles are a durable wall finish and frequently used in areas such as bathrooms and kitchens. They are made from clay with additives for colour and hardness. Glazed tiles are relatively high in embodied energy content due to the firing process (Anink,1996). The indoor air impact depends on the selection of adhesives. The environmental choice for tile adhesives is one with little or no organic solvent content: mortar for floors and water-based for walls.

Wood

The use of wood as a wall or ceiling finish material is less common outside domestic applications, but the comments about wood in floors largely apply here also (3.76) .European softwood is environmentally benign but softwood ceilings may need an applied finish and the impact on indoor air will depend on its composition.

Floors

Floor finishes are available in a wide range of natural and synthetic materials such as stone, wood, tile, vinyl and linoleum sheet, wool or nylon carpet. Concerns relate to the source of the material (renewable or non), the embodied energy content and the effect on the indoor air quality as a result of the composition of the material and the use of adhesives. The low-price end of the scale is dominated by synthetics which are petroleum-based, mass-produced and used in the form of carpet tiles and vinyl. But these mask the hidden cost of environmental damage and health hazards (Green Building Digest, 1995).

Stone

The advantage of stone (such as slate, marble or terracotta) is its extreme durability and attractive appearance. The environmental impact of stone-based products is less than that of most other materials although granite does emit a higher level of radon than most other construction materials (Martinez, Barroso et al 1996). The small amount of granite used inside buildings is unlikely to be a cause for concern.

Granolithic floors

Aggregates bedded in concrete (a poured terrazzo floor for example) are extremely hard-wearing, and require no adhesive or sealant finish after laying. Any environmental concern about these relates to the use of concrete (Refer ELEMENTS; Materials).

Wood

Wood, if recycled or from a certified sustainable source, is a non-polluting material, but it is usually protected or coated to increase its durability, and may be fixed down using adhesive. Wood finishes may be carcinogenic (Martinez, Barroso et al 1996). The degree of toxicity will depend on the amount of ventilation and the extent of harmful synthetic coating. Finishes should be specified which are based on wax, oils or eco-friendly varnishes.

Wood dust from working with timber may be toxic, immuno-damaging or carcinogenic (Green Building Digest, 1995); safety at work legislation in the UK limits exposure to hardwood dust.

Wood-based products such as plywood, blockboard, chipboard, and fibreboard contain phenol and urea formaldehyde resins, which will increase the levels of toxicity of the indoor air. Medium density fibreboard (MDF) contains a high formaldehyde content (about 14%); other particle boards and plywoods, about 10% (Talbott, 1993). However according to Ove Arup and Partners (1993) 'the health hazard created by properly manufactured products is minimised by processing and conditioning techniques, and the principle hazards relate to the release of fibres or dust on installation.' The Findhorn Trust used Karlit board and fibre board instead of plywood for sheathing because it contains no formaldehyde or toxic glues. However it does not have the same qualities as other boards in bending or water resistance.

3.76 Softwood timber panelling, the Irish Energy Centre, Dublin

Architects: Energy Research Group, University College Dublin

Floor coverings which are least likely to add to the quantity of pollutants in the indoor air are:

- *Smooth coverings: lino, cork in tile or sheet form, latex (rubber) matting.*

- *Stone, and ceramic tile e.g. quarry tile.*

- *Timber from a renewable resource or particularly recycled.*

- *Natural carpet, on a hessian backing, with felt underlay. (Carpet should be tacked in place rather than using solvent-based adhesives.)*

Wood finishes

Synthetic varnishes are more durable than natural ones, but are sources of VOCs. Non-toxic wood finishes include linseed oil, beeswax and shellac.

Carpet

Synthetic carpets are a recognised source of VOCs from the pile, adhesives and backing, and most fabric dyes are derived from petrochemicals. An extensive study of carpet emissions carried out for the US Consumer Safety Commission and quoted in Green Building Digest 9 (1996) found that under normal conditions, carpets emit formaldehyde and other volatiles at a rate resulting in concentrations below the irritance threshold of 70ppbv, but, combined with other sources of VOCs around the home, new carpet emissions could result in concentrations above threshold limit values, particularly in poorly ventilated buildings.

Nylon is often blended with wool to improve wear. Nylon manufacture is responsible for around half of the annual UK production of NO_x. It is safe during use but produces toxic fumes when incinerated. Other synthetics used in carpet manufacture and associated with toxic emissions are polyester, polypropylene, polyurethane and acrylic.

The most environmentally benign carpets are those made with animal (wool or goat) or vegetable (sisal, seagrass, coir, cotton and hessian) fibres, and on natural backings such as jute or latex, which are undyed or unbleached and which have not been treated with insecticides. However the experience of the Findhorn Foundation was that because wall-to-wall carpets are harder to clean properly they can encourage micro-organisms (Talbott, 1993).

PVC/Vinyl

The main environmental impact of vinyl flooring production is the emission of large quantities of toxic waste; the raw ingredients are known carcinogens and powerful irritants (Green Building Digest, 1995). PVC is discussed in detail in ELEMENTS; Materials.

Cork

Cork is a relatively benign material in terms of its harvesting and production. Cork granules are moulded using binding agents. Cork flooring will require a protective coating to prevent discolouration from dirt. The specifier should beware that natural binders may be replaced by those containing formaldehyde, with effects on indoor air quality. Some composite products incorporate vinyl backing or surface coatings. In conclusion, cork is only a good organic material if oil or wax coating is used.

Lino

Lino is made with cork, linseed oil, wood flour, pigments and hessian. It performs as well as vinyl for comparable cost. It is a completely natural and environmentally benign material, which even contains a naturally occurring bactericide.

Adhesives

One critical environmental dimension of the specification of wall and floor finishes is the use of adhesives. Most adhesives in common use are synthetic and chemical, with out-gassing both during application and immediately following installation, usually from inorganic solvents. In addition some adhesives can cause skin irritation during application. Rubber, cellulose, animal or vegetable derivative adhesives may be substituted. There are naturally derived products available to suit paper, cork, tile, lino, parquet, carpet, rubber sheeting and laminates (Hall and Warm, 1994).

SERVICES, EQUIPMENT AND CONTROLS

A building's energy performance depends to a considerable extent on interactive effects between its fabric and services equipment. Thus energy-efficient building design requires good communication between the architect and the building services engineer, ideally from the very start of the design process (3.77). This is particularly true in the case of buildings designed for passive solar heating, daylighting, natural ventilation and natural cooling. Good integration of mechanical and electrical services with passive systems is required to obtain maximum benefit from ambient energy (3.78, 3.79, 3.80).

In the following sections, components of energy-efficient building services systems are described, with reference to interactive effects as appropriate.

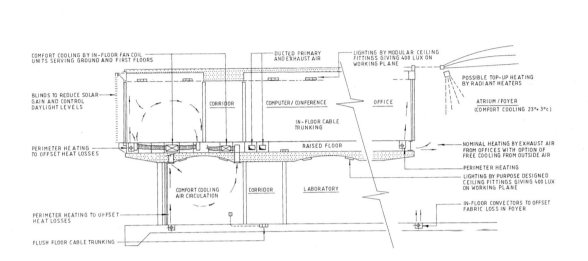

BUILDING SERVICES

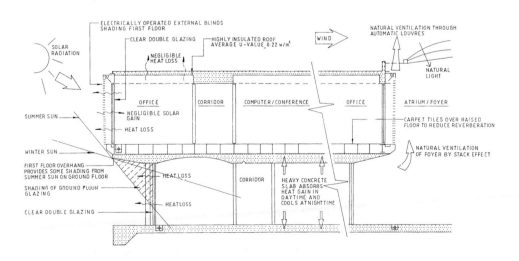

BUILDING PHYSICS

3.77 Diagramatic section of Schlumberger Research Building, Cambridge

Architects: M. Hopkins & Partners, Engineers: Büro Happold

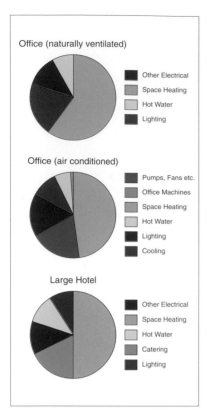

3.79 Typical breakdown of energy use in the UK for a naturally ventilated office building, an air conditioned office building and a large hotel

CO₂ emissions per unit of energy for different fuels

Fuel	kg CO₂/kWh
Natural gas	0.20
Oil	0.27
Coal	0.30–0.35

3.80

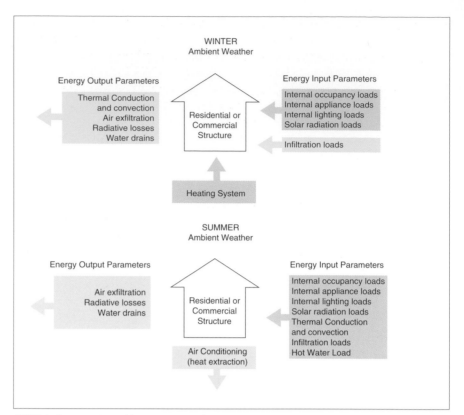

3.78 Typical energy gains and losses in winter and summer

Heating

Fossil-fuel heating systems

Where circumstances allow a choice of fuels for conventional heating systems, consider the pollution produced by burning the fuel, and the efficiency with which it can be used in available heating equipment.

Emissions of CO_2 per unit of energy are as shown in the box. SO_2 emissions are negligible for gas; for oil and coal they depend on fuel composition. NO_x emissions can be minimised by selecting a boiler with a low-NO_x burner. The energy and pollution inherent in processing and transport should also be a factor, but information on these is not readily available.

Condensing boilers

Condensing boilers are the most efficient type of boiler available, with seasonal efficiencies typically in the region of 85%. In conventional boilers, about 10% of the heat energy available in the fuel goes up the flue as latent energy in water vapour. Condensing boilers have additional heat exchanger surface area to condense the water vapour in the flue gases, extracting this latent energy.

Condensing boilers must be plumbed to a drain to carry away the condensate. The market for condensing boilers operating on gas is more developed than that for oil.

System sizing

A well-insulated building shell, along with a good level of envelope air-tightness, will not only reduce heat loss, but will also reduce the required capacity of the mechanical heating system. This will yield savings in heating system capital costs.

Increasing south-facing glazed areas above conventional levels will increase passive solar gains but will also increase transmission heat loss. However, in relation to heating system design, two further effects of increasing glazed areas are as follows.

- A larger heating system will be required to meet demand at times when passive solar gains are not available, resulting in higher capital costs.
- The boiler will operate at lower loads in relation to its size i.e. its average load factor will be lower. For some boiler installations, this will result in a lower seasonal efficiency (3.81).

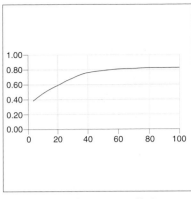

3.81 Example of efficiency curve of boiler.

Control of heat emission

Radiators and other heat emitters should be controlled so that heat is emitted only when it is required. If passive solar gains are sufficient to heat a room to the desired temperature, a control system incorporating a thermostat should cut off the supply of heat to the room. East-facing rooms will tend to benefit most from solar gains in the morning, while west-facing rooms will benefit most in the afternoon. Thus zones with windows facing in different directions should be provided with independent temperature control.

Responsiveness

The rate of passive solar heating of a room can change quickly, e.g. when the sun comes out from behind clouds. The heating system should be able to respond to these changes quickly, otherwise the room will overheat and the solar gains will be wasted. Systems with radiators of low thermal capacity tend to respond quickly, while under-floor heating systems embedded in concrete tend to respond only slowly. The latter are not considered appropriate for rooms with large south-facing windows.

Heat pumps

A heat pump can be used to extract usable heat from a low temperature source such as the earth, outdoor air, or water. These are, of course, renewable resources, but, because the pump uses electricity for compression and circulation, the financial and primary energy implications need careful assessment. The economics of heat pumps where there is a simultaneous demand for refrigeration and space heating are favourable and well established.

Cooling

Natural cooling

Natural cooling systems have the potential to maintain comfortable conditions in summer in a wide range of buildings and climates. If natural cooling alone is not adequate, then ventilation rates may be increased mechanically. If this is not sufficient, artificial cooling will be required.

However, before ruling out natural cooling as an option, all means of reducing internal and solar gains and enhancing natural ventilation during peak temperature conditions should be assessed. Naturally cooled buildings tend to have lower capital and operating costs, and, provided they can meet thermal comfort requirements, many occupants prefer them. Furthermore, effective management is critical for air conditioning systems. Without it, efficiency falls and discomfort increases. Natural cooling systems do not normally require such a commitment in terms of operation and maintenance.

If mechanical ventilation or artificial cooling is required, consideration should be given to combining it with natural ventilation in a 'mixed-mode' system. This may involve the provision of natural cooling in some parts of the building, and mechanical ventilation/cooling in others (zonal mixed-mode). Alternatively, both natural and mechanical systems may be installed in the same zone, with the mechanical system being used only when the natural cooling system is unable to meet requirements (seasonal mixed-mode).

Ceiling fans

The air movement generated by a ceiling fan may produce the same cooling effect as a temperature reduction of 2–3°C, and at only a fraction of the energy consumption of a typical air conditioning system. Air speeds below such fans should remain within acceptable limits.

Mechanical ventilation

Mechanical extract fans may be used to enhance natural ventilation. For example, in an atrium designed for stack-effect ventilation, an extract fan may be installed in the roof, and activated when internal temperatures rise above a pre-set level.

Ducted mechanical ventilation systems may also be used for cooling. However, because of the relatively high flow rates which may be required for cooling, pressure drops in the system will be correspondingly high, and additional fan power will therefore be required to drive these air flows.

Artificial cooling

Air-conditioning is energy-intensive. A fully air-conditioned building may consume two to three times the energy used by a similar naturally ventilated one. If air-conditioning must be used, it should be specified only for those parts of the building where it is essential.

If artificial cooling is unavoidable, factors which can minimise the required capacity and operating hours include a shallow plan, a well-insulated building shell, an air-tight construction (Refer STRATEGIES; Envelope), energy-efficient and well-controlled lighting and equipment to minimise internal gains, and solar control. Excessive amounts of glazing on facades exposed to the summer sun should be avoided.

Many artificial cooling systems use refrigerants containing ozone-depleting chemicals. HCFC (hydrochlorofluorocarbon) refrigerants are not as bad as the now banned CFCs (chlorofluorocarbons), but are still damaging to the ozone layer. HFC (hydrofluorocarbon) refrigerants do not damage the ozone layer but are powerful greenhouse gases, so still give rise to concern. Alternative refrigerants, which do not deplete ozone and which are not greenhouse gases, include ammonia, propane, and water, though the market for these is not as well-developed as for the fluorocarbon types above.

The efficiency of an artificial cooling system may be expressed in terms of the ratio of the heat removed from occupied spaces to the electricity consumed by the complete system. Seasonal average values in the region of 2 kW of heat removal per kW of power consumption are common in existing systems. A layout which minimises the lengths of ductwork and pipework required so as to minimise resistance to flow increases system efficiency. Locating plant rooms close to the areas of greatest cooling load may be useful in this regard.

Most of the chillers in use in artificial cooling systems are of the vapour compression type, and the comments above refer to these. Another type is the absorption chiller, which is driven by heat rather than electricity. These have been around for a long time, but have attracted increasing interest in recent years.

Environmentally benign fluids such as water may be used as refrigerants in absorption chillers. Applications with significant future potential are the use of absorption chillers for space cooling driven either by waste heat from combined heat and power plant or by active solar thermal systems. The economics of such projects will be favoured by a demand for heat throughout the year e.g. space heating in winter, space cooling in summer and hot water during all seasons.

Design internal temperatures

Many air-conditioning systems are designed for the worst case scenario, and are therefore oversized for most of their working life. Where comfort temperatures are expressed as a range, for example 24–26° C, the system should be sized for the upper end of this range rather than the midpoint. Allowing temperatures to rise above conventional comfort levels more often can reduce plant size and energy consumption considerably (3.82).

Design internal temperatures for summer and winter are often based on data provided in ISO 7730, which is derived from laboratory-based assessments of comfort perceptions. However, as outlined in Section 2 ISSUES, field research has shown that there is often a discrepancy between the comfort conditions predicted by these methods and those observed in practice. In many cases people are satisfied with higher temperatures in hot weather, and lower temperatures in cold weather, than those suggested by ISO 7730. Particularly if opportunities for adaptive comfort are provided, the selection of design temperatures need not be as stringent as ISO 7730 would suggest.

Opportunities for adaptation tend to be more numerous in naturally cooled rather than air-conditioned buildings. Examples of design features allowing occupant control of the internal environment include adjustable thermostats, trickle vents and blinds, openable windows and a flexible layout which allows occupants to arrange the position of desks and seating to suit themselves.

Ventilation

As levels of thermal insulation improve, and as occupants' expectations regarding air quality rise, the proportion of total heat loss from buildings accounted for by ventilation has become increasingly important. Though not as straightforward as controlling fabric heat loss, much can be done to control ventilation heat loss.

Required ventilation rates depend on various factors including occupant activity and type of accommodation. For example, in non-smoking offices a ventilation rate of 5–8 litres per second (l/s) per person is sometimes recommended. Ventilation rates above those required give rise to an energy penalty. Since both the driving forces for infiltration (wind pressure and internal/external temperature differences) and the internal ventilation requirements vary, a relatively airtight building envelope and controllable ventilation rates are required to meet occupants' needs without wastage.

A basic level of ventilation is required to provide occupants with oxygen, and to dilute and remove carbon dioxide and odours. However, ventilation must also remove other pollutants (water vapour, formaldehyde, etc), thus higher ventilation rates will be required if these are present in significant quantities. An important element in an energy-efficient ventilation strategy is to minimise required ventilation rate by avoiding the emission of pollutants in the building (Refer ISSUES; Health).

Where the emission of pollutants within the building is unavoidable, it is more energy-efficient to remove these at source than to increase whole-building ventilation rates. Sources of such pollutants in office buildings include some photocopying machines and printers which emit ozone, and tea-rooms and canteens which emit water vapour. Pollutants may be removed at source either through local extract or by locating the source close to a window through which air would normally leave the building (e.g. on the downwind side).

If natural ventilation is unable to fully meet ventilation needs in particular circumstances (e.g. in very calm weather), extract fans may be used to increase ventilation rates. These fans should be controlled to ensure that they are not switched on when not needed.

Building type Room/activity	Operative temperature (°C)
Residential	
Living room	21
Bedroom	18
Staircases	16
Offices	
General	20
Private	20
Stores	15
Factories	
Sedentary work	19
Light work	16
Heavy work	13
Schools and Colleges	
Classrooms	18
Lecture rooms	18
Coffee shops and bars	18
Canteens and dining rooms	20

3.82 Recommended indoor temperatures during heating season (northern Europe)

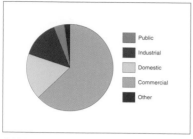

3.83 Electricity consumption for lighting in the UK

Mechanical ventilation

Mechanical ventilation systems may be categorised as supply, extract or balanced. In mechanical supply systems, air leaves the building through exfiltration, and therefore heat recovery is not feasible. Mechanical extract and balanced systems provide opportunities for heat recovery. In extract systems, heat may be recovered from the stale air leaving the building by means of a heat pump, and used for water heating. In balanced systems, heat recovered may be used to heat replacement fresh air via a plate heat exchanger or thermal wheel. The economics of heat recovery in balanced systems improve with the severity of the heating season.

Heat exchangers can have seasonal efficiencies of about 70%. However, they can only recover heat from the air leaving through them. If a building with a balanced mechanical ventilation system is leaky, much air will leave by exfiltration through the building fabric. Furthermore, infiltration will increase ventilation air supply rates above required levels. Thus, particularly in balanced ventilation systems, an air-tight construction is required for effective operation.

The ventilation system should be designed to facilitate maintenance, e.g. parts that need regular cleaning should be easily accessible. Once in operation, the system should be properly maintained, with filters changed and heat exchange surfaces cleaned regularly, otherwise efficiency will fall and air quality will deteriorate. A failure to adequately maintain mechanical ventilation (and air conditioning) systems will result not only in poor air quality, but possibly also health concerns due to the growth of micro-organisms. A useful measure of the energy efficiency of a mechanical ventilation system is the electricity consumed per unit of air supplied, expressed either in Joules per litre (J/l) or more commonly in watts per litre-per-second (W/(l/s)). Typical values range from 1–3 W/(l/s), with energy-efficient systems near the lower end of this range.

Lighting

Lighting is a significant energy consumer in non-domestic buildings. In offices it can account for as much as 50% of electricity consumption, and in deep-plan buildings lighting costs can exceed heating costs. In factories, the proportion of energy used for lighting is typically around 15%, and in schools 10–15% (3.83).

The amount of energy consumed in lighting depends on the power consumption of lighting equipment and the time for which it is switched on. A reduction in either of these will reduce the energy consumption. There is considerable potential for energy and cost savings in existing buildings, with many examples of savings in the range 30–50% having been achieved. In new building designs, the optimum use of daylighting can reduce the amount of time during which electric lighting is required.

Electric lighting contributes internal heat gain to the building. This reduces the heating load in winter, but is undesirable in summer, since it adds to cooling needs and costs. An improvement in the energy efficiency of electric lighting will be offset in winter by the corresponding increase in the heating load, though since heating is usually provided by a source of lower cost and higher efficiency (in primary energy terms), there will be a net gain in both money and primary energy terms. In summer, savings on both lighting costs and cooling needs are achieved.

Electric lighting

The luminous efficacy of a light source is the light output per unit of power input. Its units are lumens per watt (lm/W). Typical luminous efficacies for different lamp types are shown alongside (3.84). Efficacy tends to rise with lumen output, that is bigger lamps are more efficient than smaller ones (3.85, 3.86).

Gas discharge lamps require a ballast, which will consume power in addition to the power consumed by the lamp itself. Thus the luminous efficacy of lamp plus ballast will be lower than that of the lamp alone.

Lamp type	Efficacy[lm/W]
Incandescent bulb	10–15
Tungsten halogen	20–30
Compact fluorescent	50–75
Fluorescent (triphosphor)	80–100
Metal halide	70–90
High-pressure sodium	70–120

3.84 Typical luminous efficacies

The use of electronic high-frequency ballasts with fluorescent lighting, rather than magnetic ballasts, improves the luminous efficacy of the lamp/ballast combination by 10–20%. Electronic ballasts also provide for smoother starting of lamps, thus extending their operating lives and reducing relamping costs. Furthermore, the high frequency reduces flicker (there is evidence that the flickering light output from older ballasts is associated with eye strain and headaches).

A measure of the efficiency of a luminaire is the luminous flux emitted by the luminaire as a proportion of the luminous flux emitted by the lamps it contains. The directional distribution of the emitted light, and the luminance of the luminaire, are also important design considerations.

Light-coloured room surfaces will reflect more light than dark ones (Refer STRATEGIES; Finishes). If surfaces of high reflectance can be assumed at the design stage, required electric lighting capacity, and thus capital costs, will be reduced.

The provision of localised lighting (task lighting) on work surfaces, with a lower level of general (ambient) lighting in other parts of the room, is more energy-efficient than general lighting only, since not all of the space needs to be lit to the high level required at workplaces.

At times of peak overheating, electric lighting will generally contribute less to internal heat gains than daylighting. This is because the distribution of light and the illuminance levels from electric lighting can be controlled to match user requirements more precisely than with daylight. This applies despite the fact that the ratio of luminous flux to energy content for daylight (about 140 lm/W), is higher than the luminous efficacy of modern fluorescent lamps (about 100 lm/W).

Item	100W tungsten	20W plce lamp
Tungsten bulbs 8 @ €0.63	€ 5.04	
Electricity costs (100W x 8000h x 9.70 eurocents)	€ 77.60	
Total	€ 82.64	
Plce lamp 1 @ €17.00		€ 17.00
Electricity costs (20W x 8000h x 9.70 eurocents)		€ 15.52
Total		€ 32.52
Saving		**€ 50.12**

3.85 Comparison of costs of tungsten and fluorescent bulbs

Energy efficiency measure	Cost €	Energy Saving (%) (years)	Payback
Replace 38mm tubes with 26mm tubes	4–6 each (same price)	8	<2
High frequency ballasts for fluorescent lamps	20–65 per luminaire	15–20	5–15
Replace tungsten lamps with compact fluorescent	15–20 each	40–70	1–3
Replace opal diffusers with specular reflectors	30–60 per luminaire	20–50	2–6
		if fewer luminaires needed	
Install automatic lighting controls	—	20–50	2–5
Localised lighting to supplement general lighting	—	60–80	4–8

3.86 Energy efficiency measures, energy savings & typical payback periods for existing lighting installations

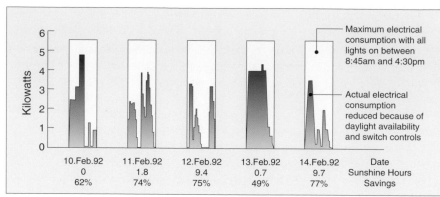

3.87 *Monitoring of controls performance*

Controls

In many buildings there is considerable potential for energy savings through switching off lamps when they are not needed. Since occupants cannot in many cases be relied upon to switch off or dim lamps as required, automatic controls have an important role to play in energy efficient lighting.

Time control can be used to switch lights off automatically when the building is normally unoccupied. Occupancy control (or absence detection control) involves the use of sensors (infrared or ultrasonic) which detect movement, and switch lamps off if no movement is detected during a preset time interval, for example 15 minutes. Daylight linking controls may be used to dim or switch off lamps in response to daylight levels. Such controls are in many cases necessary if significant daylight savings are to be achieved (3.87).

Localised switching involves the provision of opportunities to control lighting in small areas independently by means of switches which are close at hand. Lamps controlled by a single switch should be rationally related to daylight penetration and occupancy, e.g. lamps providing general lighting in an open-plan office could be controlled in rows parallel to the window wall, while lamps over each workplace could be controlled individually.

The control strategy most suitable to a particular building or room will depend on the circumstances, in particular the occupancy patterns. In many cases, the best strategy is for the controls to switch lights off only, leaving occupants to switch them on as required.

Building Energy Management Systems

As described in the sections above, automatic control of individual building services components and systems can help to effect energy-efficient operation. However, the integration of various controls as part of a Building Energy Management System (BEMS) can yield the following additional benefits:

* More sophisticated control procedures can be programmed.
* Monitoring of energy consumption, and targeting of opportunities for energy saving, are facilitated.
* Routine maintenance requirements may be flagged, helping the operator to maintain energy efficient operation and to avoid disruptive equipment failures (3.88).

Too much information can be as bad as too little, since it can cause important facts to go unnoticed among reams of data. BEMS can filter out unimportant information, and highlight where energy savings may be made. Information provided to plant operators, accountants and others can be filtered to contain only the data that each requires, and in terms that each can understand.

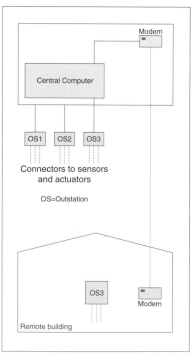

3.88 *Distributed building energy management system*

RENOVATION

'Re-using an existing building is one of the most effective sustainable strategies there is. It saves on the materials, energy and pollution costs involved in constructing a new building and also the new services and infrastructure which might be needed for a virgin site' (McNicholl, 1996).

Refurbishment of buildings currently accounts for more than one-third of construction output in the EC. It is anticipated that this figure will increase if the existing building stock continues to grow and if consciousness of the economic and environmental advantages of building renovation spreads. A large proportion of residential dwellings are blocks of apartments consisting of prefabricated concrete blocks or panels. Many of these buildings are in poor condition and need major renovations.

Any building which performs badly in terms of energy consumption, comfort conditions or environmental impact is a potential candidate for renovation. The benefits to owners and occupants of a thorough re-evaluation of a building's design and operation are potentially far-reaching; comfort, health, productivity, enjoyment, aesthetic quality, prestige and capital value, together with reduced running costs and security from energy price fluctuations. Some of these benefits are difficult to quantify, but they are nonetheless apparent to clients. The potential for architectural improvement is considerable and may extend to the reorganisation of the functional and spatial arrangement of the building or the combination of adjacent buildings and spaces.

The economics of energy-saving measures for single-family dwellings are fairly well understood, but upgrading other building types involves assessing a range of options in increasing order of cost and complexity. As with new build, an integrated approach will produce better results than a piecemeal one.

To retrofit or not ?

Sometimes there will be a choice to be made between retrofitting and commissioning or buying a better building; sometimes retrofitting will be unavoidable. In either case there are similar questions to be answered: Can the required internal environment be achieved? How much energy will be saved? What will be the reductions in CO_2, CFCs and other pollutants ? Can the proposed measures be applied at no extra risk? Will they be durable? Will additional maintenance be required? Are there other, non-energy benefits? Will the measures be cost-effective?

The cost-effectiveness of any intervention is increased if it is implemented in phase with the normal life cycle of the building and its fittings; running maintenance, routine redecoration and replacement of out-worn equipment, interior fit-out or total building refurbishment.

As a first step, the energy performance of the existing building in a 'free-running' state should be evaluated for representative periods of the day and year, together with an investigation of any building defects (such as cold bridging or condensation) to understand how the building performs and to provide a reference, base case from which to design. The thermal performance of the existing building envelope should be analysed in terms of unwanted heat loss or gain, through walls, windows, doors and especially the ground floor and the roof. Particular attention should be paid to the effectiveness of existing insulation to cold bridges, especially at balconies and floor to external wall joints where insulation may be deficient, and to energy losses due to unwanted infiltration of cold external air (or hot air during summer).

Then consider the adverse or beneficial microclimatic conditions occurring around the building. Just as with a new building, patterns of solar radiation, temperature, precipitation, wind flow and strength, topography, vegetation, surrounding buildings and the nature of local activities should be studied and interpreted in terms of environmental conditions and opportunities. The spaces between buildings may be exploited to good effect, for example, through landscaping to optimise micro-climatic conditions for energy saving and comfort, or by structures which link buildings and provide additional enclosed areas. Examples of interventions include changes to ground contours (earth berming, etc.), planting of trees and other vegetation for shelter or shading and changes in the reflective characteristics of external surfaces to improve daylight levels indoors.

Building Envelope

Alternative forms of construction for the building envelope are covered in (Refer STRATEGIES; Envelope). This section looks at the options which are likely to be relevant in renovating existing buildings.

WALLS

Insulation may originally have been placed within the wall construction and, if well fitted, may still be effective, although certain insulation types can deteriorate with age. However, it may be desirable to apply additional insulation to improve comfort and reduce energy use. In multi-storey buildings this will usually involve a choice of internal or external insulation systems.

Internal insulation should generally be used only if the facade must not be altered, occupancy is intermittent, or, in the case of multi-unit buildings, where not all the owners want to upgrade. It is usually cheaper than external insulation, but it reduces room size and involves the replacement of skirtings, architraves, pipework, wiring and any other fixed items, and, in addition, precludes the use of the building's thermal mass as a heat store. Thermal stresses in the outer skin increase the risk of interstitial condensation rises, and it is almost impossible to solve the problem of cold bridges.

Cavity fill insulation has no effect on internal or outside appearance or on room size, and can be applied without disturbing the occupants. It permits the inner leaf to function as a thermal mass and, depending on construction, can eliminate cold bridging. The insulation is well protected, and a range of proprietary systems are available. However, it must be carried out by skilled operatives and without a thermographic survey it is difficult to ensure that the wall is evenly insulated. Some zones may be impossible to insulate such as wall-to-roof or column-to-beam junctions, head and cill positions, for example. Bridging the cavity may exacerbate damp penetration.

External insulation combined with cladding or rendering systems, although sometimes initially more expensive than internal insulation, has the following advantages:

- It completely wraps the building with insulation, thus eliminating cold-bridge problems.
- It allows the thermal mass of the building to be used to moderate indoor temperature variations by acting as a heat store.
- The building can remain occupied during installation.
- It can improve the appearance and weather resistance of the building envelope.
- It can result in lower maintenance costs.
- Where renovation of the facade is necessary, the extra cost of the insulation system can often be recovered in a few years.

External wall insulation systems fall into three main categories:

Thin-layer insulation or 'coat method':
Normally the cheapest option, thin-layer insulation, usually in the form of rigid panels, is fixed to the facade and a reinforced render or plaster coat of special composition is

applied to give a weather-proof external layer with a range of possible finishes. Care is needed in detailing and installing the render coat, especially around joints, corners and window and door openings. Several proprietary systems exist.

Ventilated facade insulation

The insulation is fixed to the existing facade and finishing panels are then installed using a spacer grid. The panels have openings which allow the outside air to ventilate the space between the panels and insulation. In summer the air flows through the void cool the surface of the insulation, thereby reducing heat gains through the wall. However, these air flows can also increase heat loss in winter if unrestricted.

Pre-finished modules

Similar in thermal operation to ventilated facade insulation, pre-finished modules arrive on site ready for installation using special fixing systems which simplify the mounting operation and help to ensure a good quality of workmanship. The result is an external surface which does not require any further work.

ROOFS

Heat losses from roofs are high because of their relatively large surface area and because of night-time radiation to the sky. Adding insulation is often quite easy and pay-back periods are short. Water vapour and condensation must be controlled by appropriate use of vapour barriers and ventilation.

Pitched roof loft insulation is an easy, low-cost action where insulation material, usually fibreglass quilt, mineral wool or rigid foam plastic panels, is placed horizontally. Where the attic space is insulated the new insulation can be applied between the rafters remembering to allow for ventilation of the structure.

In general, proprietary pitched roof systems (such as the metal deck systems used in industrial premises, which may already have some insulation) can be upgraded by the application of additional internal insulation. The relatively durable decking systems are often in good condition and continue to provide an effective rain screen.

In flat roofs, cold deck construction should be avoided. Warm or inverted deck constructions allow the roof slab to act as a thermal store and the risk of interstitial condensation is reduced. An inverted deck has the advantage of protecting a sound weatherproof layer against thermal stress, but, if the existing roof finish has reached the end of its useful life, a warm deck solution may have an attractive payback period.

FLOORS

The cost of placing insulation under existing concrete floors is not likely to be justifiable unless they need to be replaced for other reasons - damp, deterioration, or inadequate load-bearing capacity, for example. Heat loss can sometimes be reduced by ensuring effective land drainage around the building perimeter and adding external insulation below ground level. Another alternative is to place insulation over an existing floor and cover it with a screed or proprietary flooring system.

Suspended floors are usually easier to insulate and proprietary systems for various forms of floor construction are available.

WINDOWS AND DOORS

In colder climates, transmission losses through glazing, cold bridging through frames, and ventilation losses through joints are all issues to be addressed. Improvements in these areas will not only reduce building heat loss but, by eliminating draughts and the 'chill factor' of cold glazing, will also reduce the room temperature needed for comfortable conditions.

The more layers of air trapped between glass panes, the lower the heat transfer through the window. It is often possible to fit secondary glazing within existing frames with only minor adaptations. This secondary unit could incorporate one of the advanced types of glazing described in ELEMENTS. If there are existing double-glazed frames in good condition, replacing the existing glazing with units which incorporate a pane of 'low-e' glass or a gas-filled cavity may be appropriate. Transparent insulation materials (TIM) are getting cheaper, and may be an option for openings where heat losses outweigh heat gains but daylight is essential. Insulated blinds or shutters are an inexpensive method of reducing heat losses after dark.

In general, but particularly in windy areas, poor air-tightness in existing window and external door frames results in heat gain or heat loss. Draught stripping can help, but where frames are seriously damaged or aged, they should be changed for new well-sealed ones.

MATERIALS

As with a new building, careful, informed selection of materials and components used in buildings can improve environmental conditions indoors, and can have a significant, cumulative effect on the health of the environment.

SERVICES

In any sustainable retrofitting programme there are two fundamental tasks in relation to services. First, reduce demand. Then make sure that where additional resources are needed they are supplied and used efficiently. Where mechanical heating or ventilation must be provided, the energy required should be supplied from renewable sources where feasible. The use of mechanical air conditioners should be avoided if at all possible.

Control systems
Better controls can have a substantial impact on energy consumption and are sometimes valid as stand-alone options. Thermostatic radiator valves save 10% over manual controls. Individual meter-based billing reduces consumption by 15% in apartment buildings (Friedemann & Johnson). A metering and recording system will give owners or occupiers the information and motivation to manage their energy consumption. Generally the more efficient a control and metering system, the higher its investment cost.

The introduction of individual meter-based billing to replace flat-rate bills provides the opportunity for significant energy savings through motivation of the consumers towards more careful use of energy. Thermostatic radiator valves typically use 10% less energy than manual controls.

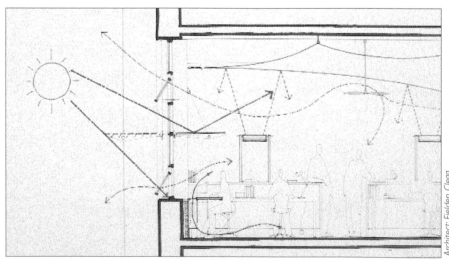

3.89 Greenpeace Headquarters, London, Environmental diagram.

Architect: Fielden Clegg

Hazards

In assessing renovation strategies, care must be taken to avoid or minimise the hazards which may arise. Renovated buildings are often occupied while work proceeds and the occupants are exposed to pollution and other hazards resulting from demolition and stripping out processes, as well as from the newly installed materials.

Problems can be identified and controlled through analysis of the potential causes of indoor air pollution. The technique will be common to all projects while the sources of pollution will, of course, be unique to the specific project in hand.

A typical sequence of management of the refurbishment project should include at least the following:

- analysis of the existing building to identify possible sources of pollutants;
- organisation and management of the refurbishment process to minimise pollution levels during demolition and disposal;
- procedures to measure and assure indoor air quality at all stages of the work.

Construction and Completion

During renovation close supervision and briefing of the construction team is essential. On completion building managers and occupants should be provided with concise, easily understood explanations of how thermal and lighting systems can be operated most effectively, information about what is required of them in using the building and the likely results of failure to operate or maintain the building and its energy systems appropriately. Sustained good management is essential.

Renovation Checklist

Space heating and ventilation

Reducing demand	• insulate fabric • reduce infiltration • utilise solar gain
Improving efficiency	• consider efficiency of heating appliances • improve controls

Space cooling and ventilation

Reducing overheating.	• reduce solar demand • improve efficiency of lighting and other heat producing equipment • use natural ventilation.
Improving efficiency	• ensure the efficiency of pumps and fans • improve controls specify efficient cooling plant (if cooling plant is unavoidable)

Lighting

Reducing demand	• improve daylighting • rationalise space usage
Improving efficiency	• redesign artificial lighting layout • specify efficient lamps, luminaires and ballasts • improve controls

Water

Reducing demand	• use water treated for human consumption only where necessary • improve water storage and pipe layout • install water meters to reduce demand
Improving efficiency	• specify water conserving fittings

Building management

Reducing demand	• educate building users • ensure good 'housekeeping'
Improving efficiency	• set targets and monitor performance • ensure effective maintenance and operation • consider a range of energy management systems

References

- Anink D, C Boonstra, J Mak (1996) *The Handbook of Sustainable Building: An environmental preference method for selection of materials for use in construction and refurbishment,* James and James (Science Publishers) Limited, ISBN 1 873936 38 9
- Athanassiou (1996) *'On the role of urban architecture towards urban sustainability'* in: PLEA 96: Building and Urban Renewal, Proceedings. de Herde, (Ed) Architecture et Climat, Louvain-la-Neuve.
- Barton, Hugh, Geoff Davis and Richard Guise, (1995) *Sustainable settlements: a guide for planners, designers and developers,* University of the west of England and the Local Government Management Board, Bristol.
- Berrutto, V and M Fontoynont, (1996) *Procedure for on-site performance assessment of daylighting systems.* Berlin, paper in 4th European Conference on Architecture, Berlin, March 1996.
- Energy Research Group, UCD (1994–95) *Living in the City.* Documentation for Architectural Competition of the same name 1994–1995, developed under the INNOBUILD project funded by DG XII for Science, Research and Development.
- Energy Research Group, UCD OPET for CECDGXVII (1994) *Daylighting in Buildings - Maxibrochure*
- Fuston, Nadel, Plaskon, Probber. (1993) *The Green Pages: The contract interior designer's guide to environmentally responsible products and materials.*
- *Going Green – The Green Construction Handbook: A Manual for for Clients and Construction Professionals* Research by Ove Arup and Partners. Bristol. JT Design Build Publication (1993) ISBN 0 9521304 0 8
- *Green Building Digest.* ACTAC Periodicals
- Hall K and P Warm (1994) *Greener Building: Products and Services Directory,* Association of Environment Conscious Building.
- Hough (1995) *Cities and natural process,* Routledge, London
- ISO 7730 1994(E) *Moderate thermal environments - Determination of the PMV and PPD indices and specification of the conditions for thermal comfort.*
- Littlefair P J, (1996) *Designing with innovative daylighting,* (BRE Report 294) UK BRE
- Martinez N C, J M G Barroso, J I de Lorens Duran, F M Reixach, P M del Rio, A P P Claveria, F. R. Camps and A. S. Barbosa (1996) *Architectural and Environmental Teaching.* For EC DG XI Environment
- McNicholl, Ann and J Owen Lewis, (Eds) (1996) *Green design: sustainable building for Ireland.* Dublin. Stationery Office.
- Murillo and de Schiller (1996) *'Sustainable urban development: obstacles and potentials'.* in: PLEA 96: Building and Urban Renewal, Proceedings. de Herde (Ed.) Architecture et Climat, Louvain-la-Neuve.
- O'Cofaigh E, J Olley and J O Lewis, (1996) *The Climatic Dwelling.* James and James (Science Publishers) Limited. For EC DG XII ISBN 1 873936 39 7
- Olgyay (1973) *Design with Climate,* Princeton. Princeton University Press
- Quah Dr L (1997) *Protocol and management information systems for indoor air quality assurance in the refurbishment of office buildings.* Paper for the Targeted Research Action, Environmentally Friendly Construction Technologies First Annual Workshop, Toulouse, France, October 1997
- *Retrofitting* - Maxi-brochure for DG XVII The European Commission.
- Roaf S, M Hancock (Eds) (1992) *Energy Efficient Building: A Design Guide.* Blackwell Scientific Publications. ISBN 0 632 03245 6
- Rocky Mountain Institute, Written by Alex Wilson (1998) *Green development: integrating ecology and real estate.* New York, John Wiley & Sons, Inc.
- Romero B (1996) *'A bioclimatic concept of public spaces.'* in: PLEA 96: Building and Urban Renewal, Proceedings. de Herde, (Ed.) Architecture et Climat, Louvain-la-Neuve.
- Russyvelt Dr P and Dr P Robinson. (1996) *The applicability of passive solar techniques to the refurbishment of non-domestic buildings in the UK* Paper for the 4th European Conference on Architecture, Berlin, March 1996
- Talbott, John L (1993) *Simply Build Green: A Technical Guide to the Ecological Houses at the Findhorn Foundation Ecological village project.* Findhorn, Findhorn Foundation Development Wing, The Park, Findhorn, Scotland, ISBN 0 905249 86 0

Section 4: Elements

COMPONENTS

Introduction

Any list of types of components used in sustainable building could be very long. Hundreds of different solutions have emerged during the history of green architecture, but few of them are well tested over many years in different situations.

Since this manual is aimed mainly at building designers approaching these concepts for the first time, we have selected technologies which are well known, at least by those familiar with green design, and widely available on the market. The non-specialist can easily apply these tried and tested solutions.

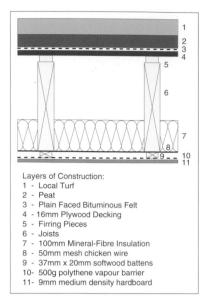

Layers of Construction:
1 - Local Turf
2 - Peat
3 - Plain Faced Bituminous Felt
4 - 16mm Plywood Decking
5 - Firring Pieces
6 - Joists
7 - 100mm Mineral-Fibre Insulation
8 - 50mm mesh chicken wire
9 - 37mm x 20mm softwood battens
10- 500g polythene vapour barrier
11- 9mm medium density hardboard

4.1 Section through the construction of a grass roof

4.2 Grass roof on the Skellig Intepretive Centre, Ireland

Architects: Peter and Mary Doyle

The Building Envelope – Opaque Elements

GREEN ROOFS

Placing soil and green plants on a flat or pitched roof to create a 'green roof' is an ancient vernacular tradition that has become popular again in recent years. However, a modern green roof is not simply a conventional roof with soil on top; it is a complex structure with multiple layers providing different functions. A typical green roof structure is illustrated below left.

The roof structure may need to be strengthened to support the extra weight of the soil, which has a density of roughly 2 t/m3. The roof deck may be flat or pitched to an angle below about 30°. Protrusions such as nail heads must be avoided. A waterproof membrane, generally made of EPDM or another synthetic rubberised material, is laid loosely over the deck. On top of the membrane is usually laid a 'geotextile mat,' which prevents soil slippage and provides a barrier to roots. The soil, typically about 200mm thick, is seeded and/or planted with whatever mix of plants is desired. The deeper the soil, the wider variety of plants can be used. A biodegradable matting is often placed on top of the soil, to prevent it from blowing or washing away before the plants are established. At the edge of the roof is a drainage zone typically consisting of a gravel-filled channel to prevent moisture build-up (Talbott, 1993).

The benefit of green roofs is mainly aesthetic. They can provide a haven for wildlife in a city and may moderate local microclimates if present in sufficient quantity. The insulation value of soil is not great, but depends on moisture content and density; values for conductance range from 0.7–2.1 W/mK, giving a U-value of 0.15–0.4 W/m²K for a 200mm thick layer. The lifespan of the roofing membrane (which is effectively the lifespan of the roof) may be longer than for other types of roofing materials, but this is probably outweighed by the high initial cost. Green roofs also cut down exterior noise, although if this is a problem then other measures such as double glazing are likely to take priority. The soil of a green roof provides a substantial amount of thermal mass, but since this lies outside the insulated building envelope it will be weakly coupled to the rest of the building.

Architectural integration
Providing access for maintenance is a possible issue. Structural design may be affected, as mentioned above.

Economics
A green roof involves considerable extra expense which is unlikely to be recouped through energy savings.

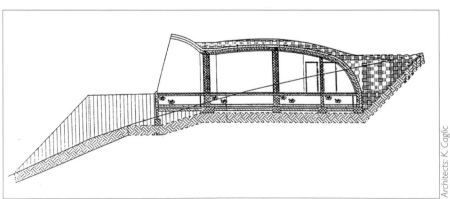

4.3 Caglic House, Slovenia

Architects: K. Caglic

Opaque Elements

TROMBE WALLS

The Trombe wall is an example of solar heating by indirect gain. It consists of a 150–500mm thick masonry wall on the south side of a building. A single or double layer of glass or plastic glazing is mounted about 10–15cm in front of the wall's surface. The exterior surface of the wall is painted a dark colour to absorb solar heat, and the glazing prevents this heat from then being lost to the outside. Thus the Trombe wall gradually heats up during the day, with the heat penetrating slowly from the exterior to the interior surface of the wall. As the interior surface of the wall heats up it radiates heat to the adjacent interior space. If the wall is the right thickness, this time lag means that the heat from the afternoon sun will start to warm the space in the evening, just as temperatures begin to drop (Mazria, 1979).

If more rapid heating is needed, vents at the top and bottom of the wall may be opened, allowing heat to circulate by convection into the interior from the glazed space in front of the wall. These vents must be closed at night to prevent the cycle reversing and heat being lost from the interior. Heat loss at night can also be reduced by drawing a curtain across the outside of the Trombe wall, inside the glazing.

Architectural integration
A full-height Trombe wall has the disadvantages of blocking sunlight from the south and of presenting a blank, dark-coloured face to the outdoors. It is worth considering a half-height Trombe wall from this point of view, since it would permit sunlight to enter the space. The loss of usable floor space caused by a thick Trombe wall is also worth considering from an architectural viewpoint.

Economics
A Trombe wall may or may not be an economical investment, depending on many factors including construction type, cost of materials and energy prices.

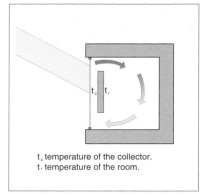

t_c temperature of the collector.
t_r temperature of the room.

4.4 Trombe wall - typical loop

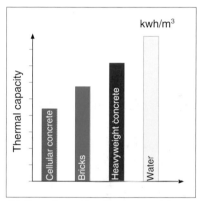

4.5 Thermal capacities of storage materials

The Building Envelope – Transparent Elements

ACTIVE (DOUBLE-FAÇADE) CURTAIN WALLS

Description
The active or double-façade curtain wall is an architectural technology designed to combine the aesthetic benefits of a high glazing ratio (over 90%) with the energy efficiency and comfort of a solid envelope.

Buildings of the last 40 years, particularly office buildings, are noted for using large areas of external glass in a non-load-bearing 'curtain wall'. This is mainly an aesthetic device, made possible by cheap energy, steel or aluminium frames supporting a non-structural envelope and comfort-control technologies, particularly air conditioning. Today's designers are more conscious of the need to save energy, while maintaining aesthetic quality. A number of architects have responded to this by designing curtain walls which will still perform adequately from an energy efficiency standpoint.

The double façade typically consists of two separate glass skins with an air space between. One or even both skins may be double-glazed. Shading and light directing devices may be situated between the two skins, and ventilation air circulates in this space. If well designed, the outer façade should protect the interior from wind, rain and noise, allowing the inner windows to be opened to provide natural ventilation. Daylighting is another benefit, although excessive light, particularly when it comes from one side of a deep space, can create glare problems. The aim is that the thermal performance of a well-designed double façade should approach that of a solid envelope.

Concerns include fire protection (because of the circulation of air between floors in the air space between the façades), and the reflection of noise between rooms.

The detail design of a double façade is critical and in the most successful examples, extensive simulation has been carried out on the envelope using computer analysis, scale models and full-scale prototypes.

Recommendations
Adequate testing is essential to achieve a design that performs well.

Double façades seem to be particularly appropriate for retrofitting office buildings.

Economics
In buildings where high glazing ratios are required, an active curtain wall has the potential for economic energy savings.

Transparent Elements

LIGHT-REDIRECTING and CHROMIC GLAZING

Redirecting light
Prismatic glazing and holographic film are products that redirect light as it passes through the glazing unit.

In prismatic glazing the direction of incoming daylight is changed as it passes through an array of triangular wedges, some of which may have specular or silvered surfaces, and whose geometry can be designed for particular conditions. It can keep out unwanted direct sunlight while redirecting diffuse daylight onto the ceiling and farther back into the room. Light coming from different angles can be handled selectively, with assemblies custom-made for site latitude and façade orientation.

Holographic film can also be designed to handle sunlight coming from well-defined angles. High-angle sun on south façades, or low-angle sun on east and west facades, for example, can be either blocked or redirected. Up to four images containing different 'instructions' can be combined in one layer. A view out is retained, but from some viewing angles there is a rainbow effect.

Chromic glass
Chromic glass is a special type of glass which when activated can turn from a clear transparent state to a dark, semi-transparent or opaque state, and vice versa. It is used to control solar radiation entering the building, preventing overheating and glare. As a result, bulky solar control measures, such as louvres and mechanical roller blinds are eliminated and maintenance costs are reduced.

Chromic glass changes its light absorption and transmission characteristics in response to changes in light (photochromic) or temperature (thermochromic), or to an electrical charge (electrochromic). Control of electrochromic glazing can be incorporated in a building energy management system. Photochromic and electrochromic glass have reached technical maturity, but costs are high.

Architectural integration
These products can be creatively used by building designers, combining performance with appearance.

Recommendations
Chromic glass which changes state without the user's intervention isn't normally appropriate for eye-level window panes, but it can be used for roof glazing or placed above and below the normal viewing level.

Economics
Prismatic sheets themselves are inexpensive to manufacture, but the overall construction cost of the window is higher than for conventional glazing. Holographic film costs are not high.

Chromic glass at present prices is likely to be an economical investment only in limited cases.

4.6 Light directing glazing at the Design Centre, Linz

4.7 Light redirecting, Bartenbach office, Innsbruck, Austria

4.8 Light redirecting, Bartenbach office, Innsbruck, Austria

Architect: Herzog and Partner

Architect: Prof J Lackner

Architect: Prof J Lackner

Single clear glass : 6mm

4.9 Clear float single glazing

Low-e film

4.10 Low E double glazing

Transparent Elements

HIGH-PERFORMANCE WINDOWS

The key performance characteristics of windows are insulation value (U-value, in W/m²K) and transmission of light. A conventional, single-glazed window with clear float glass will transmit approximately 85% of the light that falls upon it, and will have a U-value of roughly 6.0. Double glazing typically provides a U-value of around 3.0 W/m²K with a transmissivity of about 80% (Esbensen, 1998). High-performance windows are available which will greatly improve on these basic values, dealing with the three modes of heat loss: conduction, radiation and infiltration or exfiltration of air.

Gas-filled multiple glazing
Standard double- and triple-glazing units are filled with air. Sealed glazing units containing noble gases (argon and krypton) provide significantly better insulation values by reducing conduction through the unit. An argon-filled window will typically have an insulation value about 20% better than an identical air-filled unit, without affecting transmission of light (Esbensen, 1998).

Low-emissivity coatings
In a cold climate, heat from the interior space is absorbed by the glass in a normal window, which heats up and re-radiates the heat. After being absorbed and re-radiated several times the heat reaches the outside and is lost. The re-radiation process can be reduced by coating one or more panes with a low-emissivity (Low E) coating. This is a special film which substantially reduces the ability of the glass to radiate at certain wavelengths. Transmission of light is affected only slightly. A typical double-glazed unit with argon fill will have a U-value of about 1.5 and a transmissivity of light of about 77%. A comparable triple-glazed unit may have a U-value of 1.2 and a transmissivity of 70% (Esbensen, 1998).

In hot climates, Low E films may also be used to reduce incoming radiation. This means using a slightly different type of film which is specially designed for a hotter climate.

Frames
The quality of the seal around a window's edge varies depending on the frame material and the age of the window. In gas-filled windows, of course, seals have to be excellent to keep the gas in. Other windows may be rated by rate of air infiltration. The conductivity of the frame is also an issue, metal frames conducting more than wood or synthetic (RMI, 1997).

Recommendations
U-values should be specified as being for the whole unit rather than 'centre-of-glass' values which apply only to the glass itself (RMI, 1997).

Economics
As part of an integrated design, high-performance windows can provide significant cost savings, depending on energy prices.

Transparent Elements

SHADING DEVICES

Shading devices can be used to reduce glare and heat gain during the day, and heat loss at night, provided they are appropriate to location and orientation.

Interior or exterior shading?

Exterior shading is more effective in reducing heat gains (by up to 80%) because it intercepts and sheds solar beams before they strike the glass. It is more expensive to install and to maintain, but it plays a major role in the aesthetic character of an elevation.

Interior blinds tend to be cheaper and more easily adjustable. They protect a room's occupants against the immediate effects of sunlight and against glare, but are not so effective at reducing heat gains because the sunlight heats up the shades and the air around them. Reflective blinds reduce this effect by 15–20%.

Integral shading installed within a double- or triple-glazed unit, with ventilation of the void to the outside, combines the advantages of both types. Heat gains are dissipated to the outside, but the shades are protected from the severity of the outdoor climate.

Fixed or adjustable?

Fixed horizontal overhangs exclude high-angle sunlight, but reduce daylight penetration and are not appropriate for east and west orientations. Thus, they are most appropriate where light levels are high and overheating is a problem, such as in southern Europe. Continuous overhangs provide much more shade than those which extend across the width of the window only.

Light shelves can be used to redirect sunlight into the back of the room, and also to protect the front of the room from direct radiation.

Low-angle direct sunlight is more difficult to screen. Fixed vertical fins, if they are to be really effective, exclude a great deal of daylight and obstruct the view. Steel mesh sunscreens are almost 'transparent' but they too reduce the amount of daylight penetrating the windows.

Adjustable shades avoid some of these problems. Retractable awnings, adjustable exterior blades, curtains, roller blinds or venetian blinds can be left open for much of the time and closed only when the sun-angle demands it. On east or west-facing facades, horizontal louvres need to be almost completely closed to block sunlight, but vertical louvres can be left partially open to admit reflected or diffused light from the north, while still blocking sunlight. Fully automated systems, which respond to changes in sun angle, temperature and/or light levels, may be necessary, particularly for exterior systems.

Recommendations

Sun path diagrams should be used to calculate accurately the extent of the shadow cast onto the face of a building, in order to optimise performance.

Economics

As part of a good design, shading devices can be an economical investment.

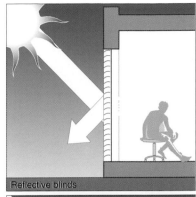

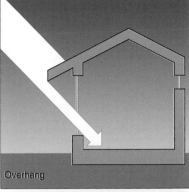

4.11 Types of external shading device

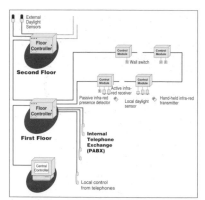

4.12 Diagrammatic layout of an integrated automatic control system

4.12 Prismatic panels, part of Siemens AG 'Daylightsystem', developed with Lichtplanung Christian Bartenbach GmbH

4.13 Apertures controlled by photoelectric cells, Arab Institute, Paris

Architect: Jean Nouvel

Electricity and Water

LIGHTING CONTROLS

In a complex or sophisticated daylight design, particularly one with exterior adjustable daylighting devices, integrated automatic lighting control systems are probably essential. In a conventionally lit commercial building, controls alone can make a 30–40% saving in lighting use. Care in the specification of control systems is necessary. Technical difficulties with the positioning and sensitivity of sensors, rapid changes in daylight levels due to fast-moving clouds, and the response of the occupants must all be allowed for (BRE, 1993).

Occupancy sensors
Occupancy sensors can help to optimise the use of background lighting. These sensors will operate the lights only when people are in the area. There are two types of occupancy sensors: infrared and ultra-sonic. Ultra-sonic sensors are best in rooms with partitions or dividers. Infrared sensors are better for open areas. Some sensors use both methods. Integrated units that include a sensor and a relay in a single housing in a standard electrical box are quite reasonably priced for residential applications.

Balancing artificial light
In rooms receiving natural light, there can be an intermittent need for artificial light depending on how bright it is outside. A fluorescent light with a 'daylighting ballast' (which includes a light-sensitive photocell) will vary light output according to the levels in the room, maintaining sufficient light at all times while eliminating the wasteful use of artificial light when daylight levels are already high.

Outdoor lighting
Photocells can also be used in outdoor lighting, for example, to activate lights at dusk and switch them off at dawn. For added efficiency, the photocell can be combined with an infrared or ultra-sonic motion detector. In this way, the lights are switched on only when daylight levels are low and there is motion in the vicinity.

Timing devices and dimmer controls
Timers turn lights on and off at predetermined times and are useful where regular cycles of light and dark are appropriate. Dimmers will only save energy when used consistently, and can often be combined with other forms of lighting control.

Recommendations
- Limit the number of light fittings controlled by any one switch.
- Provide clear and understandable layouts for light switch panels.
- Zone light fittings and controls in relation to distance from windows.
- Make light switches accessible. Hand-held remote control switches are useful where changes in partition layout are frequent. Simple local switching of this kind can produce 20% energy savings.
- Use automated controls (timers, time delay switches, movement sensors or sound detectors, daylight sensors, voltage/current controls).

Economics
Lighting controls can provide significant savings as part of a well-designed lighting scheme.

Electricity and Water

PHOTOVOLTAICS

Photovoltaic (PV) cells convert sunlight directly into electricity. They are clean, quiet, maintenance-free and efficient in their use of solar energy. The main obstacle to the wider use of PVs at present is cost: approximately 4 ECU per Watt of delivered power at peak capacity. However, this cost is falling rapidly and PVs are likely to become much more widely used in the next twenty years as costs fall still further. The amount of sunlight available to be tapped and the long-term potential of PVs are enormous. Studies in Germany and Britain have found that between a quarter and half of these States' respective electricity needs could be supplied by PVs mounted on buildings alone. (CREST, 1998)

4.14 Photovoltaics, Barcelona

Architect: BCN Cimbra Logica

Photovoltaics are used in two types of installations, known as 'off-grid' and 'grid-tied.' Off-grid or stand-alone installations are those where the photovoltaic cells and the devices which they power are not connected to a larger electricity grid. The electricity may either be used as it is generated (for example, in a solar-powered pump) or it may be stored for later use in batteries. Usually, the cost of energy storage is quite high in this type of installation. Off-grid PVs are often used in isolated rural locations for applications such as refrigeration, emergency phones and water pumps.

A grid-tied installation dispenses with the cost of storing electricity. Surplus power is supplied to the grid as it is generated and bought back when it is needed. The economics of grid-tied PV installations are governed by their legal status in the country in question, which determines whether utilities have an obligation to purchase the electricity at market rates. EU and national governments also have various programmes to encourage the use of PVs, including tax incentives, loans and grants. Further information is available from the International Solar Energy Society (http://www.ises.com), which has national branches in most EU Member States.

Architectural integration
Traditionally PV cells were installed on pitched roofs in the same way as solar thermal panels. New developments in PV technology mean that it is now possible to integrate cells into the building fabric, as part of the roof, walls, shading devices and even windows.

Recommendations
Choose experienced system designers and installers. A Guarantee of Solar Results (GSR) is often given by the company installing the system. This is a commitment that the system will provide at least a preset amount of solar energy, or the company will reimburse the cost of fuel to make up the difference. This protects the client against errors in design or installation.

Economics
At present prices, photovoltaics are likely to justify their initial cost only in limited cases.

Electricity and Water

WATER-SAVING DEVICES

Water-efficient components are available which can significantly reduce the amount of water used in a building without affecting levels of comfort. Other technologies can be used to recycle water for use in outdoor cleaning and watering plants.
(Refer STRATEGIES; Site)

Water-efficient components
Showers, toilets and taps are all available in highly efficient models that use 50% or less of the water used by standard models. Consumer surveys have shown that most users are satisfied with the performance of these appliances (Waterwiser). When calculating savings from water-efficient appliances, the savings in energy needed to heat water should be taken into account as well as the savings of metered water.

WCs
The criteria for water use is the volume of water per flush. Purpose-designed ultra-low-consumption WCs with innovative features and improved design can reduce consumption to around 6–7 litres per flush (lpf) or less, from the conventional consumption of between 15.7 and 40.5 lpf (Van der Ryn, 1995). Existing WCs may be retrofitted with low-tech devices (such as bricks in bags) to displace some of the water and thus reduce the quantity used in the flush, but this may reduce the effectiveness of the flush. The use of low flush equipment will put less pressure on a septic tank system.

In commercial buildings continuous flush urinals should be fitted with timers or sensors.

Taps
For domestic usage the key to water saving taps is careful operation. Shut-off valves and levers may be fitted which allow water to be turned off mid-operation while maintaining temperature, this is more convenient than turning both hot and cold individually off and on again in quick succession. Aeration valves may be retrofitted to existing taps to significantly reduce consumption (to around 8 lpm litres per minute) (Van der Ryn, 1995). For commercial use, infrared sensor control devices or self-closing valves will reduce wastage.

Showerheads
It is well known that showers use less water than baths. High efficiency showers are available to further improve efficiency. A conventional shower uses 13.5–36 litres per minute (lpm), while water-efficient shower heads use 11.25 lpm or less (Van der Ryn, 1995). In addition, there are savings associated with saving of hot water.

Economics
High efficiency equipment may be approximately twice as expensive as conventional. The economics of water efficiency measures vary greatly depending on scarcity of water, the level of water charges and the design of the system.

Electricity and Water

HIGH-EFFICIENCY LIFTS

Gearless disc-powered lifts consume a fraction of the energy of conventional lifts and reduce the building's environmental impact in other ways.

A typical eight-person conventional traction lift in an apartment block with a traffic intensity of 100,000 starts/year consumes roughly 3000kWh a year. A hydraulic lift in the same situation would consume 4200kWh. A gearless lift, on the other hand, would consume just 1800kWh. Lower peak loads are generated by the gearless lift, which means smaller fuse sizes and lower connection charges.

Other advantages of the gearless lift include no engine room or a smaller one, leading to space (about 12m^2 per lift) and material savings over conventional traction lifts. The machinery is supported on a metal frame, so no massive wall structures are required. The disc, which is the only moving part, has a lower rotation speed than a conventional motor (only 95rpm inspead of 1500) leading to less noise and vibration. No oil is required, compared with roughly 1–2 litres per year for a traction unit and 20–60 litres per year for a hydraulic lift. This avoids problems of disposal of waste oil.

Architectural integration
Because of the smaller operating machinery and lack of massive lift shaft walls, integration of gearless lifts is easier than conventional lifts. In areas with building height limits, this may mean an extra occupied floor becomes possible.

Economics
Depending on initial costs, a gearless lift can prove highly economical with considerable savings in running costs.

Heating and Cooling Systems

RENEWABLE ENERGY

Wind

Wind turbine technology has developed rapidly over the last 20 years or so, and wind is now one of the most cost-effective renewable energy sources. Wind turbines are mostly installed in groups in wind farms, which supply electricity to the grid like conventional power stations. Many turbines being installed at present are in the size range 500 kilowatts (kW) – 1.5 megawatts (MW).

Annual power output is dependent on the wind speed at the site. Thus the economic returns from wind turbines are much better on exposed coastal or upland sites than in sheltered areas. Planning permission and a connection to the grid are also required before a wind farm can start operating.

Wind energy is one of the most efficient energy sources in terms of land use. Only 1–2% of the land on which a wind farm stands is occupied by turbine foundations and access roads; the land between the turbines can be used for agricultural or other purposes. Offshore wind farms are also becoming common.

Biomass / waste

Heat and/or electricity may be produced from various types of waste, including agricultural wastes, forestry wastes, municipal refuse and sewage. There are many examples of commercial projects using these fuels.

Energy may also be derived from crops grown specially. For example, short rotation forestry (SRF) involves the growth of trees such as willow and poplar in relatively short cycles (often three to five years).

Water

Hydropower: Many of the best sites for large-scale hydropower have been developed, and environmental concerns may limit the development of further large-scale projects. However, there are many sites around Europe suitable for small-scale hydropower schemes (from a few tens of kilowatts up to about 5 megawatts).

Wave energy: There are enormous amounts of energy in the waves off Europe's Atlantic coasts. However, the technology to harness this energy is still at the research stage.

Tidal energy: At particular sites, the rise and fall of the tides can be harnessed to produce electricity. The most well-known scheme in operation is that at La Rance in France, which has operated successfully since 1966. However, the large capital investment required for such projects has discouraged other tidal projects. Also, they may pose a threat to delicate coastal ecosystems.

Heating and Cooling Systems

SOLAR THERMAL SYSTEMS

Description

Solar thermal systems are devices which collect the energy of the sun and deliver it as useful heat, mostly for domestic hot water. They are in widespread use all over Europe, particularly in Greece, Germany, Austria, Scandinavia and the Netherlands.

A solar thermal system contains components which collect the sun's heat, distribute it, and store it. There are three main types of solar collectors.

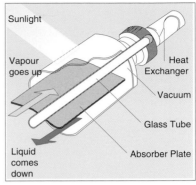

4.15 Evacuated tube solar collector: more efficient than flat plate collectors

- Unglazed collectors consist of black plastic or metal pipes through which the fluid medium is circulated. They are very simple and cheap to make but can only reach temperatures of about 20°C above ambient air temperature.
- Flat plate collectors, the most widely used type, consist of a flat insulated box, through which the fluid medium circulates. They can produce temperatures up to 70°C above ambient temperature.
- Evacuated tube collectors consist of an array of evacuated glass tubes each containing an absorber which collects solar energy and transfers it to the heat transfer fluid. These collectors can produce temperatures of 100°C or more above ambient.

Solar collectors need to be mounted so as to catch the sun, generally facing south and tilted at an angle to the horizontal that is roughly equal to the latitude of the site. In Europe, this means a tilt of 35–65°. A south-facing pitched roof is ideal.

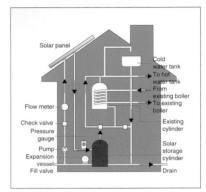

4.16 Diagram of a typical dwelling incorporating solar thermal heating

The distribution and storage parts of a solar thermal system are very similar to those of a conventional heating system. The distribution medium is usually based on either air or water. The heat storage unit will often be larger than in a non-solar system because of the need to store heat during cloudy periods. A backup heat source such as a wood, oil or gas boiler is usually necessary.

Solar thermal systems are an economical and clean source of energy. In most parts of the EU, a solar thermal system can supply at least 50% of a household's energy for hot water at virtually no running cost. A typical DHW system for a household will have 2–6m² of collector area, although less is needed in southern than northern Europe, and a 200–300 litre water tank.

Architectural integration

The impact of a roof-mounted solar thermal collector on the building's architectural appearance is no greater than that of, for instance, an attic window. Some systems, particularly in southern Europe, make use of a thermosyphon mechanism to circulate the water, which means that the tank has to be placed above the collector, on the outside of the roof. This can lead to greater architectural impact.

Recommendations

Check that shadows from surrounding buildings and trees do not obstruct sunlight falling on the collectors, especially in winter, when the sun is low in the sky.

A good quality, properly maintained system should last for 15–20 years. A Guarantee of Solar Results (GSR) is often given by the company installing the system. This is a commitment that the system will provide at least a preset amount of solar energy, or the company will reimburse the cost of fuel to make up the difference. This protects the client against errors in design or installation. Ask for a maintenance agreement (one or two inspections per year are usually enough), for at least the first five or ten years.

Information on solar thermal systems can be obtained from national solar energy associations or from the European Solar Industry Federation (ERG/ESIF, 1998).

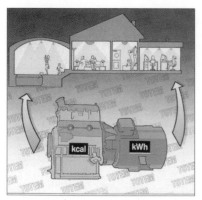
4.17 The principle of a CHP plant

Heating and Cooling Systems

COMBINED HEAT AND POWER and DISTRICT HEATING

Combined heat and power

Combined heat and power (CHP), or cogeneration, is the simultaneous production of usable heat and electricity in the same power plant.

In most power plants and generators, about 35% of the energy from the fuel is converted to electricity; the remainder is given off as heat to the environment. A further 8% of the electricity (about 3% of primary energy) is typically lost, also as heat, during transmission and distribution to the end user. It makes sense to use this heat.

A CHP plant is an electrical generator situated close to a location with a large demand for heat, such as an industrial site, hospital or hotel. Both the electricity and the 'waste' heat from the generator are usually supplied to the same end-user. The overall efficiency of a CHP process is about 86%, that is, 86% of the primary energy is delivered as heat or electricity. By comparison, a conventional power plant combined with a conventional boiler would typically have an efficiency of about 57%.

CHP can be used in almost any type of building: commercial, industrial, institutional or residential. In the industrial sector, sites with large process heating requirements, such as the chemical, brewing and paper industries, tend to be the largest and most effective applications for CHP. In offices or homes, CHP can be used in the form of 'district' or 'community' heating.

Small CHP systems, consisting of an internal combustion engine burning gas or oil with an output ranging from 15kW to 1MW electrical output, are the most common. Systems like these are developed as a complete package by a specialist firm and are located in the existing boiler room of a building (ICIE, 1992).

District heating

District heating is the common generation of heat for a neighbourhood of a group of buildings. It is usually most successful in dense, mixed-use developments. A wide range of fuels can be used effectively, including wood, straw, waste materials and solar.

Economics

The economics of CHP are very site- and machine-specific. They are governed by the site's energy demand profile, the plant's capital and maintenance costs, operating hours and energy prices. For economic viability a site should normally have an electricity load of at least 45kW and a heat load of at least 120kW. Simultaneous demands for heat and power should also be present for at least 4500 hours a year (about 50% load factor).

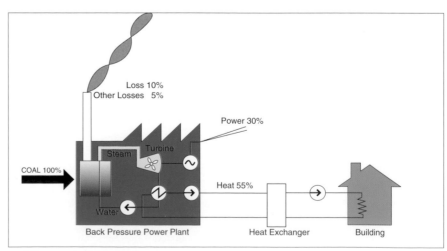
4.18 The principle of a CHP plant

Heating and Cooling Systems

GASIFICATION WOOD BOILERS

Description

Notwithstanding their use of a renewable energy source, traditional wood boilers tend to have a low combustion efficiency and produce a large amount of air pollutants, such as particulates (soot), carbon monoxide, oxides of nitrogen and sulphur and volatile organic compounds.

Gasification wood boilers overcome these and some other disadvantages connected with traditional technologies for the use of wood in heating. They also help to ensure adherence to emissions standards.

The most efficient and cleanest combustion of wood is obtained when the flame doesn't come into contact with fuel, other than that being consumed. This type of consumption is generally obtained when the flame is directed downwards at the top of the fuel. An appropriate furnace design, assisted with a small fan, provides a good air flow while inverting the flame so that it burns towards the top of the fuel. The fuel heats up, sublimes (becomes gaseous) and rises into the flame, at which point its actual combustion takes place. The result is a controlled burn that starts at the top of the furnace and progresses downwards, providing clean, efficient combustion (an efficiency of 90% and emission levels similar to those of natural gas.)

Advanced boilers can be programmed to work on standby until full heat is required, and can be loaded with wood to last up to 24 hours, depending on capacity. Gasification wood boilers typically have a peak capacity of betwen 30kW and 100kW, making them suitable for domestic, commercial and office applications. They can also be combined with fossil-fuel-based heating systems.

4.19 Gasification wood boiler

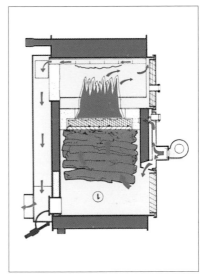

4.20 Function diagram

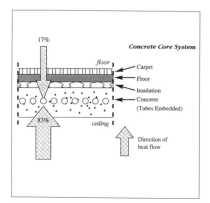

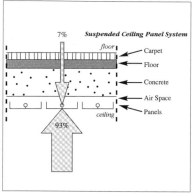

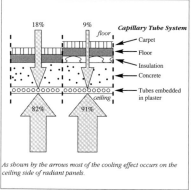

As shown by the arrows most of the cooling effect occurs on the
ceiling side of radiant panels.

4.21

Heating and Cooling Systems

RADIANT HEATING/COOLING SYSTEMS

Radiant heating/cooling systems supply both heating and cooling, in an energy-efficient manner, by changing the temperature of the walls, ceiling and/or floor of a space instead of heating and cooling the air. This works because the temperature experienced by the human body is approximately equal to the average of the radiant temperature (tr) and the air temperature (ta). The radiant temperature is the average temperature of all the objects which surround the body.

A radiant heating/cooling system generally consists of an array of pipes or tubes installed in or behind the surface of the walls, ceiling or floor of an interior space. The three main types of radiant heating/cooling systems are:

- **core systems**, where water is circulated through plastic tubes, imbedded in, for example, the slab of a concrete ceiling, wall or floor. This allows the thermal mass of the slab to be used in smoothing out heating and cooling loads.
- **panel systems**, consisting of usually aluminium panels, with metal tubes connected to their rear. The system has minimal thermal mass but a very swift response time and is often used with suspended ceilings.
- **capillary systems**, consisting of a fine grid of small-bore plastic tubes installed under wall or ceiling plaster or imbedded in gypsum board. They provide an even surface temperature and have an intermediate heat storage capacity between the other two types of system. They are ideal for retrofit applications.

Unlike conventional heating systems such as those that use wall-mounted radiators, a radiant heating/cooling system will usually occupy a large part of the total surface area of the space, such as the whole ceiling or wall. So the actual change in water temperature necessary to produce an improvement in comfort for the occupants is relatively small. The heating and cooling load is generally supplied by a low-temperature boiler, an efficient refrigeration system, a passive cooling system or a heat pump with a high coefficient of performance.

Unlike air conditioning systems, radiant systems do not detrimentally affect indoor air quality. They can significantly reduce the amount of mechanical ventilation needed to ensure comfort, and reduce the amount of ductwork needed for a conventional HVAC system by about 80%. Radiant systems can be effectively used for office or residential buildings, with or without mechanical ventilation systems.

Architectural integration
Once installed, radiant systems disappear from view; architectural integration requirements are limited to providing each room with the necessary unobstructed wall or ceiling surface.

Heating and Cooling Systems

GROUND COOLING

Ground cooling is based on the concept that the earth's temperature is lower than that of outdoor air for most of the year, and heat from the building may be stored in the ground, which has high thermal inertia and low conductivity. In Europe ground temperatures range from 8–14°C.

The exchange of heat can take place through two principal methods. The building may be designed so that a significant area of the building envelope is in direct contact with the ground; or air may be introduced into the building which has been cooled by being circulated underground: this is called earth-to-air cooling.

A typical earth-to-air cooling system consists of one or more tubes of appropriate diameter and length buried horizontally in the ground. Ambient or indoor air is drawn through the pipe, usually by electric fans.

The system of air circulation may be either open- or closed-loop. In a closed circuit, both intake and outlet are located inside the building and the indoor air is circulated through the tubes. In an open loop system the air is drawn in from outside.

The amount of temperature decrease achieved will depend on the intake temperature, the temperature of the ground around the pipes, the thermal conductivity of the pipes, the thermal diffusivity of the soil, the air velocity and the pipe dimensions (CIENE, 1994).

Recommendations

- The length of the pipes should be at least 10m.
- The diameter should be between 20–30cms.
- The pipes should be between 1.5–3m deep.
- The air velocity should be between 4–8m/s.
- Ground temperature at the depth of the pipes should be around 5–6°C lower than air temperatures.
- Tubes can be made from various materials (PVC, stainless steel, concrete, etc.) but must be completely impermeable to rainwater and soil. The material used should not release dust or toxins into the air.
- When transferring heat to the ground, the air can create condensation inside the tube. An adequate drainage system must therefore be installed and the speed of air inside needs to be calculated with particular attention to reducing the risk of condensation (CRES, 1994).

Economics

Earth to air cooling systems are simple low-cost systems, but the economics of ground cooling depends on the climate, the nature of the site and the building in question.

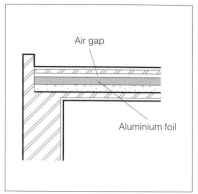

4.22 An insulated roof with a radiant barrier

Heating and Cooling Systems

RADIANT BARRIERS

A radiant barrier is used in hot climates to stop heat from external surfaces (walls and roof) from penetrating to the building's interior. The barrier consists of a sheet of reflective material (usually aluminium foil) placed in a cavity between the external surface and the insulation layer. The foil layer reflects radiant heat. For it to work properly, it is essential that there should be an air gap immediately outside the radiant barrier, otherwise heat will cross the barrier by conduction. An air stream is needed to transport heat from the foil by convection.

Where cooling is a primary design consideration the radiant barrier may be coupled with insulation as an alternative to higher insulation levels (CRES,1994). Where radiant barriers are used, the construction should not normally be airtight, and the foil should be vapour-permeable to avoid condensation within the building envelope and overheating in the attic space (Austin Green Builder, 1998; Progressive Arch., 1985).

MATERIALS

Introduction

To perform a complete analysis of the environmental impact of all the components and materials in a building would be prohibitively time-consuming and expensive. However, a responsible architect should weigh up environmental considerations alongside other criteria (Table 4.1). To do this the architect needs the intellectual tools for the job, and that is what this chapter aims to provide. For those who wish to find out more than we have space for here, there are several excellent resources available, listed at the end of this introduction.

Table 4.1 SUSTAINABILITY CONSIDERATIONS IN MATERIALS SELECTION

There are several issues that should be considered by any architect who is concerned about the environmental impact of the materials that will go into his or her building. A brief checklist might run as follows.

For materials used in quantities of 250kg or less, consider the following issues:
- impact of the material's production: habitat destruction, toxins released;
- any hazards to health or local environment during construction or use;
- life span of the material;
- eventual destination of the material after the building's life. Re-use is better than recycling, which is better than incineration or landfill;
- reduction/separation of construction waste and avoidance/careful disposal of toxic waste.

For bulk materials, consider all the above issues, but also:
- the nature of the resources involved: renewable or non-renewable, scarce or abundant;
- emissions of CO_2 (in kg/kg) during production or, if information is not available, embodied energy (in kWh/kg);
- how far and by what mode(s) the material will be transported, and emissions/energy use due to this (see Table 4.2).

The Environmental Effects of Building Materials

The design of the building as a whole cannot easily be separated from the choice of materials and components which will go into it. Their selection influences design and performance profoundly. One can consider the effect of these choices in two ways. First, there are the impacts due to the manufacture, processing, transportation, construction, maintenance, demolition and recycling or disposal of the materials themselves. Second, there is the influence of the choice of materials on the environmental performance of the whole building, seen as more than simply the sum of its parts.

Estimating the first is a matter of access to information. Studies of the environmental impact of construction materials have been performed in several countries and the results are widely available. This chapter quotes from a range of different sources, some of them listed at the end of the introduction. Readers who need more detailed information should consult these sources or seek out those produced by their own Member State.

There is still no commonly accepted standard for performing life cycle analysis (LCA) of materials. This means that a great deal of the information quoted here is anecdotal, subjective or difficult to compare. The European Network of Building Research Institutes (ENBRI), led by the UK's Building Research Establishment, is presently developing a standard methodology for LCA under the European Commission's BRITE EURAM

---

programme. However, only a small selection of materials is being studied (Viljoen, 1997). It is difficult, but clearly important, to know the relative scale of different impacts. Only then is it possible to prioritise measures to reduce them. In general, environmental effects are proportional to the physical mass of the material in question. So, the choice of structural material for the building is likely to be more important than the choice of floor covering. However, materials present in small quantities can often have disproportionate effects on the local environment; for example, indoor air pollution is often due to paints, glues and other materials present in small amounts.

The influence of components and materials on the building's overall performance is an endlessly complex subject. This chapter gives a reference guide to the properties of the materials and components themselves, as opposed to design issues surrounding them, which are covered elsewhere.

Because buildings typically last a long time (of the order of 50 years), environmental impacts in use tend to mount up. In most cases, the CO_2 emitted due to the building's energy use during the occupancy phase is the single greatest environmental impact of the building. Therefore the first priority should be to reduce ongoing energy use. Once this is done, low-impact materials come to the fore. A study of low-energy houses (Viljoen, 1997) found that 'the specification of low-embodied-energy materials, like rammed earth, is extremely significant in the total primary energy and CO_2 performance of a [low-energy] dwelling'.

Transport

Because of the sheer amount of materials used in the construction industry, the environmental impact of transporting them is a cause for concern. The energy needed to transport bulk materials is generally a function of distance travelled, mode of transport, and mass of material hauled. Materials with low density (such as insulation), however, tend to use disproportionate amounts of energy for transport, due to their bulk. Table 4.2 below gives estimates of the environmental impact of different modes of transport.

Table 4.2 TOTAL EMISSIONS AND PRIMARY ENERGY USE BY DIFFERENT MODES OF FREIGHT TRANSPORT

Emissions/g per t per km	Water	Rail	Road	Air
CO_2	30	41	207	1206
CH_4	0.04	0.06	0.3	2.0
NOx	0.4	0.2	3.6	5.5
CO	0.12	0.05	2.4	1.4
VOCs	0.1	0.08	1.1	3.0
Energy / KJ per t per km	423	677	2890	15839

Note that several important environmental impacts, such as noise, particulates, and oil spills, are not included. For the environmental impact equivalent to hauling 100 tonne-kilometres by road, it is possible to move roughly 400 t.km by rail, 700 t.km by water, or 17 t.km by air.

(Whitelegg, 1993)

Waste

Waste from the building industry forms a large fraction of all the waste produced in society. Ultimately, most building materials end up as waste that is either landfilled or incinerated, either after the demolition of the building or when packaging and surplus materials are discarded.

Demolition waste

Until recently, many materials from demolished buildings were simply re-used on the same site. However, with modern materials sich as reinforced concrete, complex assemblies of different materials, and strong adhesives, this is much harder to do. In general, modern buildings need to be designed for recycling if their materials are not to be wasted after demolition. This means assembling materials in a way that can be easily disassembled rather than destructively demolished (an example might be using relatively weak mortar so that bricks can be separated and re-used), using materials that are valuable for recycling (such as metals) rather than those that are difficult to recycle (such as many plastics) and ensuring that proper plans and records are kept so that those entrusted with demolition will know how to undertake the job.

The vast majority of demolition waste (about 95% by weight or more) consists of inert bulk materials such as brick, concrete and stone. There are often recycled into aggregate, although bricks and stone blocks can also be re-used in new building provided they can be separated and cleaned adequately. It is most important to avoid simply tipping large amounts of such waste in a convenient location; as well as often being illegal, this presents a hazard to people and wildlife.

The most valuable elements of a building being demolished are those that can be removed whole. These can range from structural elements such as trusses and girders to interior installations such as furnishings and appliances. In most areas there is a thriving market in second-hand construction elements.

Construction waste

Construction waste contains many different types of materials. Many of these are dealt with elsewhere in this chapter, with guidelines for their recycling or disposal. Often the building can be designed to use readily available sizes of material; this reduces labour (cutting and trimming) as well as minimising waste. Careful site practices can also help to avoid damaged materials. The key to successful and profitable recycling is separation of waste types at an early stage. Separate bins for different recycling categories should be maintained on site, as close as possible to the building work. Toxic waste (such as left-over paint, adhesives and chemicals) should, of course, be handled with care and disposed of according to the manufacturer's instructions.

The accessibility of information is vital to persuading professionals to research the wider effects of their building practices. Labelling systems and sources of information are covered in ISSUES; Environment. Other means of assessing the environmental performance of materials include;

4.23 Construction waste

- *Institute for Baubiologie Method*
  A schedule of materials graded in terms of ecological impact has been developed by the Institute for Baubiologie and Ecology Inc. This gives a ranking of generic classes of materials on a simplified scale. Contact: Institute for Baubiologie, Neubauern, Germany.

- *Environmental Preference Method*
  This is a widely used method developed in the Netherlands. Each of the options has been assessed for its environmental impact over its entire life cycle, from extraction as a raw material to processing of the waste material. The results are expressed as a simple ranking of different choices. Details: David Anink, Chiel Boonstra and John Mak. Handbook of Sustainable Building: An Environmental Preference Method for Selection of Materials for Use in Construction and Refurbishment. James & James (Science Publishers) Ltd., 1996.

- *Environmental Resource Guide*
  Developed by the American Institute of Architects, this provides practical, comparative information on the environmental impacts of building materials, coupled with application reports and case studies. Available from: J. R. Wiley & Sons. Tel +1 800 225 5945. Fax +1 212 850 6103.

- *Green Building Digest*
  A monthly digest providing environmental information for specifiers and purchasers of building materials. Researched and edited by the Ethical Consumers Research Association, it includes 'best buy' rankings for generic materials and environmental analyses of major building product manufacturing companies. Available from: ACTAC, 94 Mount Pleasant, Liverpool, L3 5SD, United Kingdom.

4.24 Student Hostel at Windberg

Architect: T Herzog

4.25

Wood

Wood is a highly popular building material: light, strong, durable, easy to work, beautiful and with a timeless tradition and a mature skill base. It is also a renewable resource, given proper forestry practices. However, according to WWF, the international timber trade is now the primary threat to the world's forests. Forests vary enormously in type and quality; measurements of forested area are highly misleading, equating rich natural forests with monocultural plantations. Usually, the oldest forests are the richest in wildlife, with numerous rare and indigenous species. They also contain the highest proportion of mature trees and are therefore most attractive to timber companies. Most natural forests around the world are under serious threat. The disappearance of tropical forests is well known, but temperate and boreal forests, including the few remaining old-growth forests in Europe, are also disappearing fast, mainly because of logging operations. Illegal logging is widespread in many countries, as is displacement of indigenous people to make way for forestry operations (WWF, 1998).

It is not always easy to select wood and wood products that come from suitably managed forests. Many different labelling systems and claims of 'sustainability' exist, but most are not rigorously tested and are thus meaningless. Another study by WWF found that of 80 environmental labelling systems for paper and wood products, the claims of only three could be independently verified.

The Forest Stewardship Council (FSC) is an international body that exists to verify certification systems for properly managed forestry. To carry the FSC logo, certification systems must verify that management in their forests follows the following ten principles:

- compliance with national and international law;
- documented and legally established tenure and use;
- rights of indigenous peoples respected;
- community relations and workers' rights supported;
- efficient use of the many yields of the forest;
- conservation of the biological integrity of the forest;
- existence of a management plan with long-term aims clearly stated;
- monitoring and assessment carried out;
- natural forests conserved and not replaced with other land uses;
- plantations properly managed and used to reduce pressures on natural forests.

Only products which carry the FSC logo should be treated as being from properly managed forests. Non-FSC-approved claims of 'sustainable' or 'environmentally friendly' production should be treated with great caution.

As of 1998, four European certification systems are accredited by the FSC: Skal (NL); SGS Forestry QUALIFOR and Soil Association Woodmark (UK); and the Swedish FSC Working Group's certification programme. Others are undergoing assessment. (FSC, 1998)

Wood from properly managed forests still carries a considerable environmental impact because of energy used during its extraction, transport (Refer ELEMENTS; Introduction) and processing. Air-dried timber will use less energy than kiln-dried timber (ACTAC, 1995).

An alternative to using FSC-certified wood (which is still relatively difficult to find) is to use either locally produced wood or wood reclaimed from a known source (such as a building that is being demolished.) Both have the advantage of involving less transportation energy and allowing architects to inform themselves about the provenance of the material.

Good detailing can greatly increase the life-span of wood within the building, while planning and careful sizing can maximise material efficiency and reduce waste.

Wood products

Wood is a major constituent of a wide range of products used in building. In most cases similar comments can be made for the wood-derived portion of these products as for wood itself, with the proviso that it is even less easy to be certain of the wood's provenance. Many products, such as chipboard and fibreboard and even synthetic structural beams, make use of waste off-cuts and chips of timber. While this is no guarantee that the timber itself comes from a sustainable source, it does at least ensure that the timber is being used efficiently. Plywood, however, makes use of large-dimension timber which is unlikely to be sustainably produced.

The other components of wood products vary widely. Panel products such as blockboard, plywood, and chipboard are bound together with organic resins. These do not usually have significant emissions to the indoor environment because they are effectively inert if properly manufactured. Any emissions in use will tend to be released in the first few days after installation (ACTAC, 1995).

Paper is another product that includes a significant amount of wood in its manufacture. Compared to the paper used by a building's occupants, however, the paper used in the building itself is not likely to have a serious effect on the environment. There is still considerable debate about the environmental costs and benefits of recycled paper. Paper based not on wood pulp but on other fibres such as hemp and kenaf is probably most sustainable.

4.26 School of Architecture, Lyon

Architects: Jourda and Perraudin

Forest Stewardship Council accredited certification schemes:

- Jan-Willem Heezen, Skal, Stationsplein 5, P.O. Box 384, 8000 AJ Zwolle, Netherlands. Tel. +31.38.4226 866. Fax: +31.38.4213063. email: skal@euronet.nl
- Ruth Nussbaum, SGS Forestry QUALIFOR Programme, Oxford Centre for Innovation, Mill Street, Oxford OX2 0JX, UK. Tel: +44.1865.201 212. Fax: +44.1865.790441. email: forestry@sgsgroup.com
- Jim Sandom, Soil Association Woodmark, Bristol House, 46–50 Victoria Street, Bristol BS1 6BY, UK. Tel: +44.117.914 2435/929 0661.Fax: +44.117.925 2504. email: rfp@gn.apc.org
- Jonas Rudberg, Swedish FSC Working Group, Swedish Society for Nature Conservation, P.O. Box 4625, Stockholm, S-11691, Sweden. Tel: +46 8 702 6513 Fax:+ 46 8 702 0855 email: jonas.rudberg@snf.se

European contacts for Forest Stewardship Council:

- Geert Lejeune, WWF Belgium v.z.w., Waterloosteenweg 608, B-1050 Brussels, Belgium. Tel: +32 2 340 0955 Fax: +32 2 340 0933 email: geert.lejeune@wwf.be
- Ms Anne-Marie Mikkelsen, WWF-Denmark, Ryesgade 3F, DK-2200 Kobenhavn N, Denmark. Tel: +45 35 36 3635 Fax:+45 31 39 2062 email: a.mikkelsen@wwf.dk
- Mr Harri Karjalainen, WWF-Finland, Lintulahdenkatu 10, 00500 Helsinki, Finland. Tel: +358 9 7740 100. Fax: +358 9 7740 2139 email: harri.karjalainen@wwf.fi
- Mr Tom Roche, IWFA: Irish Woodworkers for Africa, Bury Quay, Tullamore, Co. Offaly, Ireland. Tel/Fax: +353 506 23557 email: woodlife@iol.ie. http://www.iol.ie/~woodlife/
- Ms Gemma Boetekees, FoE Netherlands: Vereniging Mileudefensie, Damrak 26, 1012 LJ Amsterdam, postbus 19199, 1000 GD Amsterdam, The Netherlands Tel: +31 20 622 1366 Fax: +31 20 627 5287 email: gemma@milieudefensie.nl
- Mr Pierre Hauselmann, Av. S.-Reymondin 30, CH 1009 Pully, Switzerland Tel: +41 21 728 1387 Fax: +41 21 728 1324 email: phauselm@cyberlab.ch
- Ms Hannah Scrase, Unit D, Station Building, Llanidloes Powys, Wales SY18 6EB, United Kingdom. Tel: +44 1686 413 916 Tel/Fax: +44 1686 412176 email: hannah@fsc-uk.demon.co.uk

Internet resources:

- FSC head office: http://www.fscoax.org
- WWF Forests for Life campaign: http://www.panda.org/forests4life/index.htm

Straw and other plant fibres

Straw consists of the stems of grain crops such as wheat, oats, barley, rye and rice left over after the grain has been harvested. Straw may seem an unlikely candidate for a building material, but it is rapidly growing in popularity because of its ready availability, low environmental impact, and excellent insulating properties: straw bales have an insulation value of approximately 0.012 W/mK.

Straw can be used in building in several ways. It is used in varying proportions as a binder in earth bricks and structures (Refer MATERIALS; Earth). Since the invention of the baler in the late nineteenth century, straw bales have been used as building blocks for highly insulating walls. This practice began in Nebraska, US, where some early bale buildings are still standing; more recently it has become popular in other countries. Experience indicates that concerns about moisture and pests can be satisfactorily addressed by correct design; fire is not a problem because tightly packed, baled straw does not burn. In some buildings the bales themselves bear the weight of the roof, in others the bales are simply used as in-fill in a post-and-beam structure. The walls are usually staked together with iron or bamboo rods driven through the bales, and plastered inside and out.

Straw and other plant fibres are also used as the raw material for panel products, which can be used in a wide range of applications. The fibres are compressed together at high temperatures (about 200°C) and bond strongly without adhesives.

Reeds, straw and other plant stems are also a traditional roofing material. Thatched roofs are attractive and low-impact, but highly labour-intensive and require skilled workers.

The environmental impact of straw and other plant fibres is generally very low. They are mostly agricultural waste products, although some may be grown specially for building. Huge amounts of waste straw are either burnt (producing air pollution) or, more beneficially, tilled into the fields to improve soil structure. The main environmental impact will be due to burning fuel for haulage. The fuel needed per kilogram-kilometre will be higher than average because of the low density of the fibres. But if plant fibres are taken from a local source, their environmental impact will typically be low (EBN, 1995).

Earth

Earth consists of various grades of pulverised stone (ranging from small cobbles to silt) and clay, which is the active ingredient or 'glue' that sticks the soil together. Organic material, such as is present in topsoil, is undesirable in earth for building. Water is the other main ingredient. Clay content varies widely; most soil is likely to have too much clay (which can cause cracking as the earth dries) rather than too little (which can cause crumbling). Extra sand or straw can be added to balance excess clay. To increase the structural strength of earth it may be 'stabilised' with asphalt, lime or cement.

Earth was one of the first building materials and is still one of the most widely used; its has been claimed that one-third of the human race today live in houses made of earth. (Schumann and Sinha, 1994) Earth is freely available virtually everywhere and its environmental impact is almost nil; extraction is easy, haulage and processing are minimal and disposal couldn't be simpler.

4.27 Rammed earth construction, Mexico

Earth is used in building in several different ways. Perhaps the simplest is where it is 'puddled' with water and other ingredients and the building's walls are built up by hand without forms. This is known as 'cob' in Anglophone countries. In sunny climates, earth is molded into bricks, sometimes mechanically compressed, and sun-baked. This method, known as 'adobe' in Hispanic countries, may have originated in the Middle East as long ago as 10,000 BC, and is still used very widely. The earth can also be packed into forms in situ and compressed by machine or hand to give it great strength, a method called 'rammed earth' or 'pisé'. The forms are usually wood or metal, but even automobile tyres have been used. Rammed earth walls can resemble concrete in their hardness, strength and durability, depending on the degree of compression. Another method with a long tradition is 'geltaftan,' where a specially designed earth building is packed with fuel and used as a kiln for firing pottery, being baked to great hardness in the process. Earth walls can be a metre or more thick, or they can be no thicker than a comparable structure in brick or concrete (Schumann and Sinha, 1994).

Even if the walls are not made of earth, earth may be piled around the building (as a 'berm') or over it (as a 'green roof'), or the structure may be sunk into the ground. In each case the earth provides insulation and thermal storage. The ultimate in 'earth-sheltered' building may be dwellings that are actually artificial caves dug into the ground; there are examples in many European countries.

Earth is not a particularly effective insulator. Conductance varies with moisture and density; for a compacted block it may be 0.33 W/mK, for loose, damp earth perhaps 2 W/mK (ibid; CIBSE, 1986). It is, however, a very good thermal store. The extra structural strength needed to support a 'green roof' is likely to negate any cost savings from the use of earth as an inexpensive insulator.

Earth is a flexible and forgiving building material; clay content in particular can vary between about 10–25%, and bricks removed from old adobe buildings in the US have contained anywhere between 0–32% clay (EACI, 1998). However, as with all building materials, the techniques of building with earth are particular to the material and expert advice should be sought.

Stone

Stone forms the basis of traditional architecture in many places and is still widely used. It is particularly useful for its high thermal mass, strength and durability (depending on hardness) and beauty. Stone is non-renewable but abundant, although some types are scarce and some areas do not have much stone of building grade. The quarrying process is disruptive to natural environments, and using reclaimed stone will avoid this impact. However, the greatest environmental impact of stone is likely to be due to haulage. The natural and traditional solution to this problem is to use locally quarried stone. This also allows the architect to keep informed of any concerns about the impact of quarrying operations.

Manufactured and synthetic stone are sometimes used as a less expensive alternative to natural stone, particularly as a facing to concrete blocks. The manufacturing process for these materials is quite energy-intensive, and their overall environmental impact is probably similar to that of concrete.

Cement and Concrete

Cement

Cement is a general term for binding agents whose ingredients include lime (calcium oxide). By far the most widely used form of cement in Europe is Portland cement. To make Portland cement, calcium carbonate (usually in the form of limestone), silicates (from sand, clay or fly ash, a by-product of coal-fired power plants) and trace ingredients such as ores of aluminium or iron, are mixed together and burnt at temperatures of up to 1500°C. The result is a mixture of chemical compounds of calcium, silicon and oxygen with some iron and aluminium; the exact mix determines the properties of the cement. About 5% gypsum (calcium sulphate) is then added. Because of the high temperatures required, the process is highly energy-intensive. In addition, the chemical reaction producing lime from calcium carbonate (calcining) releases carbon dioxide.

The total amount of CO_2 emitted in the production of cement will vary depending on

4.28 Mud wall, Berlin, Germany

4.29 Stone oratory, Ireland

Architect: A Palladio

4.30 Villa Rotonda, Italy

the efficiency of the kiln and the type of fuel used. One estimate (EBN, 1993) is that a kilo of cement releases roughy 1.1 kilos of CO_2 in its production. Of this, 60% is from the burning of fossil fuel and 40% from the calcining process. On the positive side, waste fuels such as used motor oil, hazardous waste and tyres can be burned more safely in cement kilns because of the high temperatures involved. However, this relies on proper monitoring and controls being in place, and there are concerns about this (ACTAC, 1995).

Other environmental impacts of cement production are mainly due to the highly alkaline nature of cement dust. When released into the air or water (from equipment washing), it can present an environmental hazard, since alkaline water is toxic to fish and other aquatic life. It may also present dangers to workers' health through its corrosive qualities (EBN, 1993).

There is no means of rating cement by how environmentally sensitive its production is, so the main strategy of the environmentally aware architect should be to minimise the amount used. Careful design helps, for example in the use of pier foundations or pre-cast concrete; so does effective management of construction to avoid mixing excess concrete which will be thrown away. Lime and fly ash (see below) can be substituted for concrete in some applications.

Concrete
Concrete, the biggest end-user of cement, consists of roughly 12–14% cement and varying amounts of water (6–7%), sand (25–35%) and gravel, crushed stone or other aggregate (48–53%). Fly ash can be substituted for 15–35% of the cement when mixing concrete (Anink, 1996).

Water efficiency is dealt with elsewhere in the book. Sand and gravel are non-renewable resources which are quarried or dredged, involving a significant impact on the local environment. Although considerable resources remain untapped, many of these will not be developed because of environmental considerations. Crushed stone requires an additional input of energy in the crushing process. Reclaimed and recycled aggregate and industrial waste products (even crushed concrete) can be used as part of the mix to reduce quarrying and haulage. Haulage will probably be the major environmental impact of these products. However, carbon dioxide emissions from the production of the cement generally form the bulk (at least 85%) of overall CO_2 emissions due to concrete.

The other major environmental consideration in the use of concrete is disposal. Concrete forms about half of all waste from construction and demolition. It can often be crushed for reuse as aggregate, but re-use is rare.

Concrete blocks are basically identical to other forms of concrete in their environmental impact per kilogram, except that they need to be cured before use. High-pressure steam is often employed for this purpose, using more energy (ACTAC, 1995).

Specialised forms of concrete include aerated concrete, which uses aluminium sulphate powder in the mix. This reacts with the lime to produce hydrogen gas, which forms bubbles in the concrete. While the aluminium sulphate adds an environmental impact to the process, due to the large amounts of energy used in its production, the resulting concrete has a higher strength-to-weight ratio and the overall environmental impact for a given structure is likely to be lower than for ordinary concrete.

Composite insulating blocks are formed of insulating foam in between layers of concrete. The main concern here is to avoid the use of ozone-depleting CFCs and HCFCs as foaming agents in the insulation. Another possible concern is the difficulty of recycling or re-using composite blocks at the end of the structure's life, because the concrete cannot be separated from the insulating foam.

Brick, tile and other ceramics

Ceramics such as brick, tile and sanitary ware are made by baking clay at high temperature. Clay is a highly abundant, although non-renewable, material. Clay quarrying can have a detrimental impact on local environments, but the main environmental impact of ceramics is due to the fuel burnt during the firing process. The energy used in this process will vary, but a typical kiln will generally use about 2.75 $MJ.kg^{-1}$ to make brick, somewhat more for glazed ceramics (CIRIA, 1995). Assuming that a mix of solid fuel, oil, gas and electricity is used in the firing process, CO_2 emissions will be around 0.33 $kg.kWh^{-1}$. This means that the CO_2 emissions attributable to the brick will be around 0.25 kg CO_2 per kg of brick. This is only a quarter as much as Portland cement; but if concrete consists of 12–14% cement, the end result is that brick typically has twice the CO_2 emissions per kilogram of concrete. Brick, therefore, is one of the most energy-intensive of bulk building materials. Reclaimed bricks are an alternative, in which there is a thriving market in many places (ACTAC, 1995).

4.31

Glass

Glass is made from silver sand, sodium carbonate and sulphates, all of which are non-renewable resources but none of which are scarce. The manufacturing process is highly energy-intensive, releasing about 2kg of CO_2 per kg of glass produced. But the actual mass of glass in most buildings is relatively small. It has been estimated that a three-bedroomed, detached house contains about 100kg of glass, compared with over 25 tons of concrete (the main structural material) (Howard, 1991). So the environmental impact of the glass is outweighed by its importance in influencing daylighting and thermal performance. Glass is generally recyclable but only a small proportion is actually recycled.

4.32

Metals

Metals are obtained by mining, which is often detrimental to the local environment through large-scale physical alteration and toxic emissions. Most mine sites require expensive rehabilitation after closure before the land can be used for anything else. The process of extracting metal from ore is often highly energy-intensive. However, no accurate figures exist for the amount of energy used in these processes. Estimates vary widely; for example, the *Architects' Journal* (1995) gives the embodied energy of steel as 63 MWh/m^3 and aluminium as 195 MWh/m^3. (No source is given for these figures.) By contrast, the BSRIA *Environmental Code of Practice 1994* (quoted in Viljoen, 1997) gives the figures for steel as 103 MWh/m^3 and for aluminium, 75.6 MWh/m^3 Clearly, it is not possible to make a reliable estimate of the emissions due to extraction of metals based on existing figures.

4.33

Architect: Jean Nouvel

Although metals are a non-renewable resource, they are generally recyclable. Construction and demolition waste should be separated in order to facilitate recycling. Non-separated waste can be recycled but the cost is much higher. In principle these metals could be reclaimed even from mixed waste, and so it is unlikely that they will ever run out completely. Recycling saves a significant proportion of the energy used in the extraction process, although precise figures are again unavailable. The recycled content of metal is not always easy to estimate but it is a reasonably good measure of the metal's global environmental impact.

Aluminium

Aluminium is extracted by electrolysis of the ore, bauxite, a highly energy-intensive process which consequently has large environmental impacts. However, aluminium is highly recyclable and recycling only requires about 5% of the energy needed for electrolysis from ore. It is highly durable and resistant to corrosion, although specifiers should be careful to avoid contact with acids, alkalis, or other metals.

4.34 *Zinc roofing, Tallinn, Estonia.*

Copper

Copper is widely used for roofing, cladding, ornament, piping and cables. It has natural biocidal properties, which make it suitable for exterior use, but leads to toxic runoff. Copper pipes are still used in water supply, although they are banned in some places (such as Sweden); they are generally being supplanted by plastic. Copper is highly durable, corrosion-resistant and very recyclable.

Lead

Lead is a highly toxic material and a cumulative poison whose use in buildings should be discouraged. It is also a material in very short supply, although easy to re-use.

Steel

Steel is the most widely used metal in construction. Its production process is highly energy-intensive. The recycling of scrap steel is widespread, although not as easy as with other metals. Steel is not corrosion-resistant and in many situations in order to prevent rust it needs to be treated with paint or another coating, whose impact should be considered separately.

Zinc

Zinc is often used as a coating for other metals. By its nature this zinc coating has to be strongly bonded with the other metal, so neither is likely to be readily recyclable. The processes of zinc coating (galvanisation) frequently involve use of chromate solution, which is highly toxic. The coating processes are also energy intensive. However, galvanisation is a very effective way to lengthen the life of steel and other metallic components. Zinc is also used in sheet form, and is a less toxic alternative to copper for many applications.

Paints, adhesives, preservatives, sealants and cleaning agents

Paints, adhesives, preservatives, sealants and cleaning agents encompass a very diverse range of substances. They are typically present in relatively small quantities in buildings, but can have a disproportionate effect on the environment. Although their manufacture often involves the use of oil and gas both as fuel for the manufacturing process and as feedstocks, CO_2 and other fossil-fuel-related emissions are not a major environmental concern here because of the small quantities involved compared to other materials (Howard, 1991).

Toxic emissions during manufacture, use, and disposal are a greater concern. These products should be treated as toxic waste and disposed of accordingly. Also, in particular, the quality of the building's interior environment can be seriously affected by the careless use of these products. Indoor air quality (IAQ) is becoming a major concern of building designers, particularly because buildings are becoming more airtight, and the use of organic solvents, office appliances and artificial ventilation are on the increase. For further discussion of IAQ issues (Refer ISSUES; Health).

Paint

Paint consists of a solvent (the 'base'), bonding agents, fillers, and additives such as pigments, drying agents, polishers and anti-foaming agents. Each of these ingredients can potentially be hazardous to health and the environment. Some pigments, for instance, include potentially harmful heavy metals such as lead, cadmium and chromium (ACTAC, 1995; Anink, 1996; CIRIA, 1995).

Water-based paints, although not readily available for some applications, are environmentally preferable to those using organic hydrocarbons, which are hazardous to painters and occupants. Most hydrocarbon-based paints used alkyd resin as a binder. 'High solids' alkyd paint is preferable to traditional alkyd paint because it contains less organic solvent. 'Natural paint' generally consists of ingredients of biological origin, which are naturally degradable; these paints still use organic solvents such as turpentine, however, and tend to be more expensive and less effective than conventional paints. Acrylic paints are primarily water-based, containing 10% or less organic solvents, but tend to contain harmful preservatives. In all cases, high gloss paints require more solvents than those with a less glossy finish.

The EU Eco-label, and other national eco-labelling schemes (NF Environnement in France, Blue Angel in Germany, Stiching Milieukeur in the Netherlands and White Swan in the Nordic countries), include certification systems for less environmentally damaging paints. Standards vary widely and none are very high, but choosing paints with one of these labels is a good way of reducing environmental impact to some degree (ACTAC, 1995).

Adhesives

Concerns with the environmental impact of adhesives mainly focus on the release of VOCs from organic-solvent-based adhesives and curing agents, for example those used in epoxy-resin systems. Adhesives which use organic solvents should be applied with care and proper ventilation, or avoided altogether in favour of water-based adhesives or mechanical fixing systems. The widespread use of adhesives can make disassembly of the building for re-use and recycling more difficult.

Wood preservatives

Wood preservatives are available in a wide range of different forms: paints, sticks, pastes and even smokes. Their active ingredients range from the relatively mild to the highly toxic; they include compounds based on copper, chromium, arsenic, zinc, boron and fluorine; also creosote, pentachlorophenol, dieldrin, lindane, tributyl tin oxide and permethrin.

Health effects in wood treatment workers are well documented and demonstrate that most of these compounds are to some degree detrimental to health.

Decay is normally a symptom of a building defect or moisture build-up, rather than an inevitable product of time. Each source of moisture should be balanced by a means of removing it. Preservatives can often be avoided altogether, if proper detailing is observed, a durable wood is chosen and where necessary a protective finish is applied and maintained. Localised preservation with solid implants, in vulnerable places such as the corner joints of window and door frames, is preferable to overall treatment. (Table 4.3)

Table 4.3 PRESERVATIVES RANKED FROM LEAST TO MOST ENVIRONMENTALLY DAMAGING	
Least damaging	• borates • quaternary ammonium compounds, zinc soaps, azoles • chromium copper boron (CCB), zinc copper fluoride (ZCF)
Most damaging	• chromium copper arsenic (CCA), improsol (bifluoride), creosote oil
(Anink, 1996)	

Borates are the most environmentally benign form of preservative, although they suffer from leaching in the wet; where they will be in contact with water, they may need to be combined with a water-repelling treatment.
Preservation treatment should always be carried by suitably qualified operatives.

Sealants

Because of their flexibility and ease of application, sealing compounds are used very widely for sealing joints, cracks and other gaps; some might say over-used. A wide range of products is available. Sealants may be in the form of tape or other solid, or as a fluid. Fluid solvents may be plastic or elastomeric. As with all building products, the environmental impact of the sealant should be weighed against its durability, since the more often it is replaced the more impact it will have.

In general, sealants are used in small amounts and do not have very great environmental impact. The main things to avoid are: sealants that use ozone-damaging chemicals (CFCs and HCFCs) in foaming; polyurethane (PUR) and polyvinyl chloride (PVC) sealants, both of which have significant environmental impacts (Refer MATERIALS; Synthetics); and use of sealants which contain organic solvents, such as non-water-based acrylic sealant.

Cleaning agents

An often-forgotten part of the construction process is the cleaning of the building after completion but before occupancy. This is usually the responsibility of the contractor but it is often contracted out to specialist cleaning firms who may not be fully aware of previous efforts to ensure a non-toxic, healthy building. Cleaning agents that are non-toxic and biodegradable should be specified.

Synthetics

Synthetics are manufactured by a range of chemical processes, mainly from petroleum. It is also possible, although rare, to make them from plant-derived renewable resources; they are then known as bioplastics or biosynthetics. The cracking and polymerisation processes by which synthetics are manufactured can involve the release of organic materials into the environment. Other additives such as chlorine and cyanide are also used, and these may involve toxic emissions. Only a small proportion of the world's petroleum is used to make synthetics. The amount of energy used in the process is relatively large; estimates vary widely, between 50–100 Mj/kg However, the quantities used in the building process are generally quite small and this means that embodied energy is not a major concern.

Most synthetics are not readily biodegradable and this presents a long-term disposal problem. On the other hand, when they do degrade, or when they are otherwise destroyed or damaged by fire, UV radiation and so on, the resulting products in some (not all) cases are a toxic hazard. Recycling is possible in some cases but not in others, and generally only where waste is separated.

Synthetics are extremely useful in many applications; they are mostly waterproof, flexible and inexpensive. In most cases, their environmental impact is not serious enough to outweigh their usefulness, but disposal should be considered carefully because their non-degradable nature can lead to problems. In the case of PVC, however, there are serious questions about whether its use is appropriate at all (Greenpeace, 1992).

Bitumen

Bitumen is widely used in roofing and weatherproofing. It is produced from low-grade petroleum fractions. It is theoretically recyclable as long as it is not polluted with other materials, but this is usually the case; normally it is mixed with rock dust or applied to cloth, glass fibre or polyester sheeting to form mastic, sheeting or or shingles. It does not generate environmental problems during use. Care must be taken with hot bitumen/asphalt application with respect to the health and safety of workers.

EPDM (Ethylene-Propylene-Diene Monomer)

EPDM sheet is used in flat roofs, for lining reservoirs, and in gaskets and flashings. It is produced by polymerising and then vulcanising the ethylene, propylene and diene monomers. Various organic solvents, which could cause environmental hazards if released, are used in the process. It cannot be recycled although 'down-cycling' to form low-grade filler is possible.

EPS (Expanded Polystyrene) and Extruded Polystyrene

Polystyrene is used in insulation and sheet glazing. Th eproduction of polystyrene involves some emissions of styrene and benzebe, moderately harmful organic compounds. The blowing process by which EPS is expanded uses pentane (a moderately toxic organic solvent). In some cases CFCs and HCFCs may still be used for blowing extruded PS.

References

- ACTAC (1995–1997) Green Building Digest.
- Anink David, Chiel Boonstra and John Mak (1996) *Handbook of Sustainable Building: An Environmental Preference Method for Selection of Materials for Use in Construction and Refurbishment.* James & James (Science Publishers) Limited 1996.
- Architects' Journal, 8 May 1995.
- Austin Green Builder Programme (1998) *Sustainable Building Sourcebook,.* Austin TX. http://www.greenbuilder.com/sourcebook/
- BRECSU-OPET/DG XVII. (1993) *Energy Efficient Lighting in Offices* 'Maxibrochure'
- Casado Martinez, N., et al. (1996) *Architectural and Environmental Teaching.* DG XI.
- CIBSE (1986) *Guide, Volume A.*
- CIENE (1994) *Natural Cooling: Mid-Career Education Package.*
- CIRIA (1995) *Environmental impact of materials,* CIRIA Special Publication 116.
- CRES/DG XVII, (1994) *Natural and low energy cooling in buildings:* Maxibrochure.
- CREST (1998) Residential Indoor Water Efficiency: Water Efficient Fixtures. http://crest.org/environment/gotwh/general/res-water/html
- CREST (1998) *The Sun's Joules.* http://solstice.crest.org/renewables/SJ/index.html
- Earth Architecture Centre Internations, EACI (1998) http://www.earthbuilding.com/eaci-FAQ.html
- EBN (1993) *Environmental Building News.* West River Communications, Inc., http://www.ebuild.com.
- ERG/ESIF (1998) *Solar Thermal Systems in Europe:* Information Booklet.
- Esbensen Consulting Engineers. (1998) *Energy Comfort 2000 Information Dossier No 5.*
- Forest Stewardship Council. http://www.fscoax.org
- *Going Green - The Green Construction Handbook.* (1993). Research by Ove Arup and Partners. Bristol. JT Design Build Publication, 1993.
- Greenpeace. (1996) *Building the future: a guide to building without PVC.*
- Greenpeace. (1992) *PVC: Toxic waste in disguise.*
- Howard Nigel. (1991) *Energy in balance.* Building Services Journal.
- ICIE/DG XVII. (1992) Small-scale cogeneration in non-residential buildings.
- Lewis, J. Owen, Goulding John R. (Eds.) (1995) Light and shade: optimizing daylight design. Nick Baker in: *European Directory of Sustainable and Energy Efficient Building*, Published annually since 1993. London. James & James (Science Publishers) Limited
- Mazria, Edward. (1979) *The Passive Solar Energy Book.* Rodale Press.
- Progressive Architecture 4: 1985.
- Rocky Mountain Institute. (1997) *Home Energy Briefs No 2: Windows.* http://www.rmi.org/hebs/heb2/heb2.html
- Schumann and Sinha (1994), Earth building today, in *Architects' Journal.*
- Talbott L. (1993) *Simply Build Green: A Technical Guide to the Ecological Houses at the Findhorn Foundation.* John Findhorn Foundation.
- UCD-OPET for DG XVII. (1995) *Daylighting in Buildings.*
- Viljoen A. (1997) *Low-energy dwellings and their environmental impact.* in: European Directory of Sustainable and Energy Efficient Building, London, James & James (Science Publishers) Limited
- Waterwiser, various dates. http://www.waterwiser.org/
- Whitelegg, John Prof. (1993) *Transport for a Sustainable Future: the Case for Europe.* Belhaven Press,
- WWF Global Network. http://www.panda.org.

References for Metals

- Anink David, Chiel Boonstra and John Mak. (1996) *Handbook of Sustainable Building: An Environmental Preference Method for Selection of Materials for Use in Construction and Refurbishment.* James & James (Science Publishers) Limited 1996.
- CIRIA (1995) *Environmental impact of materials.* CIRIA Special Publication 116.
- *Going Green - The Green Construction Handbook.* (1993). Research by Ove Arup and Partners. Bristol. JT Design Build Publication, 1993.

References for Synthetics

- Anink David, Chiel Boonstra and John Mak. (1996) *Handbook of Sustainable Building: An Environmental Preference Method for Selection of Materials for Use in Construction and Refurbishment.* James & James (Science Publishers) Limited 1996.
- CIRIA (1995) *Environmental impact of materials.* CIRIA Special Publication 116.
- *Going Green - The Green Construction Handbook.* (1993). Research by Ove Arup and Partners. Bristol. JT Design Build Publication, 1993.
- Green Building Digest. (1995–1997) ACTAC.

References for Waste

- Casado Martinez, N., et al. (1996) *Architectural and Environmental Teaching.* DG XI.

Further reading
Environmental effects of building materials

- ACTAC, *Green Building Digest*, ISSN 1357-3098.
- BRECSU & European Commission DG XVII, (1995) *Environmental Assessment of Buildings*.
- Environmental and Conservation Services Department, (1993) *Sustainable building sourcebook: supplement to the green builder program.* Austin, TX.
  http://www.greenbuilder.com/sourcebook/SourcebookContents.html
- *Environmental Building News*, West River Communications Inc, 1993– ISSN: 10623957.
  http://www.ebuild.com.
- Greenpeace, (1996) *Building the future – a guide to building without PVC.* London, UK.
- Lewis J O, J R Goulding (Eds) *European Directory of Sustainable and Energy Efficient Building*, Published annually since 1993, James & James (Science Publishers) Limited, London, UK.
- Pearson, David, (1996) *The natural house catalog: everything you need to create an environmentally friendly home*, Simon & Schuster Inc, ISBN 0684801981.

Section 5: Evaluation

INTRODUCTION

Owner, user, designer, authority and public all evaluate proposed or realised buildings, with regard to comfort, functionality, cost, aesthetics and many aspects of performance. Evaluation of environmental performance is necessary for good design. At the design stage, alternatives can be considered and the best solution chosen. The architect frequently evaluates environmental performance: energy, daylight, indoor comfort, heat loss or gain and materials. Simulation-based evaluation is often useful and, in large or complex buildings, indispensable. Monitoring the completed building can involve assessing comfort, energy and water inputs and waste outputs. This section of the book provides advice on environmental evaluation methods.

DESIGN EVALUATION TOOLS

Introduction

Design evaluation tools can be manual or computer-based. Some tools are associated with early strategic decisions; others predict performance of detailed proposals. Table 5.1 gives an indication of which tools are most suitable for different evaluation. In most cases simple or intermediate level tools can provide the required analysis. Many tools are available free or at minimal cost. Complex tools can require specially-trained staff expert in carrying out simulation studies. A smaller practice which cannot afford such staff may employ specialist consultants.

Table 5.1 DESIGN TOOLS AND ENVIRONMENTAL EVALUATION

•E -Early, •I - Intermediate, •D - Detailed

Design tool:	Drawing	Manual Calculation	Computer Calculation	Scale model	Computer simulation
Issue:					
Insulation		•E	•I		•D
Overshadowing	•E			•E	•I/D
Thermal performance		•E	•I		•D
Daylighting		•E	•I	•E	•D
Ventilation		•E	•I		•D
Infiltration		•E	•I		•D
Comfort			•E		•D
Building fabric		•E	•I		•D
Services Systems		•E	•I/D		•D
Energy Consumption		•I		•D	
Total performance					•D

Environmental issues are inter-related, in that they can directly or indirectly affect both one another and overall performance. The aim is to achieve the optimum balance. No one tool can do this automatically, as most answer specific questions. Evaluation forms part of an iterative process involving design expertise and appropriate tools.

For example, to know how alternative forms of wall construction will perform, the architect must select materials, dimensions and obtain thermo-physical characteristics for each alternative. Each construction must be input and the results calculated. Only then can results be compared and the better one selected. If the design tool has a database of materials or constructions matching those to be compared, the input required is reduced.

Data output varies considerably. Simpler tools often provide only an outline of results to act as design pointers, but which strategically may be very valuable. The choice of data output increases with the complexity. Generally, when considering energy analysis design tools, output in the form of energy requirements or as heat loss or gain per unit area are most common. More sophisticated tools allow the user to customise the output format and provide a range (such as temperatures, comfort indices and light levels) from which to select .

Input

Climatic data
Energy performance is affected by altitude, latitude and longitude, ground topography and surrounding structures, local microclimate, etc. External temperature is a basic requirement for most tools analysing energy-related matters, but can be required as hourly, daily or monthly values. Other data may include wind speed and direction, solar radiation and humidity. Efforts have been made to develop standard weather data sets (e.g., Test Reference Years), but these are not widely used in professional practice.

Building geometry
Simpler tools only accept vertical wall and window elements, horizontal floors and flat, sloping or pitched roofs. However, as sophistication increases, the complexity of the geometric model accepted by the tool generally increases also.

Orientation is important, particularly in respect of solar irradiation and wind. Zone control is important in more detailed studies. Many simpler tools only consider 'single zones', where the model assumes the building is represented as a single room. This is often sufficient for simple and intermediate analyses of domestic buildings, but otherwise limiting.

Perhaps the most important element of geometrical data input is the building material description. More developed tools often provide built-in databases of the properties of typical materials as individual components, or as typical constructional elements such as walls, windows, etc.

Standard calculations
There are many different theoretical calculation methods to study energy use/consumption, lighting, daylighting, ventilation, infiltration, running costs, etc. It is essential to use a method acceptable to national or European standards. The differences between comparative methods are often negligible, but some regulatory bodies require particular standards to be used, particularly when demonstrating compliance with Building Regulations.

Services systems
Many intermediate and high level tools offer a wide range of systems describing services within a building. However, for detailed study of services systems, specific tools are probably more appropriate.

Computer aided design
Some CAD applications include three dimensional modelling tools which allow the architect to study lighting distribution.
Efforts are being made to integrate design tools and CAD so as to exchange data in a

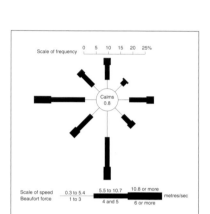

5.1 Wind rose diagram

common format. These would present to the user as a single design system with built-in CAD facilities. One example is the ZIP modeller, used by several design tools to provide a graphically based geometric input. Typically, a geometrical model is constructed within the CAD package and, when complete, imported into the energy analysis software in a specified file format, normally DXF.

Systems allow visualisation of 3-D building models through rendering software and can be linked to databases and other software.

Accuracy and validation

Results from a design tool are never exact, as the model upon which a tool is based incorporates assumptions and approximations and is to some degree a simplified representation of the building. Even the most detailed calculations demonstrate varying degrees of error compared to a physical test environment. Furthermore, it is rare that actual results exactly match design calculations. For example, the heat loss performance of building fabric in the built fabric can be up to three times higher than predicted U-values, due to poor workmanship. Thirdly, users may misuse a tool as a result of inadequate understanding. Despite these sources of error, many tools provide sufficient accuracy to satisfy the architect's needs.

Validation, so as to have greater confidence in the accuracy of results, is important. When choosing a model, enquiries should be made as to the results of any testing and validation studies. This would apply to all levels of computer based design tools and not only the more advanced simulation packages.

Selection and use

Architectural model
Architectural scale models of card or other materials, when built to represent the site and surroundings, can be used to study insolation and overshadowing. When used with a simple hair dryer and a fine grained powder such as light sand, site models can be helpful in identifying exposed and sheltered external areas in the prevailing wind. When reasonably carefully constructed, internal models can give a good representation of daylight distribution and of relative daylighting levels.

Stereographic sun chart
To assess solar availability on a site, shading from adjacent buildings and vegetation must be determined. The chart projects a view of the sky onto a horizontal plane. For each latitude there is a specific stereographic diagram, used to indicate which sections of the sky are free of obstructions and, consequently, the relative importance of the periods when solar light will be blocked.

The LT Method
The LT Method (available in manual and computer-based form) uses energy performance curves drawn from a mathematical model where most parameters are given assumed values. Only a few key design variables relating to building form and facade design, glazing ratio, surface to volume ratio, etc., are left for the user to manipulate. The resulting energy breakdowns of heating, cooling and lighting give a picture of the relative importance of various energy components.

New Method 5000
New Method 5000 is a manual or computer based tool for determining quickly and approximately the performance of passive solar buildings. It predicts the auxiliary heating required to meet comfort conditions for buildings heated solely by direct gain and those using other techniques for any specified month. This is done by subtracting the useful heat gains and heat losses (both in kWh) for a given month.

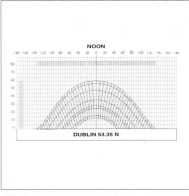

5.2 Stereographic sun chart diagram

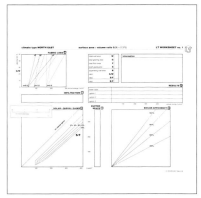

5.3 The LT Method

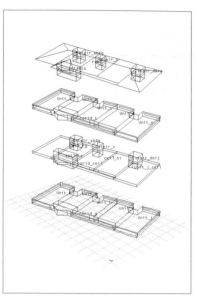

5.4 ESP-r

Passport

PASSPORT evaluates heat requirement in residential buildings. The method is based on a steady-state energy balance for the building zone, with allowance for external temperature variations and a utilisation factor taking account of the dynamic effect of internal and solar gains. Some of the main features include provision for free gain utilisation, intermittent heating and multizone passive solar buildings.

Lightscape

The LIGHTSCAPE Visualisation System combines proprietary radiosity algorithms with a physically based lighting interface.

ESP-r

ESP-r is a dynamic thermal simulation environment which may be used to explore a range of issues including building fabric, mass flow, ideal and detailed plant systems, separately or in combination, at varying time steps.

Further information

* European Resource Guide: Compiled over several years and updated biannually, with numerous references to design tools as well as other energy-related material. Available on disk (currently for Macintosh only): Energy Research Group, University College Dublin, Richview, Clonskeagh, Dublin 14, Ireland Fax: +353.1-283 8908, e-mail:jolivetp@richview.ucd.ie, www:http://erg.ucd.ie

* Info Energie: Liste der Software/Liste des Logiciels: A comprehensive listing (in German and French) of internationally developed software with contact details for each design tool: Bundesamt für Energiewirtschaft, CH-3003 Bern, Fax: +41.31-352 7756

* Guidance on Selecting Energy Programs: A publication by the Construction Industry and Computing Association, with detailed information to assist in the selection of energy related software available in the UK: CICA, Guildhall Place, Cambridge CB2 3QQ, United Kingdom Fax: +44.1223-62865

* BSRIA - Software for Building Services - a selection guide: Valuable information on a wide range of software packages, many of which are concerned with energy: Building Services Research and Information Association, Old Bracknell Lane West, Bracknell, Berkshire RG12 7AH United Kingdom Fax: +44.1344-487575

* Interior lighting calculations: a guide to computer programs, IP 16/98 published by the Building Research Establishment, Garston, Watford WD2 7JR, United Kingdom, Fax +44.1923 664 098 is published to help lighting designers select appropriate interior lighting calculation software by focusding not on individual programs but on the issues common to all such programs and their underlying algorithms.

Procedures to assess the environmental impact of proposed development, whether of building or infrastructure, have developed as a consequence of the EU Directive on Environmental Impact Assessment, 85/337/EEC and subsequent revisions. The thresholds at which the procedures must be observed vary between Member States. When a proposed development exceeds the thresholds for a given project type, or when a regulatory authority requires an Assessment of Environmental Impact, an Environmental Impact Statement must be prepared and made available to the authorities and the public in respect of the proposals.

Many types of development covered by the Directive are outside the normal scope of services. These include, above varying size thresholds, forestry, land reclamation, poultry and pig rearing, fish farming, mining, and infrastructural proposals: large roads, railways, waste treatment plants and other civil engineering work. However, many industrial projects, including food industry packing, canning, brewing, confectionery and other industrial types; and many general building projects, including industrial estates, urban developments and holiday villages are also covered by the Directive.

The material to be provided in an environmental impact statement includes a description of the proposed development, the reasons for proposing it, and a non-technical summary. It should provide the data needed to assess the main likely environmental effects (whether permanent or temporary, positive or negative) on people, flora, fauna, soil, water, air, climate, landscape, the interaction between the foregoing, material assets and cultural heritage. It should identify significant adverse effects, and describe measures to avoid, reduce or remedy those defects. Where relevant, a description of the industrial production processes should be provided.

Without limiting the architect's role in the preparation of Environmental Impact Statements, that role will include knowing when an EIS is needed, briefing specialist consultants, and assessing visual impact, noise emissions and traffic flows.

TOTAL BUILDING ENVIRONMENTAL PERFORMANCE

Methods to assess the overall ecological performance of the building design have been developed in recent years in several Member States. These apply point-scoring ratings under many different criteria to the design for the site, building envelope, systems and components. Two such methods are:

* *Ecological Building Briteria for Viikki,* developed by Helsinki City Council in Finland for the Viikki ecological neighbourhood
  and
* *BREEAM 98 for Offices: An Environmental Assessment Method for Office Buildings,* developed since 1990 by the Building Research Fstablishment in the United Kingdom.

Ecological building criteria for Viikki

Introduction
Ecological Building Criteria for Viikki defines minimum ecological levels for building and assess a project's ecological performance. Minimum levels are defined in a way to enable their implementation at reasonable additional cost. Through fulfilling the criteria, cost savings in use are also achieved.

The criteria examine projects from several perspectives. Pollution is given the greatest importance, and is reduced by building more efficiently, and using durable and recyclable buildings. Natural resources are conserved by building better and less, and by using renewable and recyclable materials. Health is improved by creating a favourable external

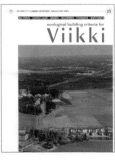

We are indebted to the Helsinki City Council for permission to include extracts from the 'Ecological building criteria for Viikki'. The material in this book is a summary of the checklist and is provided so that the reader can appreciate the scope of issues covered in this environmental audit. The full material is available from Helsinki City Planning Dept. Publications, Kansakoulukatu 3, FIN-00100 Helsinki; Tel: +358. 9 16914460 Fax +358. 9 16914484, email: elina.wiberg@ksv.hel.fi

microclimate as well as by healthy indoor conditions. Natural diversity is enhanced by leaving as large a part of the land unbuilt as is possible, and by arranging access for the animal population into and through the area. Future demolition should be anticipated if the area is later needed for food production.

Pollution

Emission loads to air or soil, and the quantity of non-recyclable waste generated by the building, must not exceed approved values. Values are calculated per gross square meter of floor area. Atmospheric pollutants, such as oxides of carbon, sulphur and nitrogen, are released primarily by energy use. All these emission quantities yield parallel correlation with energy use; for that reason, only limits for carbon dioxide are set. The carbon dioxide emissions for the reference building over a 50 year period are set at 400 kg/m^2, to take account of production of building materials, 50 years of servicing and emissions caused by maintenance. Construction site emissions are outside the scope of the examination.

The quantity of waste water is described by consumption during occupation. There is generally a direct correlation between incoming and waste water. Recirculation/ purification systems reduce both to the same degree. The correlation weakens if, for instance, rainwater is used directly as household water without recirculation. Consumption of the reference building is 160 l/resident/day. Reduction must be shown in the sanitary drawings and metered during follow-up by apartment-specific remote-read meters which monitor hot and cold water without recirculation. The service manual required for each building explains the correct use of water saving devices.

Construction site waste is measured in kg/m^2 of gross floor area. It does not include surplus earth. The reference building's estimated quantity is 20 kg/m^2. The amount can be reduced, for example, by sorting building waste, using pre-cut materials and employing re-usable equipment. Decreases in waste quantities will be indicated in the building specification.

The solid waste load during occupation is measured through the quantity of mixed waste. The reference building's mixed waste quantity is 200 kg/resident, year. Reduction is shown in the waste management plan (possibility for sorting with adequate space allocation) and is monitored in follow-up.

Pollution can be limited by giving preference to materials meeting the criteria for Nordic or EU Eco labels. The use of materials meeting the Eco label criteria will be shown in building specifications.

Natural resources

More moderate use of natural resources can be achieved though building less, through durable and recyclable building or by using renewable natural resources. Reducing energy consumption conserves non-renewable fossil fuels.

Fossil fuel consumption is measured by the total primary energy used: heating (including hot water) and electrical energy purchased during occupation, embodied energy of materials and the energy needed for maintenance over 50 years. The calculation takes account of energy loss during production. The reference heating energy consumption is 160 kWh/m^2 year, calculated using 'Motiwatti' software. Follow-up is by apartment-specific remote-read meters. The reference electrical consumption (housing corporation and resident electricity) is 45 kWh/m^2 year. If the use of electrical energy leads to significant reductions in total energy consumption, minimum requirements may be waived.

The reference building's primary energy consumption is 37 GJ/m^2, 50 years. Primary energy consumption is measured using BEE software.

Floor plan flexibility, common space use and multi-functionality of spaces

Increasing residential density can have a significant effect on use of natural resources. A floor plan satisfactory for a small number of residents, yet permitting family growth without significant change, can serve the family in different situations, conserve natural resources and allow increased residential density if necessary. By increasing shared use of spaces, it is possible to remove functions such as clothes washing, drying or sauna bathing from individual apartments. Multi-use spaces permit services and workplaces to be situated closer to housing, reducing the need for traffic. The local 'Area Co-operation group' performs the evaluation on request.

Health

The interior climate must be comfortable, and healthy: Goals are set for interior climate, building works and finishes according to Classification of Indoor Climate, Construction, and Finishing Materials 95 (Finnish Society of Indoor Climate and Quality). The fulfilment of criteria is shown in the building specification.

The management of moisture risks is indicated in design documents. The Building Regulation Department of Helsinki evaluates moisture risks on request.

To achieve good sound insulation levels, compliance with recent norms is recommended (Ministry of the Environment proposal, 1996). The fulfilment of criteria is shown in building specifications.

The local 'Area Co-operation Group' evaluates insolation and site layout on request.

Living comfort can be improved by increasing housing diversity with alternative floor plans.

Natural biodiversity

The natural vegetation types of site and surroundings form the basis for selecting plants. Species-rich solutions featuring domestic varieties create a durable natural diversity. Micro-organisms and the plant population should be able to exchange genes with the natural surroundings through nature corridors. It should be possible for certain animals (hare, squirrel, birds), to live in the area. As large a quantity of clean (not from road surfaces for example) storm water as is possible should be used on the site without drainage.

The existing area is composed of fields reserved for cultivation of a single plant species. Because it is not possible to support the existing plant population, the points system is specially tailored for Viikki's conditions. The local 'Area Co-operation Group' evaluates planting and storm-water performance on request.

Food production

The solution enables the continuation of production of food. Utilisation of composed humus and rainwater are required. The solution should enable the site to be returned to production at a later stage.

VIIKKI: THE PIMWAG EVALUATION METHOD

Pollution (10)

Type	Points available	Difference from reference	Max	Score	(x10/10=) PIMWAG
CO_2	Minimum 1 2	3200 kg/m², 50 years (- 20%) 2700 kg/m², 50 years (- 33% 2200 kg/m², 50 years (- 45%)	2		
Waste water	Minimum 1 2	125 l/resident/day (- 22%) 105 l/resident/day (- 34%) 85 l/resident/day (- 47%)	2		
Construction site waste	Minimum 1 2	18 kg/m², 50 years (- 10%) 15 kg/m², 50 years (- 25%) 10 kg/m², 50 years (- 50%)	2		
Residents' waste	Minimum 1 2	160 kg/residence, year (- 20%) 140 kg/residence, year (- 30%) 120 kg/residence, year (- 40%)	2		
Eco labels	Minimum 1 2	No requirements Floor coverings and glues, or interior paints, and lacquers fulfilling criteria Floor coverings and glues, and interior paints and lacquers fulfilling criteria	 2		

Natural Resources (8)

Type	Points available	Difference from reference	Max	Score	(x8/8=) PIMWAG
Heating energy	Minimum 1 2	105 kWh/m², year (- 34%) 85 kWh/m², year (- 47%) 65 kWh/m², year (- 59%)	2		
Electrical energy	Minimum 1 2	45 kWh/m², year + poss. for local adjustment (- 0%) 40 kWh/m², year (-11%) 35 kWh/m², year (- 22%)	 2		
Primary energy	Minimum 1 2	30 GJ/m², 50 year (- 19%) 25 GJ/m², 50 year (- 32%) 20 GJ/m², 50 year (- 46%)	2		
Flexibility common use	Minimum 1 2	Conventional solution 15% of flexible or housing functions concentrated in common spaces 15% of flexible or housing functions concentrated in common spaces, and multi-purpose spaces designed for buildings	 2		

Healthiness (6)

Type	Points available		Max	Score	(x6/9=) PIMWAG
Interior climate	Minimum	SI Interior climate, Class 2 PL Purity, Class 1 ML Purity of finishing materials, Class 2			
	2	SI Interior climate, Class 1 ML Purity of finishing materials, Class 1	2		
Moisture risks	Minimum	Conventional adequate solution			
	2	Moisture risks well under control	2		
Noise	Minimum	No additional requirements			
	1	New norms (under preparation)			
	2	Insulation clearly exceeds norms	2		
Wind protection, solar impact	Minimum	Adequate solution			
	1	Excellent solution	1		
Alternatives	Minimum	Conventional solution			
	1	15% of apartments with alternative			
	2	30% of apartments with alternative	2		

Biodiversity (4)

Type	Points available	Difference from reference	Max	Score	(x4/4=) PIMWAG
Plants	Minimum	Plants based on identified vegetation			
	1	Plenitude of species and multiple layers characterise vegetation.			
	2	Garden design has created new vegetation types that increase natural diversity.	2		
Storm water	Minimum	Conventional solution			
	1	Only water from building foundations' drainage is discharged			
	2	Rainwater used to create enriched ecosystem	2		

Food Production (3)

Type	Points available	Difference from reference	Max	Score	(x2/3=) PIMWAG
Planting	Minimum	Conventional solution			
	1	1/3 of planted bushes and trees are useful			
	2	Residents have chance to cultivate plots	2		
Topsoil	Min.	Topsoil used in Viikki area			
	1	Topsoil used on the site	1		

TOTAL: [   ]

BREEAM 98 for offices
Roger Baldwin · Alan Yates · Nigel Howard · Sushmel Rao
BREEAM

BREEAM: Building Research Establishment Environmental Assessment Method

Introduction

The *Building Research Establishment Environmental Assessment Method (BREEAM)* was originally launched in 1990. The current assessment, applicable to new and existing office buildings, comprises three parts: core, design and procurement, and management and operation. The main objectives of the assessment are:

- to distinguish buildings of reduced environmental impact in the market place;
- to encourage best environmental practice in building design, operation, management and maintenance;
- to set criteria and standards going beyond those required by law and regulations;
- to raise the awareness of owners, occupants, designers and operators of the benefits of buildings with a reduced impact on the environment.

Step 1 Complete the checklist of credits by adding the number of points in the checkbox under the appropriate columns. Shaded areas indicate that the issue is not assessed in that column

Step 2 Sum the total number of points in the **Building Performance Score** (BPS) and transfer to Box A in the **Design and Procurement** column OR the **Management and Operation** column as appropriate. Also transfer this score to Box C below.

Step 3 Sum the total number of points achieved in the column being assessed (including BPS transferred above) and enter in Box B, and also transfer this score to Box C below.

Step 4 Calculate the Building Performance Score in Box C by using the scale given. The environmental Performance Index is given on a scale of 1 to 10.

Step 5 Use Box D to predict the final BREEAM Rating by comparing the final number of points achieved with the minimum required number of points in the rating matrix.

BREEAM 98 FOR OFFICES: ASSESSMENT PREDICTION CHECKLIST

Management

	Points	Building Performance	Design & Procurement Assessments	Management & Operation Assessments
Client commitment to efficient operation of all services	30			
Established company policy on the environment to include scope, action plan, responsibilities and nominated people, strategic and short-term targets, annual review, and a commitment to report the results of review and performance	30			
Verifiable environmental purchasing policy	30			
Verifiable environmental management system	30			
Building operating manuals available	30			

Health and well-being

	Points	Building Performance	Design & Procurement Assessments	Management & Operation Assessments
Cooling tower locations allow ease of access for cleaning/ replacement or no cooling towers	6			
Actions taken to minimise risk of Legionellosis	6			
At least 30% of windows openable	6			
No steam humidification	6			
Air intakes/outlets over 10 m apart to minimise recirculation and avoid sources of major external pollution	6			
At least 30% fresh air is provided in a/c mech vent systems or trickle vents provided	6			
At least 80% of net lettable area adequately daylit	6			
Controllable blinds to prevent glare	6			
High frequency ballasts are installed in general luminaries	6			

Health and well being

	Points	Building Performance	Design & Procurement Assessments	Management & Operation Assessments
Lighting meets BCO Specification for Offices recommendations for lighting levels	6			▓
Control of lighting relates to circulation space, daylighting and is broken down to provide separate control for groups	6			▓
All workstations have view out	6			▓
Local temperature control in office areas	6			▓
Cooling towers/systems accord with HSG70 & TM13 or no cooling towers	6	▓		
Assessments of thermal comfort at design stages, used to evaluate appropriate servicing	6	▓		
Ambient noise levels below: – 40 dB LAeqT in small offices – 45 dB LAeqT in large offices	6	▓		
Policy to operate maintenance schedules: Heating/cooling; ventilation/humidification; lighting; domestic hot water	6		▓	▓
Safety survey of dhws carried out and appropriate steps to minimise risks. Where building < 3 years old design to TM13	6	▓	▓	
Smoking ban	6	▓	▓	
Maintenance schedules include high performance cleaning of carpets and soft furnishings	6	▓	▓	
Collect and record occupant feedback	6	▓		
Improvement targets relating to occupant satisfaction	6	▓		

Energy

	Points	Building Performance	Design & Procurement Assessments	Management & Operation Assessments
Total net CO_2 emissions will be predicted. Credits given based on scale below: Total net emissions as follows: *(select one)*			▓	▓
• CO_2 emissions 160 – 140 kg/m²/yr	8		▓	▓
• CO_2 emissions 139 – 120 kg/m²/yr	16		▓	▓
• CO_2 emissions 119 – 100 kg/m²/yr	24		▓	▓
• CO_2 emissions 99 – 90 kg/m²/yr	32		▓	▓
• CO_2 emissions 89 – 80 kg/m²/yr	40		▓	▓
• CO_2 emissions 79 – 70 kg/m²/yr	48		▓	▓
• CO_2 emissions 69 – 60 kg/m²/yr	56		▓	▓
• CO_2 emissions 59 – 50 kg/m²/yr	64		▓	▓
• CO_2 emissions 49 – 40 kg/m²/yr	72		▓	▓
• CO_2 emissions 39 – 30 kg/m²/yr	80		▓	▓
• CO_2 emissions 29 – 20 kg/m²/yr	88		▓	▓
• CO_2 emissions 19 – 10 kg/m²/yr	96		▓	▓
• CO_2 emissions 9 – 5 kg/m²/yr	104		▓	▓
• CO_2 emissions 4 – 0 kg/m²/yr	112		▓	▓
• CO_2 emissions < 0 kg/m²/yr	120		▓	▓
Sub-metering for substantive energy uses	8		▓	▓
Check-metering of tenancy areas	8		▓	▓
Energy policy endorsed by Board and available to staff	8	▓		▓
Energy audit at least every three years	8	▓	▓	
Quarterly dissemination of information on energy use and savings	8	▓		
Energy /CO_2 monitoring using historical data	8	▓		
Energy/CO_2 targeting using historical data	8	▓		
Evidence showing movement towards energy /CO_2 targets over time	8	▓		
Actual energy consumption figures are less than established good practice	8	▓		
Maintenance schedules that cover regular cleaning of lighting installations and phased replacement of luminaries	8	▓		

	Points	Building Performance	Design & Procurement Assessments	Management & Operation Assessments
Transport				
RURAL location with typical public transport connections	0		■	■
EDGE OF TOWN location with typical public transport connections	16		■	■
TOWN/SMALL CITY location with typical public transport connections	24		■	■
SMALL TOWN location with typical public transport connections	32		■	■
URBAN CONURBATION location with typical public transport connections	48		■	■
NATIONAL TRANSPORT NODE location with typical public transport connections	64		■	■
Public transport connections are good and car parking is restricted by at least 20% from LA standard	16		■	■
Where provision of cycling facilities: Sheds, Showers and changing facilities	8		■	■
Actions to encourage use of public transport to and from site (passes/loans etc) and discourage cars	8	■		■
Actions to encourage use of public transport for business travel	8			■
Good access to public transport within 500 m, 15 min frequency to local urban centre	8			■
Good access to public transport within 500 m, 30 min frequency to major transport node	8			■
Water consumption				
Predicted water consumption 20–10 m³ per person per year			■	■
Predicted water consumption 9–5 m³ per person per year			■	■
Predicted water consumption 20–10 m³ per person per year < 5 m3			■	■
Water meter installed to all supplies			■	■
Leak detection system installed			■	■
Proximity detection shut off provided			■	■
Maintenance Procedures covering all water systems, taps, sanitary fittings and major water consuming plant		■		■
Consumption monitoring at least once every quarter		■		■
Materials				
No asbestos or where survey has been carried out and asbestos either removed or contained and identified			■	■
Dedicated storage space for materials within building or on site skips with good access for collections			■	■
Major Building elements evaluated against specifications in Green Guide to Specification as follows:		■		
• At least 80% by area of upper floor slab specifications achieved "A" overall rating		■		
• At least 80% by area of external wall specifications achieved "A" overall rating		■		
• At least 80% by area of roof specifications achieved "A" overall rating		■		
• At least 80% by area of window specifications achieved "A" overall rating		■		
Timber for key elements comes from sustainable managed sources		■		
Specifications of timber panel products use only timber that complies with above requirements		■		
Reuse of > 50% of existing facades		■		
Reuse of > 80% of major structure by building volume		■		
Use of crushed aggregate or masonry for use in structure, slabs, roads etc		■		
Policy and procedures for collection and recycling of consumables		■	■	■
Information on presence of hazardous materials available for staff and contractors		■		■

	Points	Building Performance	Design & Procurement Assessments	Management & Operation Assessments

Land use

	Points	Building Performance	Design & Procurement Assessments	Management & Operation Assessments
Where site has been previously built on or used for industry in last 50 years	16	░		░
Where Land is 'contaminated' adequate steps taken to contain or clean site prior to construction	16	░		░

Ecology

	Points	Building Performance	Design & Procurement Assessments	Management & Operation Assessments
Where land is defined as of low ecological value	16	░		░
• Where change in ecological value of site is minor and negative	16	░		░
• Where change in ecological value of site is neutral	32	░		░
• Where change in ecological value of site is minor and positive	48	░		░
• Where change in ecological value of site is significant and positive	64	░		░
Seek and act on advice from Wildlife Trusts (AWTC) or member IEA on enhancement	8	░		░
Trees over 100 mm trunk dia, hedges, ponds, streams etc maintained and protected from damage during construction	8	░		░

Pollution

	Points	Building Performance	Design & Procurement Assessments	Management & Operation Assessments
Refrigerant type has ODP of zero or no refrigerants	14		░	░
Refrigerant leak detection system covering high risk parts of plant or no refrigerants	14		░	░
Automatic refrigerant pump down to coil or storage tanks with isolation values or no refrigerants	14		░	░
Absence of Halon based fire fighting systems	14		░	░
Burners in boiler plant (except standby) have maximum NOx emission levels:				
• Emissions are 200–100 mg/kWh delivered heating energy	14		░	░
• Emissions are 99–70 mg/kWh delivered heating energy	28		░	░
• Emissions are 69–40 mg/kWh delivered heating energy	42		░	░
• Emissions are < 40 mg/kWh delivered heating energy	56		░	░
Site facilities reduce run off to natural and municipal watercourses by 50% and where on site treatment is present	14		░	░
Specification of insulants avoids ozone depleting substances	14	░		░
Policy to operate maintenance schedules covering BOILER/BURNER systems including regular checking of controls, filters and cleaning	14	░	░	░

		Building Performance	Design & Procurement Assessments	Management & Operation Assessments
Sum points achieved in each column assessed		☐	☐	☐
A	**Building Performance Score (BPS)** Transfer Building Performance column total to this box Also transfer to Box C below and calculate Building Performance Index		☐	
B	**Total number of points achieved (incl. BPS in Box A)** Transfer to Box D on below and predict final rating using the matrix given (Design and Procurement OR Management and Operation assessment only)			☐

C

Building Performance Score (BPS)
from Box A above ☐

Probable Environmental Performance Index (EPI)

BPS
0   100   200   300   400   500

1 2 3 4 5 6 7 8   9   10
EPI

D

Final Score from Box B ☐

Probable BREEAM Rating

	Final Score from Box B	Minimum No of Points required	
		Design & Procurement Assessments	Management & Operation Assessments
☐ Pass		200	160
☐ Good		300	280
☐ Very Good		380	400
☐ Excellent		490	520

LIFE CYCLE COST

Introduction

At present many building environmental costs (emissions of greenhouse gases; the consumption of finite resources such as hardwood and metals; and the creation of construction waste) are not reflected in either initial construction cost or in ongoing building servicing cost. Water, waste and energy taxes are gradually changing this and make green building increasingly attractive economically. To enable the client assess a financial return over the building's life of an initial investment in energy-saving or other resource-conserving measures, life cycle cost analysis is necessary.

Life cycle cost

The objective is to optimise the value of a construction project over its lifetime, having regard to all the project costs, both direct and indirect. This involves selecting an appropriate lifetime for the building. However, with maintenance, any building can last almost indefinitely, and it will be easier to assign a lifetime to replacement date for individual systems and components. For example, depending on specification, floor finishes might have a lifetime to replacement of from 10 years (inexpensive thin sheet flooring) to 30 years (hardwood strip). When annual operating and maintenance costs are added, this lifetime to replacement can help determine the life cycle cost. For a full environmental evaluation, it is necessary to ascribe costs to the otherwise not costed environmental facotors: pollution, resource depletion.

The *Green Guide to Specification: An Environmental Profiling System for Building Materials and Components*, published by the UK Building Research Establishment, gives estimated replacement intervals for a wide range of building materials and components, over a 60-year building design life cycle, which takes account of maintenance and refurbishment.

Payback period and life cycle to replacement

The simplest way to calculate the cost-effectiveness of an investment is to determine payback period. The ultimate objective is to identify the value of a construction component or project over its lifetime, to enable selection based on life cycle cost. For commercial investment appraisal, future income and expenditure is discounted to a present value using an appropriate rate. The appropriate discount rate to use is the real rate of return required on the investment. For domestic consumers, this rate may be the difference between the after-tax interest rate on bank deposits and the rate of inflation. Rates vary with time and country, but with a 2% inflation rate and a 5% after-tax interest rate, the domestic discount rate is 3%. A higher rate of return is normally required in the commercial sector.

Discounting to present value

In the case of low-energy or sustainable design, consideration of life cycle costs from the outset is essential. The balance between construction cost and cost-in-use is fundamental to the architecture of the building. For example, the design of a window will have implications for heating, cooling, ventilation and artificial lighting, pollutant emissions, plant size and maintenance costs.

The length of payback periods needs consideration. The payback periods used in different organisations and EU Member States vary considerably, from as short as three years to ten years or longer. Plainly this one element has critical consequences for the evaluations of solar low-energy strategies. Far-sighted clients, particularly those who will be owner/occupiers, may be willing to consider longer payback periods.

Passive Solar

- Colombo, Landabaso and Sevilla, (Eds) 1994 *Passive Solar Architecture for the Mediterranean Area: Design Handbook*, Joint Research Centre for DG XII of the Commission of the European Communities, Brussels.
- ECD Partnership (1991) *Solar Architecture in Europe*, UK-London Prism Press 2 South Street, UK - Bridport   DT6 3NQ   England
- Fitzgerald and Lewis, (Eds) (1996) *European Solar Architecture. Proceedings of a Solar House Contractors' Meeting*, Energy Research Group, Dublin, for DG XII of the Commission of the European Communities.
- Foster, Scheer (Eds) (1993) *Solar Energy in Architecture and Urban Planning: Proceedings of the Conference on Architecture.* . H. S. Stephens and Associates, Bedford, UK for Commission of the European Communities.
- Goulding, Lewis and Steemers (Eds) (1992) *Energy in Architecture: The European Passive Solar Handbook*, B T Batsford, London, for DG XII of the Commission of the European Communities. ISBN 0 7134 69188
- Goulding, Lewis and Steemers (Eds) (1994) *Passive Solar Resource Guide,* Energy Research Group, Dublin.
- Mazria (1980) *The Passive Solar Energy Book*, Franco Muzzio Editore, Padova.
- Zold and Santamouris, *Fundamentals of Passive Solar Heating*, Central Institution for Energy Efficiency in Education (CIENE), Athens

Renewables

- Böttger and Schoen (Eds) (1995) *Building with photovoltaics* Ten Hagen & Stam, Den Haag, NL.
- Colombo, Gilliaert, and Landabaso, (Eds) (1991) Life Cycle Cost Analysis of Solar Heating and DHW Systems in Residential Buildings, Commission of The European Communities Office for Official Publications.
- Derrick, Barlow, McNelis and Gregory, (Eds) (1993) *Photovoltaics: A Market Overview* James & James (Science Publishers) Ltd, London.
- Imamura, Helm and Palz (Eds) (1992) *Photovoltaic System Technology: A European Handbook,* H.S. Stephens & Associates, UK.
- Office of Official Publications of the Commission of the European (1996) *Communities Energy for the future: renewable sources of energy - Green paper for a Community Strategy*, Luxembourg.
- Sick, Friedrich and T Erge (1996) *Photovoltaics in buildings: a design handbook for architects and engineers,* James and James (Science Publishers) Ltd, London.

Site and Urban Design

- Alexander et al. (1977) *A Pattern Language: Towns, Buildings, Construction.* Oxford University Press, New York.
- Rocky Mountain Institute (1998) *Green development: integrating ecology and real estate,* Wiley, New York.
- Barton, Hugh, Geoff Davis and Richard Guise (1995) *Sustainable settlements: a guide for planners, designers and developers,* University of the West of England and The Local Government Management Board, Bristol.
- Building Research Establishment (1990) *Climate and Site Development.* BRE Digest 350 Parts 1–3. Garston, UK.
- Building Research Establishment, (1988) *Microclimate and The Environmental Performance of Building,* Garston, UK.
- Energy Technology Support Unit (1990) *Estate Layout for Passive Solar Housing Design.* UK Dept of Energy Contractors Report, Ref No ETSU S1126, Oxfordshire, UK.
- Hough (1995) *Cities and natural process,* Routledge, London.
- Littlefair P J (1991) *Site Layout Planning for Daylight* (BR 209) Building Research Establishment, Garston, UK..
- Littlefair P J (1992) *Site Layout Planning for Sunlight and Solar Gain.* (Information Paper IP 4/92). Building Research Establishment, Garston, UK.
- Lynch and Hack (1984) *Site Planning* MIT Press, Cambridge, Mass. ISBN 0 262 1206 9
- *Urban energy planning guide* (1994) Energie-Cités , France.

Further Reading

General

- Baker (1995) *Energy and environment in non-domestic buildings: a technical design guide,* Cambridge Architectural Research Ltd, Cambridge.
- BRECSU Energy Technology Support Unit (1993) *Best Practice Guides,* Garston, UK.
- Gallo C, M Sala and A M M Sayigh (Eds) (1998) *Architecture - Comfort and Energy,* Pergamon
- Givoni (1982) *Man Climate and Architecture* Applied Science Publishers, London.
- Goulding, John R, J Owen Lewis and Theo C Steemers, (Eds) (1992) *Energy Conscious Design: a Primer for Architects,* B T Batsford Ltd London for DG XII of the Commission of the European Communities. ISBN 0 7134 69196
- Green Paper for a European Union energy policy, Office for Official Publication of the Commission of the European Communities, Luxembourg, 1995
- Halliday, Newton, Venables et al (1995) *A Client's Guide to Greener Construction.* UK Construction Industry Research and Information Association (CIRIA) ISBN 0 86017 4239
- Hawkes D, (1996) *The Environmental Tradition: Studies in the architecture of environment.* E & F N Spon, London.
- International Environmental Yearbook, SPA, Madrid, Spain
- Lewis, J Owen, John R Goulding (Eds) *European Directory of Sustainable and Energy Efficient Building,* Published annually since 1993, James & James (Science Publishers) Ltd, London.
- Littler J and R Thomas (1984) *Design with Energy: the Conservation and Use of Energy in Buildings.* Cambridge University Press, Cambridge. ISBN 0 521 245621
- Local Agenda 21 and Rio Declaration, United Nations Conference on Environment and Development (UNCED), Rio, 1992
- Lopez, Barnett and Browning, (1995) *A Primer on Sustainable Building,* Rocky Mountain Institute Green Development Services, Snowmass, Colorado. ISBN 1 881071 05 7
- Markus, Morris et al. (1980) *Buildings, Climate and Energy,* Pitman, London.
- O'Cofaigh E, J Olley and J O Lewis, (1996) *The Climatic Dwelling,* Energy Research Group, UCD and James & James (Science Publishers) Ltd, London. ISBN 1 87 3936 39
- Olgyay V, (1973) *Design with Climate,* Princeton University Press, Princeton.
- Roaf and Hancock (Eds), (1992) *Energy Efficient Building - A Design Guide,* Blackwell Scientific Publications, Oxford. ISBN 0 632 03245 6
- Thomas R (Ed) (1996) *Environmental design: an introduction for architects and engineers,* E & FN Spon, London.
- Union Internationale des Architectes, (1993), *Declaration of Interdependence for a Sustainable Future:* UIA/AIA World Congress of Architects, Chicago, 18–21 June 1993
- United Nations World Commission on Environment and Development, (1987) *Our Common Future* (the Bruntland Report), Bruntland.
- Woolley, Kimmins and Harrison (1997) *Green Building Handbook* Thomson Professional, London.

Building Types

- Architectural Association Graduate School (1994) *Solar Architecture Resource Material: Educational Buildings,* Environment and Energy Studies Programme, London.
- Building Research Establishment (1998) *BREEAM 98 for offices* (BRE Environmental Asessment Method) Watford, UK.
- Cambridge Architectural Research Ltd, (1994) *Case study: offices (Case studies of energy-efficient non-domestic buildings).* Cambridge, UK.
- Cambridge Architectural Research Ltd, (1994) *Design guide: colleges (Design guides for energy-efficient non-domestic buildings).* Cambridge, UK.
- Cambridge Architectural Research Ltd, (1994) *Design guide: hospitals (Design guides for energy-efficient non-domestic buildings).* Cambridge, UK.
- Cambridge Architectural Research Ltd, (1994) *Design guide: schools (Design guides for energy-efficient non-domestic buildings).* Cambridge, UK.
- Energy Research Group, UCD, (1995) *Solar Architecture Resource Material: Residential Buildings.* James & James (Science Publishers) Ltd, London.
- Greenpeace (1995) *Unlocking the power of our cities: solar power and commercial buildings,* London, UK.
- Hestnes Anne-Grete, S Robert Hastings and Bjarne Saxhof (Eds) (1996) *Solar Energy houses: strategies, technologies, examples,* James and James (Science Publishers) Ltd, London, UK. ISBN 1 873936 69 9
- Instituto Cooperativo per l'Innovazione (ICIE), (1995) *Designing healthy energy efficient office buildings,* A Thermie Maxibrochure, for the European Commission, Rome, Italy.
- Laing A, F Duffy, D Jauntzenz and S Willis, (1998) New environments for working (BR 341) Building Research Establishment, Watford, UK.
- NBA Tectonics for the Department of the Environment, (1986) *Energy Efficient Renovation of Houses: a Design Guide,* Her Majesty's Stationery Office, London.
- Santamouris (1995) *Energy retrofitting of office buildings* (3 vols). CIENE, Athens.
- Universite Catholique de Louvain (1994) *Solar Architecture Resource Material: Tertiary Buildings.* Architecture et Climat, Louvain-la-Neuve.
- Wastebusters (1997) *The green office manual: A guide to responsible practice,* Earthscan Publications Ltd, London, UK.
- Yannas (1994) *Solar Energy and Housing Design. Vol: Principles, Objectives, Guidelines; Vol 2: Examples.* AA Publications, Bedford Square, London.

Climate

- Page, Palz and Greif, (Eds) (1996) *European solar radiation atlas: solar radiation on horizontal and inclined surfaces,* Springer Verlag, Berlin.
- Palz (Ed) (1989) *European Wind Atlas,* Dept. of Meteorology & Wind Energy, Risø National Laboratory, P.O. Box 49, DK-4000, Roskilde, Denmark, for Commission of the European Communities.
- *Tables of Temperature, Relative Humidity and Precipitation for the World: Part 3 - Europe & The Atlantic Ocean, North of 35° N.* (1975) Her Majesty's Stationery Office, UK.

Envelope

- Building Research Establishment (1989) *Thermal Insulation: Avoiding Risks*, Ref. BRE 143, Garston, UK.
- Chartered Institution of Building Services Engineers (CIBSE) (1987) Applications Manual: Window Design, London.
- DG XVII of the Commission of the European Communities (1988) *Windows: the Key to Low Energy Design*. Energy Comfort 2000 Information Dossier No 5.
- Heat Losses through Ground Floors, Ref. BRE 145 Building Research Establishment, Garston, UK.
- 'Maxibrochure' (1993) *Transparent Insulation Technology*, The Franklin Company, ETSU-OPET, Harwell, UK, for DG XVII of the Commission of the European Communities
- Littlefair P J (1996) *Designing with innovative daylighting*, BRE Report 294, Building Research Establishment, Garston, UK.

Health

- Curwell, March and Venables (1990) Healthy Construction: The Rosehaugh Guide to The Design, Construction, Use and Management of Buildings, RIBA Publications, London.
- Commission of the European Communities (1989) *Sick Building Syndrome: A Practical Guide*. Report 4, European Collaborative Action: Indoor Air Quality and its Impact on Man, Brussels.
- Levin (1993) 'Best sustainable indoor air quality practices in commercial buildings', in *Environmental Building News*, EBN, Vermont.
- Potter (1988) Technical Note 4/88: Sick Building Syndrome, Building Services Research and Information Association (BSRIA), Bracknell.
- Pearson (1989) *The Natural House Book*, Conran Octopus, London.
- Ranson (1991) *Healthy Housing - A practical guide*, E & FN Spon, London for the World Health Organization Regional Office for Europe.

Heating, Ventilation, Cooling and Services

- Andersen (1992) 'Maxibrochure' *Basic aspects of application of district heating*, CENTEC Energy Centre Denmark, Copenhagen, for DG XVII of the Commission of the European Communities.
- Chartered Institution of Building Services Engineers (CIBSE) (1989) *Application Manual AM3: Condensing Boilers*, UK,
- DG V of the Commission of the European Communities (1992) *Guidelines for Ventilation Requirements in Buildings*, Report 11, European Collaborative Action - Indoor Air Quality and its Impact on Man, Brussels.
- Givoni (1980) *Passive Cooling of Buildings - An Overview*. Miami, USA.
- Liddament (1996) *A Guide to Energy Efficient Ventilation*, Air Infiltration and Ventilation Centre.
- Liveris, (Ed) (1994) 'Maxibrochure' *Natural and Low Energy Cooling in Buildings*. Centre for Renewable Energy Sources (CRES), Pikermi, Greece, for the Commission of the European Communities.
- Santamouris M and D Asimikopolous (Eds) (1996) *Passive cooling in buildings*, James and James (Science Publishers) Ltd, London.

Lighting

- Baker (1995) 'Light and Shade: Optimising Daylighting Design' in *European Directory of Sustainable and Energy Efficient Building*, James & James, London, for the Commission of the European Communities
- Baker N, A Fanchiotti and Steemers, (Eds) (1993) *Daylighting in Architecture: A European Reference Book*, James & James (Science Publishers) Ltd, London for the Commission of the European Communities.
- Bell and Burt (1995) *Designing Buildings for Daylight*, Building Research Establishment, Garston, UK.
- British Standards Institute (1992) *BS 8206:1992 Part 2: Code of Practice for Daylighting*, London.
- Chartered Institution of Building Services Engineers (CIBSE) (1993) *Lighting Guide LG7: Lighting for offices*, UK.
- CIBSE Code for Interior Lighting. Chartered Institution of Building Services (CIBSE), London, 1984
- Crisp, Littlefair, McKenna and Cooper (1985) *Daylighting as a Passive Solar Energy Option (BR 129)* Building Research Establishment, Garston, UK.
- *Energy Efficient Lighting in Schools* (1992) *Energy Efficient Lighting in Industrial Buildings* (1992)
  Energy Efficient Lighting in Buildings (1992) *Energy Efficient Lighting in Offices* (1993)
  Energy Efficient Lighting Practice (1994) BRECSU-OPET, Garston UK, for the Commission of the European Communities.
- *Energy Efficient Lighting in Buildings*, Building Research Establishment (BRE), Garston, UK for DG XVII of the Commission of the European Communities, 1991
- Littlefair, *Average Daylight Factor, A Simple Basis for Daylight Design*, Building Research Establishment (BRE), Garston, UK.
- McNicholl, Ann and J. Owen Lewis (Eds) (1994) *Daylighting in Buildings*, UCD-OPET, Dublin, for the Commission of the European Communities.

Materials and Waste

- Anink, David, Chiel Boonstra and John Mak, (Eds) (1996) *Handbook of Sustainable Building: an Environmental Preference Method for the Selection of Materials for Use in Construction and Refurbishment* James & James (Science Publishers) Ltd, London. ISBN 1-873938-38-9
- CSIRIA (Construction Industry Research and Information Association (1995) *Environmental impact of materials: Volume A - Summary*, London, UK.
- Goumans, van der Sloot and Aalbers, (Eds) (1994) *Environmental Aspects of Construction with Waste Material*, Elsevier Science, NL.
- Howard Nigel, David Shiers and Mike Sinclair (1998) Green guide to specification: an environmental profiling system for building materials and components, Building Research Establishment, Watford, UK.
- Talbott (1993) *Simply Build Green*, Findhorn Foundation, Scotland.
- World Resource Foundation (1995) Information Sheet, *Construction and demolition wastes*, Tonbridge, Kent.

Table 5.2 COST CONSIDERATIONS FOR DESIGN INCLUDE:

Direct and indirect: initial, life cycle, and environmental

Initial:
Construction: supply and installation
Design

Life cycle:
Daily, weekly and annual maintenance including cleaning, repair, redecoration
Replacement, including removal, waste disposal, replacement
Running cost for energy consuming components

Environmental:
Resource depletion and environmental pollution:
Extraction, manufacture, transport, use and disposal: to air, ground, water
Indoor environmental quality

Table 5.2 above lists different cost types to be considered when evaluating life cycle and environmental cost. This does not deal with the issue of component quality. If, over say 50 years, the cost of a PVC tile floor finish is equal to the cost of a high quality hardwood strip floor, the architect might also ascribe an extra value given to the user by the visual and olfactory pleasure of the high-quality component over that produced by the cheap one.

Comparison of initial and life cycle cost: Worked example

Incandescent light bulb as against compact fluorescent • Discount rate 3% / yr • No cost included for • environmental cost of additional CO_2 and SO_2 emissions: estimated at 750 kg and 8kg over working life (Browning and Romm, 1995) • labour involved in bulb replacement • contribution to higher heat contribution (whether useful or surplus) of incandescent bulb.

			100W incandescent	23W compact fluorescent
Initial cost, €				
Supply and install			€1	€7
Running cost: 1000 hr/yr, €0.1/kwh			€10 /yr	€2.3 /yr
Life expectancy			1000 hours	8000 hours
Life cycle comparison for 8-year period:				
Initial capital cost			€1	€7
Replacement cost, discounting at 3%/yr				
Factors:	Year 1	0.971		
	Year 2	0.943		
	Year 3	0.915		
	Year 4	0.888		
	Year 5	0.862		
	Year 6	0.837		
	Year 7	0.813		
	Total	6.229 x € 1	€6.229	0.00
Running cost over 8 years				
Years 1–7, as above	6.229			
Year 8	0.789			
Total	7.018		x €10 = 70.180	x €2.3 = 16.141
Total life cycle cost over 8 years			**€77.409**	**€23.141**

CALCULATION OF PAYBACK PERIOD FOR INVESTMENT

Total extra initial investment: €6

Return on Investment over 8 years, discounted: €77-23 = €54 or €6.75 /yr

Payback period: **11 months**

Further reading

- Aaltonen-Gabrielsson-Inkinen-Majurinen-Pennanen-Wartiainen, (1997) *Ecological building criteria for Viikki,* Helsinki City Planning Department Publications, Serial Number: 1998. 6, 25 May 1997, 36 pp., ISBN 951-718-092-6

- Baker N and K Steemers, (1995) *The LT Method Version 2.0: An energy design tool for non-domestic buildings,* Cambridge Architectural Research Ltd.

- Building Research Establishment, (1998) *BREEAM 98 for offices: an Environmental Assessment Method for office buildings,* Building Research Establishment, Garston, Watford, United Kingdom. ISBN 1 86081 2384

- Building Research Establishment, (1998) *The Green Guide to Specification: An Environmental Profiling System for Building Materials and Components,* Garston, Watford, United Kingdom. ISBN 1 860812 42 2

- Energy Research Group, UCD, (1997) *Mid-career education: Solar Energy in European Office Buildings: Building Economics:* Energy Research Group, University College Dublin for Alterner Programme, European Commission Directorate-General XVII for Energy, 1997, published on the Internet at http://erg.ucd.ie / mid-career/mid-career.html